Agatha Christie Goes to

Agatha Christie has never been substantially considered as a war writer, even though war is a constant presence in her writing. This interdisciplinary collection of essays considers the effects of conflict, particularly the Second World War, on the social and psychological textures of Christie's detective fiction and other writings, demonstrating not only Christie's textual navigation of her contemporary surroundings and politics, but also the value of her voice as a popular fiction writer reflecting popular concerns. *Agatha Christie Goes to War* introduces the "Queen of Crime" as an essential voice in the discussion of war, warfare, and twentieth century literature.

Dr. Rebecca Mills is a lecturer at Bournemouth University.

Dr. J.C. Bernthal is a guest lecturer at the University of Cambridge.

Routledge Interdisciplinary Perspectives on Literature

100 **Make it Work**
    20th Century American Fiction and Fashion
    Jan Ellyn Goggans

101 **Haunted Europe**
    Continental Connections in English-Language Gothic Writing, Film and New Media
    Edited by Evert Jan Van Leeuwen and Michael Newton

102 **Challenging Memories and Rebuilding Identities**
    Literary and Artistic Voices that undo the Lusophone Atlantic
    Edited by Margarida Rendeiro and Federica Lupati

103 **Literature with a White Helmet**
    The Textual-Corporeality of Being, Becoming, and Representing Refugees
    Lava Asaad

104 **The Birth of Intertextuality**
    The Riddle of Creativity
    Scarlett Baron

105 **Doubles and Hybrids in Latin American Gothic**
    Edited by Antonio Alcalá and Ilse Bussing

106 **The Feminist Architecture of Postmodern Anti-Tales**
    Space, Time and Bodies
    Kendra Reynolds

107 **Agatha Christie Goes to War**
    Edited by Rebecca Mills and J.C. Bernthal

For more information about this series, please visit: https://www.routledge.com

Agatha Christie Goes to War

Edited by
Rebecca Mills and J.C. Bernthal

NEW YORK AND LONDON

First published 2020
by Routledge
605 Third Avenue, New York, NY 10017
and by Routledge
2 Park Square, Milton Park, Abingdon, Oxon, OX14 4RN

First issued in paperback 2021

Routledge is an imprint of the Taylor & Francis Group, an informa business

Copyright © 2020 Taylor & Francis

The right of Rebecca Mills and J.C. Bernthal to be identified as the authors of the editorial material, and of the authors for their individual chapters, has been asserted in accordance with sections 77 and 78 of the Copyright, Designs and Patents Act 1988.

All rights reserved. No part of this book may be reprinted or reproduced or utilised in any form or by any electronic, mechanical, or other means, now known or hereafter invented, including photocopying and recording, or in any information storage or retrieval system, without permission in writing from the publishers.

Trademark notice: Product or corporate names may be trademarks or registered trademarks, and are used only for identification and explanation without intent to infringe.

Publisher's Note
The publisher has gone to great lengths to ensure the quality of this reprint but points out that some imperfections in the original copies may be apparent.

Library of Congress Cataloging-in-Publication Data
Library of Congress Control Number: 2019951961

ISBN 13: 978-1-03-223994-1 (pbk)
ISBN 13: 978-0-367-20852-3 (hbk)

Typeset in Sabon
by codeMantra

The editors would like to dedicate *Agatha Christie Goes to War* to the Agatha Christie Conference once and future regulars.

Contents

Acknowledgments   ix

Introduction   1
J.C. BERNTHAL AND REBECCA MILLS

1 Mapping War, Planning Peace: Miss Marple and the Evolving Village Space, 1930–1962   11
SARAH MARTIN AND SALLY WEST

2 Christie's Wartime Hero: Peacetime Killer   28
PAULA BOWLES

3 Writing through War: Narrative Structure and Authority in Christie's Second World War Novels   46
BRITTAIN BRIGHT

4 Taking on Hitler: Agatha Christie's Wartime Thrillers   63
MERJA MAKINEN

5 "When She Eats She Will Die": Informal Meals and Social Change in *Sad Cypress* and "And Then There Were None"   81
J.C. BERNTHAL

6 "A Worrying, Nerve-Wracked World": Agatha Christie's Emergence as a Playwright during and after the Second World War   95
JULIUS GREEN

7 "There Are Things One Doesn't Forget": The Second World War in "Three Blind Mice" and *The Mousetrap*   109
FEDERICA CRESCENTINI

8 Displaced Persons: *A Murder Is Announced* and
 the Condition of Postwar England 124
 CHRISTOPHER YIANNITSAROS

9 Detecting the Blitz: Memory and Trauma in Christie's
 Postwar Writings 137
 REBECCA MILLS

10 "The Thrill When It Suddenly Went Pitch Black!":
 Blackout Cultures in *A Murder Is Announced* and
 The Mousetrap 155
 ROGER DALRYMPLE

Notes on Contributors 167
Index 171

Acknowledgments

The editors would like to thank the following Christie fans and scholars in particular for their support, enthusiasm, and inspiration during the process of devising and collecting this volume: Gill Plain, Merja Makinen, Mia Dormer, Mark Aldridge, Sarah Martin, and Tina Hodgkinson.

We would like to thank all of our contributors for their patience and support, as well as their thoughtful and insightful essays. We also owe many thanks to Jennifer Abbott, Mitchell Manners, and the team at Routledge.

Jamie would like to thank Alan Bernthal-Hooker, and Rebecca would like to thank her family, as always, and Max Gee, Bronwen Thomas, Sam Goodman, and the rest of the W322 crew at Bournemouth University.

Jamie wishes to thank Rebecca, the perfect partner in crime, and Rebecca wishes to thank Jamie for his kindness, friendship, and collaboration since they first met while she was nervously waiting for her viva in 2014.

Introduction
J.C. Bernthal and Rebecca Mills

After the varying degrees of anxiety and ambivalence felt in the United Kingdom regarding Adolf Hitler's rise to power in Germany and annexation of territory in the 1930s, and the disillusionment of British Prime Minister Neville Chamberlain's appeasement policy, Great Britain and France declared war against Nazi Germany on 1 September 1939. Following the tensions of the Phoney War between September 1939 and May 1940 (when expected air raids and poison gas attacks on civilians failed to materialize), the Dunkirk evacuations of May 1940, the Battle of Britain, the Blitz, and Winston Churchill becoming Prime Minister, the Second World War had settled in for its grim duration when Agatha Christie published her only thriller dealing explicitly with the conflict. *N or M?* (1941) features bombs, evacuees, fifth columnists, and an English coastline riddled with spies and under threat of invasion, but it was an element of the novel's comic relief that caused genuine concerns around national security. According to the codebreaker Dilly Knox, the British secret service organization MI5 was so concerned that a minor character in the book, a Major Bletchley, indicated some secret knowledge of the covert intelligence operations at Bletchley Park that they investigated her. Christie is said to have explained later that this was all a misunderstanding, and that, being "stuck at Bletchley [railway] station", she "found the place so boring that she thought it the ideal name for the tiresome old major" (Smith 32).

There is a sense in which this anecdote reflects the trajectories of critical scholarship of Christie and her work. In her lifetime—and encouraged by Christie herself—scholarship and media reviews and commentary tended to highlight the works' escapist irrelevance: puzzle was everything, and every other element an example of "animated algebra", to use journalist Francis Wyndham's 1966 term. The major is just a major. There have been subsequent earnest attempts to link Christie with prominent movements and events surrounding her work: just as the name Major Bletchley rang alarm bells, some researchers have used miniscule pieces of evidence as jumping-off points for direct interventions into modernist, feminist, and political movements. However, two decades into the twenty-first century, academic treatments of

Agatha Christie, far from excusing or qualifying her popular status by finding tenuous relationships to more credible discourse, are starting to consider the relevance *in* her playful populism. Major Bletchley was named for a boring town; surely Bletchley Park was also selected for its innocuous location. The major *might* be only a major, but the way he came to be created is grounded in a context of national duplicity and the war effort. Christie's self-conscious interaction with the real world means that war—and other things—are present throughout her work, whether or not the texts appear escapist.

Christie's first novel, *The Mysterious Affair at Styles* (1920), written and set during the First World War, introduced Hercule Poirot as a Belgian refugee and his companion Captain Hastings as a soldier. The Poirot canon and the broader Christie canon are bookended by war. It is not simply that the last novel published in Christie's lifetime, *Curtain: Poirot's Last Case* (1975), was written during the Second World War and, while intended to appear timeless, is clearly set in a landscape indelibly marked by the conflict. There is also Christie's posthumously published autobiography, in which she devotes whole chapters to "War", "The Second War", and her adventures with her archaeologist husband unearthing evidence of ancient conflicts, as well as offhand remarks framing her own life with reference to the structuring principle of war in shaping collective and international identity:

> "I suppose," a well-educated girl says with interest, "that you remember *all* about the Crimea?"
> Rather hurt, I reply that I'm not quite as old as all that. I also repudiate participation in the Indian Mutiny. But I admit to recollections of the Boer War—I should do, my brother fought in it. (12, emphasis original)

Thinking about these remarks, one wonders how colorless the stereotypical "old majors" in Christie's fiction—recognizable club bores and monocled raconteurs—really are. War is not simply a state of affairs one remembers, but a memory in itself, with strong personal connections like the "brother [who] fought in it". Christie did not merely make war a backdrop but wrote occasional thrillers in which major international conflict directly informs the plots, from the communist and republican uprisings in *The Secret Adversary* (1922) to the stirrings of the Cold War in *They Came to Baghdad* (1951) and the increasingly plausible threat of neo-Nazism in the once-ridiculed *Passenger to Frankfurt* (1970).

Historian Robert Mackay opens *The Test of War: Inside Britain 1939–1945* (2003) by observing that "'Never again' was the feeling at all levels of society in 1918; and yet, here again, when the memories of that time were scarcely faded, the call to total war went out" (1). This sense of cyclicality is encountered in Christie's autobiography:

And so we were back again in wartime. It was not a war like the last one. One expected it to be, because I suppose one always does expect things to repeat themselves. The first war came with a shock of incomprehension, as something unheard of, impossible, something that had never happened in living memory, that never would happen. This war was different. (482)

And yet, despite the differences globally—advanced technologies of war, Blitzkrieg, the threat of "a new Dark Age made more sinister, and perhaps more protracted, by the lights of perverted science" (Churchill, 1940)—and the different effects on Christie's own life and family, including displacement, having their home requisitioned by the military, and suffering a bombing, there were parallels between Christie's own situations. In the First World War, Christie nursed wounded soldiers in Torquay and worried about Archie Christie, who she had married in a hasty war wedding in 1914. In the Second World War, Christie wrote to her second husband Max Mallowan, who had been posted abroad, and her daughter Rosalind rapidly married Hubert Prichard, who was deployed abroad and eventually killed. In both wars, she wrote detective novels. The trajectory and environmental and psychological textures of Christie's fiction, plays, and life writing show a negotiation of the legacy of war, and apprehension for its return.

The impact of the First World War on the social and material settings and dynamics that informed Christie's interwar writing, and that of her peers, has been significantly reassessed in the last thirty years. The myth of the Golden Age "curiously sanitized and bloodless corpse" (Scaggs 43) has been laid to rest, as has the notion that the detective fiction of this period entailed purely cerebral clue-puzzles and resisted engagement with its contemporary milieu. In this volume, we take for granted that Christie's work can be read within its time; our starting point is that detective fiction is a rich resource for investigating the social, psychological, and political concerns that inflect cultural and literary memorializing of war.

Broadly, there are two critical strands in the study of British detective fiction during and after the Second World War: one that presents a narrative of crisis followed by malaise, and another that incorporates detective fiction into the study of intermodernist,[1] middlebrow,[2] and popular women's writing of this period, acknowledging what Phyllis Lassner calls the genre's "innovative aesthetics with enough political, cultural and social critique to go around" (115). While this collection is positioned to build on the recuperative work of scholars such as Lassner, Light, Gill Plain, and Petra Rau, examining the terms of the former strand offers insight and potential complication of the parameters of the Golden Age itself.

The Golden Age is widely understood as bordered by the First and Second World Wars. The sense of a gulf between 1939 and after has persisted, heightened by the fact that key Golden Age author Dorothy L. Sayers stopped writing detective novels at the outset of the Second World War, while Ngaio Marsh and Margery Allingham incorporated the espionage thriller into their wartime detective fiction. As Lassner writes of Allingham (and Helen MacInnes), these generic conventions are merged to "question relationships between the ethics of detecting and spying and the urgency of saving Britain in a necessary war" (114). With the exception of *N or M?*, Christie's wartime output focused on detection rather than espionage, and this question of ethics rarely surfaces, even in her post-war thrillers.

The continuity of Christie's detective fiction across the Second World War makes her work central to studying the evolution of the genre. Martin Priestman observes a shift from the conventions of the "brilliant" (173) private detective to novels of "espionage or psychological suspense" (173), and eventually the police procedural later in the century (174), noting that

> [a] mapping of how this change came about in the decades between 1940 and 2000 seems particularly needed for British crime fiction, on whose post-war developments there has been very little synthesizing criticism since Symons, and which is still too often seen as an indecisive hangover from the privileged fantasy-world of the pre-war "Golden Age", or as palely reflecting trends which really belong to America. (173)

This collection aims to use Christie's work as a tool in creating this map, and makes the case that her postwar work is not merely a hangover from the Golden Age but demonstrates both the resilience of the genre in its inherently "British" mode and its adaptability into what we argue here is war writing, with its ellipses, uncertain chronology and authority, and knowing reconfiguration of genre conventions to allow for social and global as well as familial and individual instability. Victoria Stewart argues that, "Detective fiction might have traditionally served as a means of encompassing or controlling the apparently uncontrollable—violence, death—in wartime, this function becomes both more urgent and more difficult" (93). This anxiety around containment becomes particularly evident in Christie's post-war detective fiction, as essays here discuss. This collection, we hope, will form a starting point for further study of this liminal period. Indeed, some of the recent publications from the British Library Classics series that recovers "lost" crime fiction texts are labeled Second World War novels, such as Michael Gilbert's *Death Has Deep Roots: A Second World War Mystery* (1951) and E. C. R. Lorac's *Murder by Matchlight* (1945), suggesting that further critical reevaluation of the Golden Age and its aftermath is on its way.

Christie's own negotiation of the Second World War has been comparatively little studied, with scholarly discussion of Christie and conflict tending to focus on the aftermath of the First World War in her Golden Age novels. This may be because, as Stephen Knight has famously observed,

> Christie's [1939–1945] wartime mysteries superintend contemporary battles from a distance and with an Austenesque pattern of radical displacement, not recognizing the war as itself, but representing its effect in terms of disruptions to the normal balance of gender and social power. (163)

As Gill Plain suggests, this implies that "in the case of a writer like Christie, the dislocations of crime fiction symbolize, in manageable form, the alienating impact of war" (*Literature of the 1940s* 135). These socially disruptive and alienating effects of the Second World War are frequently recurring themes in feminist criticism that aims to recover forgotten women's writing from the first half of the twentieth century, as well as criticism designed to assert the value of middlebrow and popular fiction as revelatory of their context as well as objects of literary study. Kristine A. Miller, for instance, positions Christie, alongside Margery Allingham and Graham Greene, as a twentieth-century voice providing sometimes allegorical perspectives on the "complicated myth of the Blitz" (126). Gill Plain observes that the 1942 Miss Marple novel "*The Moving Finger* is firmly designed to assert stability in the face of change and to keep wartime trauma under control" ("A Stiff is Still a Stiff" 113). Jenny Hartley proposes a metaphorical rather than a direct relationship between Christie's writing and the Second World War, suggesting that, "[i]n a time of increased vulnerability, identity could be fragile" (170), and linking both detective narratives and Christie's pseudonymous novels exploring the fractured nature of women's identities to the raging conflict. While Plain's scholarly work in particular has been vital in broadening critical understandings of what constitutes war writing, commentary that deals with the intersection of detective fiction and social and historical context has tended to focus on gender. As Plain points out, bombs and "the 'war machine' had profound effects on domestic life and perceived gender roles, making explorations of "the perceived cultural disjuncture between [domestic] 'women' and [violent] 'war' vital for contemporary writers and subsequent scholars" ("Women Writers and the War" 166). The present volume uses the Second World War as a springboard to discuss broader themes of identity, history, and psychology in Christie's work and milieu, including but not limited to questions around gender.

As Plain, Light, and others have discussed, Christie's interwar fiction can be read as an ambivalent and elliptical response to the First

World War; Plain and Hartley suggest the same of the Second World War, which is indeed a tempting reading. What this collection identifies, however, is the complexity of these texts and their situation. Some of Christie's novels during the Second World War can be read as primarily escapist or nostalgic in nature; the seaside holidays of *Evil Under the Sun* (1941) and the country house of *The Body in the Library* (1942) come to mind. *N or M?* (1941) is the only novel to be situated as clearly within the Second World War as *The Mysterious Affair at Styles* is in the First. This is one reason they remained popular. As Plain observes, "By 1945, Britain was tired, and it sought distraction from its exhaustion in the pleasures of popular film and fiction" ("Escaping 1945" 34). Certainly, compared to the work of her contemporaries Marsh, Greene, and Allingham, which explicitly engage with the danger and privation of the Home Front and global theaters of war, Christie's wartime writing displays Knight's notion of "radical displacement". As demonstrated by chapters in this collection, then, a variety of readings are possible. These chapters examine how anxieties of social change, disruptive violence, and individual and communal survival generated during the First World War and its aftermath persisted in Christie's work into the 1950s and beyond, subtly shifting into concern about nation and isolation, recurring trauma, and rootless and unfixed identity. These preoccupations are shared by Christie's contemporaries—Lorac's *Murder by Matchlight*, for instance, hinges on the ease of assuming a false identity by purloining an identity card in the chaos of the Blitz, a theme that Christie picked up later in *Taken at the Flood* (1948) and *Mrs McGinty's Dead* (1952). Paula Bowles and Rebecca Mills suggest psychological themes of continuity between the First and the Second World War, for instance, while Brittain Bright argues for a moment of "drastic doubt" in the author's—and the detective's—authority during the Second World War.

In considering Christie as a war writer, the academy lags behind popular culture. Even the arch-conservative ITV television series *Agatha Christie's Poirot* (1989–2013) with David Suchet, which started out presenting a nostalgic vision of the interwar years untroubled by conflict beyond murders behind closed doors, spent its final series exploring national loss, grief, and the coming of a second war. More recently, the BBC has produced a series of dark, gritty Christie adaptations that foreground the presence and impact of war in the world they depict. In *And Then There Were None* (2015), characters were given backstories in which the First World War had directly damaged their psyches: actor Sam Neill followed the BBC line when promoting the program by stating, "[t]his book is set on the cusp of the Second World War and that must have been very much on Agatha Christie's mind when she wrote this book" (BBC). In *The ABC Murders* (2018), Poirot's immigrant status is prioritized, as he faces frequent abuse and harrowing memories in the course of his investigations. Christie's long-running West End play

The Mousetrap (1952), which has undergone frequent reinventions, now emphasizes its roots in immediate postwar British culture in promotional materials (Petty), and the themes of loss, trauma, and rationing are frequently picked up by reviewers over and above the traditionally interesting matter of the plot twist (Flutsch).

The contributions to this volume, therefore, open up new avenues of scholarship, some of which have already been explored beyond the academy, and introduce spirited debates alongside rigorous interdisciplinary analysis. In these pages, Christie is considered as a genre novelist, a propagandist, a playwright, a social commentator, and a figure of national unity. What unites contributors is an unwavering conviction that it is time to understand the best-selling novelist of all time as a key voice in the literature of war. Our focus is on the Second World War, during which Christie was at the height of her commercial success, even as the "Golden Age" of crime fiction waned. We have encouraged contributors to explore the buildup and aftermath because war, like so many topics of literature, cannot be easily limited to the dates we learn in school.

In "Mapping War, Planning Peace: Miss Marple and the Evolving Village Space, 1930–1962", Sarah Martin and Sally West establish Christie as a novelist concerned with the impact of war on community space, exploring three Marple novels set in villages reeling from international war. Exploring the First and—especially—Second World Wars' geographic, psychological, and social effects on village space, Martin and West consider how middle-class crime shifts and changes in insular responses to broader conflict. Paula Bowles, in "Christie's Wartime Hero: Peacetime Killer", also looks across a temporal span. Bowles examines Christie's presentation of ex-military servicemen in interwar texts and uncovers a nuanced approach to a stock character type.

Brittain Bright's "Writing through War: Narrative Structure and Authority in Christie's Second World War Novels" focusses on crime novels published during the Second World War, tackling the fraught question of modernity and its relationship to the past, at a time when both those concepts are being radically overhauled. Looking at Christie's experimental approach to memory and how this goes beyond thematic observation to inform the structure of plots and puzzles, Bright suggests a moment of crisis, while insisting that Christie negotiated the war for sensitive readers with candor and strategy.

War can be allegorical; it can also be direct. Merja Makinen makes the case for Christie as a forthright polemicist who highlights and undermines the manipulative power of dictators. Christie's little-studied thriller, Makinen insists, are "haunted by the figure of Hitler and how his evil oratory can persuade particularly the young to an orgy of destruction". Often overlooked by critics, Christie's thrillers have developed a reputation for being dashed-off and even confused, as they mingle the totalitarian threats of communism and fascism, but Makinen reveals a strategy underlying the presentation of apparently complicated yet fundamentally simple ideologies and their impact on shifting generations of youth. J. C. Bernthal argues not only that Christie was socially engaged but that this engagement accounted for a great deal of her success during the Second World War, bucking broader publishing trends that turned against the apparently escapist nature of puzzle-based crime fiction. Comparing Christie's presentation of food and rationing at the outset of the Second World War with comparative scenes in a late-war dramatization, Bernthal suggests that "informal meals provide textual spaces for attitudes to social change to reach a point of passionate crisis, where social coding is at its frailest".

Julius Green highlights Christie's productivity in the theater during and after the Second World War, noting that more than a demand for escapism underlay her emergence as a playwright. Examining how Christie "broaden[ed] her personal, socio-political, and intellectual frame of reference" partly through work as a "modern playwright" whose directly and self-consciously war-conscious scripts challenged as well as entertained their audiences. Christie's most famous play is the world's longest-running, *The Mousetrap* (1952), which, along with the novella it is based on, forms the basis of Federica Crescentini's contribution "'There are Things One Doesn't Forget': The Second World War in 'Three Blind Mice' and *The Mousetrap*". Crescentini identifies a "darkening" of adapted material despite the well-known maxim that mystery plays are lighter and more escapist than mystery stories. The darkness of *The Mousetrap* lies not only its direct mapping of a postwar environment, but also in its return to the real crime that inspired the plot. Darkness is not always a question of narrative style; sometimes, the most troubling and unsettling aspect of an escapist narrative can be how well and knowingly it sits in the real world.

In "Displaced Persons: *A Murder is Announced* and the Condition of Post-War England", Christopher Yiannitsaros revisits the much-discussed postwar masterpiece to consider a character too often politely ignored in discussions of Christie's work. Mitzi, a Jewish refugee who now works as a maid in a postwar English village, is apparently presented as a compulsive fantasist whose chief role in the fabric of the novel is to provide comic relief. However, Yiannitsaros probes deeper to consider "the dystopian reality of life lived in immediate post-war England", where promises that individuals can carve new identities are shown to be compromised by a struggling but surviving hierarchy of social prejudice.

Rebecca Mills examines texts produced further after the Second World War, but with no less psychological difference. In her analysis of the Blitz as it lingers in the memory of Christie, her characters, and her readers, Mills unearths a "dynamic of absence and resurfacing", as the traumatic upheavals of 1940–41 are never over and, despite the whodunit narratives, never neatly resolved. The collection closes with

"'The *Thrill* When It Suddenly Went Pitch Black!': Blackout Cultures in *A Murder is Announced* and *The Mousetrap*", in which Roger Dalrymple takes the study of the Blitz in a different direction. Linking what he calls the "gift to crime writers" of sudden plunges into darkness with the much more traumatic reality of blackouts, Dalrymple considers the gothic memories of war underlying blackout scenes in Christie's postwar work. Christie's engagement with the war here is also her negotiation of it; a blackout on stage or in the pages of a book does not represent an unknown or international enemy, but a single, already present, and soon to be unmasked criminal. Dalrymple, therefore, proposes a conscious and productive relationship between the public and the personal, society and community, the unknown and the intimate.

In 2005, Charles Rzepka noted that

> war, the Holocaust, the atomic devastation of Hiroshima and Nagasaki, all had demonstrated the limited impact of reason when pitted against the powers of darkness, and Golden Age authors now had to acknowledge the transformation of their tidy world of country villages and manor houses, of eccentric sleuths and convenient fingerprints. (227–28)

A focus on war and its echoes in Christie's work challenges this narrative of the Golden Age's "tidy world" definitively and indeed the concept of a temporally limited Golden Age itself. Christie's postwar—and interwar—work does indeed often take a "darker turn"; one reason for this is because it is often a belated expression of collective and individual war trauma, but another is an expression of paradoxical creativity and innovation amid the aftermath of ruin that confronts the destabilization and inadequacy of authority, rather than the exhausted limits of a cozy puzzle-based genre. War is not a backdrop but a structuring principle in Christie's prolific career, and Christie emerges from this volume as an essential voice in the discussion of war, warfare, and twentieth-century literature.

Notes

1 For more on intermodernism, see Kristin Bluemel's *Intermodernism: Literary Culture in Mid-Twentieth-Century Britain* (2009).
2 For more on women's middlebrow writing, see Nicola Humble's *The Feminine Middlebrow Novel 1920s to 1950s* (2001).

Works Cited

BBC. "And Then There Were None: General MacArthur". 2016. www.bbc.co.uk/programmes/profiles/23Ssp4TsTHWtRNyK1PxF0H5/general-macarthur Accessed 1 Jun. 2019.

Bluemel, Kristin, ed. *Intermodernism: Literary Culture in Mid-Twentieth-Century Britain*. Edinburgh University Press, 2009.

Christie, Agatha. *An Autobiography*. 1977. Collins, 2011.

Churchill, Winston. "Their Finest Hour" [Speech to the House of Commons]. 18 Jun. 1940. https://winstonchurchill.org/resources/speeches/1940-the-finest-hour/their-finest-hour Accessed 28 Jun. 2019.

Flutsch, Catherine. "Review: The Mousetrap". *Plays to See*, 3 Mar. 2019. www.playstosee.com/the-moustrap-2 Accessed 1 Jun. 2019.

Hartley, Jenny. *Millions Like Us: British Women's Fiction of the Second World War*. Virago, 1997.

Humble, Nicola. *The Feminine Middlebrow Novel 1920s to 1950s*. Oxford University Press, 2001.

Knight, Stephen. "Murder in Wartime". *War Culture: Social Change and Changing Experience in World War Two*, edited by Pat Kirkham and David Thoms, Lawrence & Wishart Ltd., 1995, pp. 161–72.

Lassner, Phyllis. "Under Suspicion: The Plotting of Britain in World War II Detective Spy Fiction". *Intermodernism: Literary Culture in Mid-Twentieth-Century Britain*, edited by Kristin Bluemel, Edinburgh University Press, 2009, pp. 113–30.

Mackay, Robert. *The Test of War: Inside Britain, 1939–1945*. UCL Press, 2003.

Miller, Kristine A. *British Literature of the Blitz: Fighting the People's War*. Palgrave Macmillan, 2009.

Petty, Moira. "The Mousetrap: Secrets of the World's Longest-Running Play Revealed". *Daily Express*, 25 Nov. 2017. www.express.co.uk/entertainment/theatre/884205/The-Mousetrap-Agatha-Christie-worlds-longest-running-play-secrets Accessed 1 Jun. 2019.

Plain, Gill. "Escaping 1945: Popular Fiction and the End of the War". *Long Shadows: The Second World War in British Fiction and Film*, edited by Petra Rau, Northwestern University Press, 2016, pp. 33–56.

———. *Literature of the 1940s: War, Postwar and 'Peace'*. Edinburgh University Press, 2013.

———. "'A Stiff is Still a Stiff in this Country': The Problem of Murder in Wartime". *Conflict, Nationhood and Corporeality in Modern Literature: Bodies-at-War*, edited by Petra Rau, Palgrave Macmillan, 2010, pp. 104–23.

———. "Women Writers and the War". *The Cambridge Companion to the Literature of World War II*, edited by Marina MacKay, Cambridge University Press, 2009, pp. 165–78.

Priestman, Martin. "Post-war British Crime Fiction". *The Cambridge Companion to Crime Fiction*, edited by Martin Priestman, Cambridge University Press, 2003, pp. 173–90.

Rzepka, Charles. *Detective Fiction*. Polity, 2005.

Scaggs, John. *Crime Fiction*. Routledge, 2005.

Smith, Michael. *Bletchley Park: The Code-Breakers of Station X*. Shire, 2013.

Stewart, Victoria. *Narratives of Memory: British Writing of the 1940s*. Palgrave Macmillan, 2006.

Wyndham, Francis. "Agatha Christie Writes Animated Algebra: Dares One to Solve Buried Basic Equation". *Waterton New York Daily Times*, 1966, pp. 4, 9.

1 Mapping War, Planning Peace
Miss Marple and the Evolving Village Space, 1930–1962

Sarah Martin and Sally West

In his essay "The Guilty Vicarage" (1948), W. H. Auden famously delineates the structural features of the detective story in an attempt to "throw light [...] on its magical function" and account for his own self-confessed addiction to the genre (406). Auden identifies certain "rituals" associated with the classic detective novel, one of which is the "milieu", or setting, which he divides into "human" and "natural" (407–08). The human milieu should be a closed society of some description, for instance, a "closely knit geographical group (the old world village)" (407). During the course of the story, this "natural" element of the milieu will be navigated by its "human" inhabitants, therefore: "In the detective story, as in its mirror image, the Quest for the Grail, maps (the ritual of space) [...] are desirable" (408). While Auden's concern is to identify the features that combine to create the perfect detective story, of which setting is one, his use of the term "ritual" can be explored not simply as a formal feature of the genre but a process that takes place in the action of the novel itself.

In Agatha Christie's Marple novels, the setting of the English "old world village" allows characters to enact "the ritual of space" in a particular way; the battle between murderer and detective is frequently waged in not merely geographical but psychogeographical terms. Guy Debord defines psychogeography as the "specific effects of the geographical environment, whether consciously organized or not, on the emotions and behavior of individuals"; characteristics of physical space thus affect the thoughts and behavior of those who inhabit it (10). This chapter argues that in the village milieu of the Marple novels, supremacy in the battle between detective and criminal is dependent on who has better control of this enclosed space and therefore possesses a clearer understanding of its inhabitants and their behavior. However, the character of village space in the Marple novels undergoes significant shifts in tone and texture as the twentieth century develops, at least in part in response to the traumatizing effects of two World Wars. Our investigation seeks to characterize the nature of some of these changes, focusing on the different ways in which the village terrain is "mapped", both by its inhabitants and by the external forces of town planning. In doing so, a picture emerges of Christie as an author who, far from writing as if "the Great War had never happened" (Scaggs 48), was intimately engaged with the local effects of shifting social changes brought about by global conflict.

From the interwar period of the 1930s to the postwar capitalist setting of the 1960s, we can identify significant cultural shifts in the meaning of maps. To appreciate the wartime attitude toward maps in Britain, the position of Germany provides a useful juxtaposition. In *History of the World in Maps*, Philip Parker observes that, in Germany, "the art of mapping for political purposes [...] was refined during the period [...] after 1933", as maps came to be used as "tools of state propaganda" (180). This reflects how a map's meaning can be culturally constructed, giving it more significance than its primary or assumed purpose of outlining mere geographical boundaries in an objective manner. Through the aid of maps, a Greater Germany could be conveyed in an image of ownership and power. Britain, however, accorded maps a very different symbolic meaning in a culture of war. Rather than a tool of propaganda to be celebrated and distributed, maps become, in a British context, a potential weak point in the war effort and their use and publication were strictly controlled. Amy Bell notes that "representations of London—in detailed maps or photographs—were restricted or forbidden during war time" due to growing "concerns [...] over who had access to information that might help the enemy" (157). Bell observes how fears regarding the enemy's knowledge of the space of Britain are apparent in the control of map orders under the War Measures Act, 4 July 1940, which decreed: "no person will acquire a map of any part of the UK or Isle of Man drawn to scale [...] except under authority of a licence [...] no alien shall have in his possession after 10th of July 1940 any map of the UK or Isle of Man" (157–58). This attention to the "intimate details of the UK's Geography" (Bell 158) marks the terrain of Britain as vulnerable and requiring protection, which could be exploited and manipulated by the enemy.

This way of seeing a landscape also aligns with Britain's own use of the intimate details of enemy space as a tool in wartime strategy. Peter Chasseaud notes that "a crucial part of the intelligence push to prepare for the [D-Day] invasion was the production of detailed maps" (189). That Britain used maps and studied the geography closely, using photographs and postcards to look at the features of the terrain as well as the geographical environment, begins to paint a picture of how the space of an area, the contours of its geography, the very terrain and details of landscape, can form a strategic tool. Space can be used, exploited, and manipulated. Moreover, maps symbolize knowledge in British culture, and this becomes exclusive knowledge, available only to those few granted the privilege of handling maps as war time strategy. With Chasseaud's suggestion that aerial photos were key additions to the maps, we can begin to see how the geographic strategy of war needed multiple perspectives in order to possess a spatial advantage. As W. Balchin observes, "it is the intelligent use of geographical knowledge that outwits the enemy and wins wars" (160). Balchin further notes how the development of geography as a discipline expanded rapidly in the interwar years, as a consequence of the subject's strategic utility in the First World War.

Via the central importance of village space to both committing and detecting crime in Agatha Christie's novels, there is an increased focus on the meaning of geographical, objective place and the more metaphysical, subjective perspective of space through technical geography and mapping in the interwar years. The relationship between the superficially domestic world of Christie's villages and the context of global devastation, and painful reconfiguration brought by two World Wars, has been critically recognized, but frequently dismissed as merely exhibiting an "ideological motivation to recover, or return to, a previous period characterized by stability and order" (Scaggs 47). Commenting on the social unreality of Christie's fictional worlds, Scaggs continues: "the physical and social settings are so isolated from post-war depression that it is as if the Great War never happened" (48).

However, it is possible to find distinct engagements with the context of war in Christie's texts. Gill Plain suggests that the conflict between detective and criminal in wartime and postwar crime fiction can be read as a microcosmic version of the conflict between nations on the global stage. Because of the detective's successful identification and eradication of the criminal, "the reading of crime fiction offers both vicarious agency and a fantasy of resolution in the face of [the] almost unbearable uncertainty" of war (Plain 138). In the years following the First World War, Plain argues, writers sought to produce a "narrative of explication" characterized by "a desire to reconfigure criminal responsibility as something more excusable, or, at least, something that might be rehabilitated" (241). In this context, Christie's "physical and social settings" deserve a reassessment in terms of how they reflect twentieth-century postwar contexts. This reassessment can be achieved by observing how the inhabitants of these spaces, in particular Christie's spinster detective, Miss Marple, interact with, attempt to control, and "map" their local physical environments post–First World War, post–Second World War, and in the context of developing town planning in the 1960s.

The Ritual of Space: Defining the Village

The dislocating effects of the First World War were still being felt in the collective psyche when Christie published *The Murder at the Vicarage* in 1930; the futile devastation was still a recent memory, and the promise of a second war was a growing reality. The delineation of war-conscious modernity is evident only sixteen years prior to the publication of

Christie's first Marple novel with Wilfred Owen asking, in "Anthem for Doomed Youth", "what passing bells for these who die as cattle?" (1). This registers an increased introspection, a turn to the significance of the individual human subject, in the context of the trauma of war, the likes of which we see displayed in Christie's texts. As Alison Light observes, the type of interwar fiction produced by Christie and her Golden Age contemporaries was "embracing of modernity, shaped by the experience of dislocation after the First World War and fueled by essentially pacific rather than aggressive urges" (11). The study of the social anxieties of a close community through the vehicle of the cozy blanket of "popular fiction" offers a perfectly microcosmic stage on which to anatomize a destabilized world. Christie's map of St. Mary Mead symbolizes this introspective vision of society.

The presence of the compass in the left-hand corner of the map in British editions of *The Murder at the Vicarage*, along with the details of house sizes and the positioning of trees, gates, and gardens, allows an intimate and exclusive view of the space, fixing, and clarifying details available in the text. This perspective provides the amateur detectives in Christie's readership with a spatial advantage akin to that sought by those behind the drive toward increased geographical mapping during the First World War. The presence of the map functions akin to Yi-Fu Tuan's suggestion that

> the map is God's view of the world since its sightlines are parallel and extend to infinity [...]. The landscape picture, with its objects organized around a focal point of converging sigh-lines, is much closer to the human way of looking at the world. (123)

Perhaps the most striking piece of information, which the map provides, is the central position of Miss Marple's house within the village, highlighting the way in which her perspective straddles both objective and subjective perspectives of space. While the map alludes to her "god like" perception, she is still at the very heart of the village social space, subject to the everyday "human way of looking at the world".

Like the guard in Jeremy Bentham's Panopticon, Marple is granted, by virtue of her physical position, her an all-encompassing vision.[1] The presence of the map in *The Murder at the Vicarage* reifies, in this physical presentation of the space, the social centrality of Miss Marple to the village community so apparent in the text. As the novel's narrator Leonard Clement informs us, "Miss Marple always sees everything. Gardening is as good as a smoke screen, and the habit of observing birds through powerful glasses can always be turned to account" (26). It is the combination of spatial location and social observation that affords Marple the knowledge to solve the crime.

If we consider the cultural significance of the map in wartime, then, Christie appears to offer her readers a tool to navigate the fictional and microcosmic territory of St. Mary Mead and potentially "defeat the enemy" in the form of the novel's criminal. The presence of the map, therefore, enhances the "vicarious agency", which, Plain argues, detective fiction offers to a disempowered interwar readership. More than this, however, the map and the position of Marple's house in it become symbolic of her ability to view and thus detect. As she reminds us, from her "little garden [...] one simply cannot help seeing anything that is going on next door" (101).

If, as Plain has suggested, the effects of the First World War created a more introspective consciousness (3), the map's limited scope and apparently distinct boundary could be read as symbolic of a feeling of togetherness in the face of adversity and a certainty about the social identity of those included in the close-knit community. In this context, it is significant that the map cannot encompass Old Hall, home of the Protheroes, its existence only indicated by a road snaking off to the west. As Old Hall is the home of both the first victim and one of the murderers, the construction of village space represented by the map visually anticipates the necessary ejection of undesirable elements from the community. Of course, interestingly, Redding's property is also similarly and symbolically peripheral and detached. As the plot develops, we become aware of the network of vision, "the detective instinct of village life" (47), which exists, at least in part, as a result of the geography of the space. Christie's map crystallizes the network of surveillance existing in the vision and knowledge of old women in the village, as "there is no detective in England equal to a spinster of uncertain age with plenty of time on her hands" (47). The vicar's wife, Griselda, articulates how this spinster surveillance operates:

> Mrs. Lestrange went out at a quarter past eight and hasn't come in yet [...] it isn't to Dr. Haydock's, Mrs. Wetherby does know that, because she telephoned to Miss Hartnell who lives next door to him and who would have been sure to see her. (18)

Notable here is the interconnectedness of the village; its networks of snooping and gossip are enabled through physical proximity: through geography and intimate knowledge of space. Notably, this network of surveillance also functions as Mezei suggests: "The spinster is nevertheless uniquely situated as an instrument of surveillance precisely because of her marginal and indeterminate position" (104).

The interconnectedness of village space functions as a part of both Marple's detection *and* Laurence Redding's criminal plot. In her analysis of the plot to kill Protheroe, Marple notes that both conspirators "realized [that she is] a noticing kind of person" (362). Marple acknowledges here that members of the community, especially those with nefarious intent, understand they are subject to her gaze as a consequence of her spatial and social centrality. Anne Protheroe and Redding attempt to subvert and exploit the vision and informal surveillance she practices over the space and try to match Marple through a spatially constructed social performance. First, Anne deliberately passes Miss Marple's garden, stopping to speak to her "so as to give [Miss Marple] every opportunity of noticing that she has no weapon with her and also that she is quite her normal self" (362). Second is the performance of leaving Redding's studio, where, apparently, the lovers break off their relationship. This is a display for Miss Marple's benefit because, as she notes: "I'm afraid they realize that I shan't leave the garden till they come out again" (363).

However, the social performance of the murderers does not match their presupposed more intimate one: "In reality, they made a mistake. Because if they had really said goodbye to each other, as they pretended, they would have looked very different" (363). It is Marple's central position in the map of the village that offers her a commanding view across the terrain and of the activities of its inhabitants. However, it is her understanding of spatial and social performance that enables her to penetrate the misdirection of the suspects. Anne and Redding are aware that they are subject to the gaze of Marple's detection; however, while they recognize her detective instinct or observation, they do underestimate her powers of understanding spatial performance. While the criminals attempt to construct their own performance, Marple's physical and psychological mastery of the village space allows her to solve the crime. It allows her to distinguish a staged and mannered (theatrical) performance from real life, owing to her own psychogeographical ability. She is aware of how her gaze affects others' behavior in the space, which allows her to assess the veracity of their performance: "human nature being what it is" (363), she could not help but *observe*.

In *The Murder at the Vicarage*, we can observe a development in the mapping of postwar village space. The safe and circumscribed physical map, which delineates both the geographical and social borders of St Mary Mead, is revealed to have complex, more psychological submaps superimposed upon it; Redding and Anne Protheroe attempt to chart a physical course that will ensure that their social performance is accepted and that their crime thus escapes detection. Miss Marple, however, reveals a better knowledge of her village's geography, of "human nature" and, importantly, of how these things are intimately connected. As Auden observes in "The Guilty Vicarage", both committing and solving crime requires an intimate knowledge of the rituals of the given environment: "The murderer uses his knowledge of the ritual to commit the crime and can be caught only by someone who acquires an equal or superior familiarity with it" (408). In line with the aims of cartographers at the forefront of developing mapping as war strategy during, and following, the First World War, Marple is commander of her terrain and defeats the enemy. Two decades and another war later, the village space will have transformed again and require a new kind of cartography for its navigation.

The Hidden Map: Cartographical Subversions

In Christie's presentation of the second post–World War period of twentieth-century Britain, gone is the certainty of the fixed, physical map to accompany the text; a new uncertainty necessitates a new means of interacting with physical space. In *A Murder Is Announced* (1950), Christie depicts the impact of the Second World War on ideas of community and national identity. As John Curran comments, the novel is "a convincing picture of an England stumbling out of post-war austerity [...] The shadow of rationing and bartering, deserters and foreign 'help', ration books and identity cards hovers over the book" (487). On a global scale, the map of Europe is altered through shifting borders and immigration, while in the microcosm of the village, we see a transformation in the individual's relationship with space, both physically and psychologically, caused by the trauma and dislocation of war. Perception of belonging—or not—in a given space affects the experience of national, personal, and social identity. In place of the real map presented in *The Murder at the Vicarage*, we see the development of the interior or, as Lili Pâquet terms it, cognitive map in *A Murder Is Announced* (53). Though Pâquet does not discuss the cognitive map in relation to the text specifically, the notion of a "cognitive map", an internalized map superimposed over the physical space, recalls the feelings of introspection in the wake of the First World War; the exterior geography is navigated via an inner collective consciousness. Once again, in the aftermath of war, questions of identity and the individual's significance or place in the world are raised, with the human subject as the core of the examination through the vehicle of the crime story. This is charted through the characters' relationships with space, this time symbolized in the cognitive map.

In the St Mary Mead depicted in *The Murder at the Vicarage*, "no one [...] lock[s] their house up" (138). By the time of *A Murder Is Announced*, the practice of unlocked doors in a village has gained a further practical advantage: open houses allow the surreptitious exchange of goods on the black market. Such freedom of movement is, of course, frustrating in the case of a murder investigation. As Mrs. Swettenham blithely admits to Sergeant Fletcher, "We all walk in and out of each other's houses, sergeant, nobody dreams of locking a door until it's dark" (185). Networks of cognitive maps are superimposed on the village space through open houses, which enable the exchange of goods within the postwar community. Such maps are again a source of knowledge and power; knowing who has what to exchange allows an added insight into the day-to-day lives of the inhabitants of Chipping Cleghorn. That the community "all walk in and out of each other's houses" dismantles the concept of public/private spaces and creates communal pathways, through houses, around the space. These pathways, however, are not accessible to all; the exclusive cognitive map of the village is accessible only to those belonging to the black-market network of exchange and barter.

The map of open houses creates ways of traversing the village space without suspicion through the exchange of goods, which provide an agenda for navigating the space of people's private housing. Mrs. Harmon enlightens Inspector Craddock regarding a cryptic note from Miss Blacklock about leaving something for her *"in the usual place"* (276, emphasis original). She says:

> It's all a bit hush hush, you know, a kind of local scheme of barter. One person gets butter, and sends along cucumbers, or something like that [...] you know the sort of thing. Only one can't, very well, say it right out to the Police. Because I suppose quite a lot of this barter is illegal—only nobody really knows because it's all so complicated. But I suspect Hinch slipped into Little Paddocks with a pound of butter or something and had put it in the *usual place*. That's a flour bin under the dresser, by the way. (277, emphasis original)

Craddock's bemusement at Mrs. Harmon's revelation indicates the exclusivity both of the village's network of exchange and of the cognitive map that allows that network to function. In this instance, both Miss Blacklock and Miss Hinchcliffe enact the ritual of space; they are aware of the identity of *"the usual place"*, of the unlocked doors that enable goods to be left there, and of the safest times to do so. In Craddock's professional experience, an individual's presence in a space without a clearly expressed reason is suspect. However, as Miss Marple points out, "You must make allowances for the times we live in, Inspector" (276), times when surreptitious barter and exchange allow the continuance of this rural economy.

Looking at people's motives for their presence within the space allows an insight into a community reshaped by war and by the commodification of people through exchange value. The ways in which the members of the community negotiate their movement through the public/private space of people's houses are directly influenced by the exchange value of goods and, by extension, of the people who produce those goods within the closed space of the village. The blurred boundary between public and private space allows the network to manipulate the way in which space usually constructs social identity—in this case, the normality of casual social calls—but it also restructures the identity of community members in a different way through their commodification. Their exclusive membership of the network is gained only through the exchange value of their produce. A person's presence within a space, and the very nature of the routes through that space, start to become defined by a new capitalist hegemony that exists as a direct consequence of war.

We can argue that Christie is exploiting the new black-market economy, which flourished in response to rationing to enhance the traditional Golden Age plot device that all "suspects must be guilty of something" (Auden 409) or, at the very least "have something to hide" (Knight 89). The disinclination of certain members of the village network to admit involvement in this illegal system of exchange leads Craddock and Fletcher to erroneous suspicions, prolonging the official police investigation and thus delaying the revelation of the true culprit (276). It is true that freer movement through the postwar space and the uncertainty over fixed identity that ensues grants Christie wider opportunities in terms of plot. In *A Murder Is Announced*, Miss Marple offers her detective services to Craddock thus: her "snoop[ing]", natural to the old lady, can help the police "to find out if people are who they say they are" (163):

> [T]hat's really the particular way the world has changed since the war. Take this place, Chipping Cleghorn, for instance. It's very much like St. Mary Mead where I live. Fifteen years ago one *knew* who everyone was. [...] They were people whose fathers and mothers and grandfathers and grandmothers, or whose aunts and uncles, had lived there before them. If somebody new came to live there, they brought letters of introduction, or they'd been in the same regiment or served in the same ship as someone already there. If anybody new—really new—really a stranger—came, well, they stuck out—everybody wondered about them and didn't rest till they found out. (163–64)

Here, Marple articulates the network of familial or professional connections that bind the inhabitants of a rural community to its space. Prior to the Second World War, a village like Chipping Cleghorn was composed of the known and those securely connected to the known. The dislocation of war threatens the integrity and insularity of the rural space, but the danger, as Craddock muses, is that old habits die hard: "the subtler links that held together English social rural life had fallen apart. In a town nobody expected to know his neighbor. In the country now nobody knew his neighbor either, *though possibly he still thought he did ...*" (165, emphasis added).

In this context, the security of the network of movement and exchange of goods that maps the space of Chipping Cleghorn is potentially a dangerous illusion. It is no longer certain that "people are who they say they are", but the open doors and communal knowledge of the location of secret domestic spaces necessitated by the black-market exchange network demonstrates that the community is behaving as if that certainty still exists, taking people at their "own valuation" (164). It is significant that the first suspects in the case are Rudi Schertz and Mitzi, the novel's representations of the foreign, as Christopher Yiannitsaros discusses elsewhere in this volume. Wendy Webster notes that after the Second World War, Eastern Europeans in particular were seen as a threat, as "migration to Britain brought fear of the collapse of boundaries" of the home and of the country (152). Here, the concept of boundaries has both social and spatial significance. Myrna Harris's comment in *A Murder Is Announced* that "you never know where you are with foreigners" (63) expresses succinctly this casual postwar xenophobia, but also implies a connection between the "where" and the "who", suggesting that the "foreign" elements cannot be entrusted with knowledge of exclusively English networks. It is notable, for instance, that Mitzi seems to play no part in the black-market network of exchange in the novel, regardless of the fact her position requires her to acquire and make use of all kinds of rationed goods.

In the reconstructed cognitive map of the village, Christie thus reveals the dangerous insularity of rural environments like Chipping Cleghorn and St Mary Mead, where residents believe that they can identify an outsider from accent and appearance. That the map is "cognitive" or imagined suggests that so too is this ideal of the inviolable English community. The village's attempt to maintain a lost sense of "Englishness", an exclusivity that binds a community together in the face of global fragmentation, is shattered by murder. This reveals Christie's recognition of the constructed nature of such communities that refuse to adapt postwar. As Ackershoek observes,

> The danger inherent in believing in things and people that are not what they seem and of clinging to an illusory reality that does not adapt to change is central to Christie's work. It may well have had its roots in the dramatic changes World War I brought to British society. (127)

A Murder Is Announced suggests that, after the Second World War, the inhabitants of rural settings are still failing to adapt to the inevitability of social and spatial change, as the reconstructed map of the village is revealed only to provide an illusory sense of safety. The threat, of course, does not come from without, but from within. This community insularity regarding the inevitable expansion of social and cultural boundaries cannot be maintained, however. A little over a decade later, Christie's engagement with the consequences of expanding village and suburban spaces is more explicitly presented in Miss Marple's encounter with "the Development" in *The Mirror Crack'd from Side to Side* (1962).[2]

Mapping the Future: The Development

As the Marple novels moved into the 1960s, Christie used her detective to reflect upon the changing nature of village space as the country began to gain a little more confidence in its peace. At the beginning of the novel, Marple states, "One had to face the fact: St. Mary Mead was *not* the place it had been [...] nothing was what it had been. You could blame the war (both of the wars)" (11, emphasis added). The rural society depicted in this novel still exhibits some of war's lingering influences, but also looks forward, if ambivalently, to the influence of town planning policies, which were to significantly reconfigure social space. Altered space requires altered means of mapping in order to traverse its contours and in this, as in so much else, and despite increasing age, Miss Marple proves adept. If the immediate postwar rural economy of *A Murder Is Announced* required a shared cognitive map to navigate the village space, the world of *The Mirror Crack'd* explores the effects of the external imposition of housing developments and commercial spaces on the community.

Space affects behavior. Where that space is designed by external authorities, for the use of a diverse community, any individual's identity in that space will be contingent on the competing identities of others coexisting there. Town planning is, in essence, social engineering. Henri Lefebvre's *The Production of Space* (1974) develops a theory that connects physical, mental, and social spaces, and is concerned with the power dynamics inscribed in precisely the relationship between spaces as *conceived* by an external agency and spaces as *lived* by its inhabitants. For Lefebvre, social space is a social product and therefore a potential "means of control, [...] of domination, of power" (26). Borrowing terms from Chomsky, Lefebvre argues that we each possess spatial "competence" and enact spatial "performance" as part of our daily routine (33). We have already suggested that Christie engages with what could be called spatial performance in Redding and Anne Protheroe's unsuccessful attempt to subvert Marple in *The Murder at the Vicarage*. Thirty years on, *The Mirror Crack'd* engages much more explicitly with the potential of engineered social space to construct and manipulate social identity.

Initiatives like the "New Towns for Old" project of 1942, which outlined the development of new towns, gained an increased urgency in the context of the destruction brought by war. In addition to increasing housing stock, the project also intended, through planning the shape and structure of the new towns, to engender "a sense of community life" as a means of combatting the fear of fractured communities following increased movement out of city space ("New Towns for Old" 7).[3] The aims of this project thus accord with Lefebvre's theories of social space: there *was* actually an agenda in postwar society to recreate not only a physical place to live, but a *community* in which the individual felt a sense of belonging. Moreover, we can describe this as a psycho-geographically implemented sense of community—an inorganic sense of belonging to the space and society. The very space is cultivated in order to control the way the inhabitants of the society think, feel, and behave.

A visual model from the "New Towns for Old" project presents the sort of idealized reconstruction of new towns after the war, demonstrating how the government was attempting to implement a sense of community through the geographical organization of towns and human beings into "sections". The model is in the form of a wheel split into wedges. Three "Residential" sections are interspersed with three of "Green Wedge", one "Commercial", one "Industrial", and one "Bazaar". A railway link is indicated at one end of the space, running through the industrial and one of the residential sectors. The intended effect seems to be a fruitful balance of human habitation, commercial business of one form or another, and relaxing green space. However, in its shape and structure, the model suggests a distinctly panoptical town space. It is designed with the intention that individuals living within the space are supposed to be peering into each other's lives, in order to enforce a feeling of community; without choice, neighbors are displayed to neighbors.

Envisaged in 1942, reconstruction of this type was to have taken a minimum of ten years. In 1962, Christie provides an insight into just such a spatial and social reconfiguration of rural space in the form of "the Development" in *The Mirror Crack'd*, which "had an entity of its own, and a capital letter" (325). Miss Marple, still residing in the "old" St Mary Mead, reflects on the difference between being outside and inside this newly socially constructed space:

> [S]he had seen the Development from the Market Basing Road, that is, had seen from afar its Closes and rows of neat well-built houses, with their television masts and their blue and pink and yellow and green painted doors and windows. But until now it had only had the reality of a map, as it were. She had not been in it and of it. (331)

Christie's description here registers a tension between the uniformity imposed by town planners and the desire for individuality expressed by the residents of the Development. Only the differing colors of the painted woodwork indicate individual ownership and taste. Furthermore, this description registers Marple's position as outsider. To her, the Development had only the two-dimensional quality of a "map", and she "had not been in it and of it". The ideology driving the New Towns project aspires to what Michel Foucault called a heterotopic space. Foucault explains: "[Heterotopias] present society itself in a perfected form, or else society turned upside down, but in any case these utopias are fundamentally unreal spaces" (Foucault 3). Marple reflects that this "brave new world [...] was like a neat model built with child's bricks. It hardly seemed real. [...] The people, too, looked unreal" (*Mirror Crack'd* 331). The social space created by the Development is an "unreal" yet "ideal" space in its inorganic but idealized (re)production of society.

In town planning initiatives like the Development, the map comes first; imposing a spatial structure on the terrain creates the resulting social structure. That community space is something produced and commodified suggests a blurred boundary between reality and a mere simulation of it, to use Jean Baudrillard's term (1–42); the inorganic production of community affects the ways in which that community functions and social identity is produced. As we have seen in the map of St. Mary Mead, which accompanies *The Murder at the Vicarage*, originally Marple lay in the very heart of the space, with a sweeping vision across the village from the vantage point of her garden. However, the sprawling development of this rural community compromises her view of the totality of the area and posits a new center to the panopticon of social visibility. As a consequence, Marple must adapt her methods of relating to this new space in order to understand its nature and that of its inhabitants. In doing so, she is able to acquire the knowledge that will prove vital in unravelling a future crime.

Marple possesses a source of information about the Development in the form of Cherry Baker, who does—or tries her best to do—Marple's housework. Cherry's language in relation to Marple's personal signposts in microcosm the difference in their spatial experiences. Cherry "always called Miss Marple's old-world overcrowded drawing-room the lounge" (326). That the very signifier used to describe the same space has transformed, emphasizes the temporal shift in attitudes toward the intimate space of the home, and, by extension, other social spaces as well. At the start of *The Mirror Crack'd*, Cherry is Miss Marple's link to the uncharted territory of the Development. Christie tells us of Cherry Baker, that

> Miss Marple liked her very much [...] She was one of the detachments of young wives who shopped at the supermarket and wheeled prams about the quiet streets of St. Mary Mead. They were all smart and well turned out. Their hair was crisp and curled [...] They were like a flock of happy birds. (326)

Here, Christie identifies how town planning reproduces social identity; the "happy flock of birds" are all visually uniformed, and their routes through the Development defined and predictable. They embrace the new supermarket (which is treated with much suspicion by the older residents of the village) and manifest visually, in their "smart" clothes and "curled" hair, a comfortable and comforting uniformity. These "detachments of young wives" represent in microcosm precisely the manifestation of community, which was the aim of the "New Towns for Old" project.

Marple's relationship with Cherry gives her some vicarious access to the world of the Development, but she is not content with second-hand knowledge. So it is that Marple, "[w]ith the feeling of Columbus setting out to discover a new world" (*Mirror Crack'd* 331), takes on the role of psychogeographer, exploring the terrain of the Development, giving herself up to the influence of the space. That the space is a "new world" confirms the uncharted nature of this new part of St. Mary Mead, but that Miss Marple is characterized as "Columbus" indicates that the space is one which she will soon understand and uncover for herself; it will become an equally "owned" space through her voyage of discovery. Psychogeography posits a dialectical relationship between human behavior, emotion, and experienced identity and the spaces and places in which that individual exists. While created spaces can impose their social structure upon inhabitants, individual wanderings about the terrain can be revelatory of individual psychology; how one interacts with one's landscape, the details one notices, and, importantly, the route one chooses to take through that landscape, all reveal something of the self. In contrast, then, to Lefebvre's focus on the potentially constraining properties of the urban landscape on the behavior of its occupants, the individual psychogeographer challenges official representations of space and opposes any authority that seeks to restrict, physically or mentally, the individuality of the wanderer. We have seen in *A Murder at the Vicarage* that Marple has mastery of her space through familiarity. Now she must begin a voyage to integrate herself into the new space of the Development. As Marple travels through the space of the housing estate, we are presented with a psychogeographical map of its contours as she forges an individual route through it: "Miss Marple passed over the bridge, continued on the path and within four minutes was actually in Aubrey Close" (331). Now she is both "in" and "of" the space.

It is a constant in Christie's Marple novels that her detective capitalizes on the social stereotypes associated with elderly spinsters. Assumptions about scattiness, unworldliness, and the limitations imposed by increasing physical decrepitude make the elderly spinster an ideal undercover detective. By the time of *The Mirror Crack'd*, Marple is feeling her age and thus experiences the change in her community with some melancholy and bemusement. However, her instinct to consider these changes close up by broaching the physical space of the Development allows a realization that her detective powers have not been dulled by age and that her mind can adapt to the changing space. Her initial impression of the unreality of the Development's inhabitants gives way to "her usual series of recognitions" (331); body language and overheard snatches of conversation reveal to her that "[t]he new world was the same as the old. The houses were different, the streets were called Closes, the clothes were different, the voices were different, but the human beings were the same as they always had been" (332). She begins to notice similarities between the residents and people she has known before; human nature, she realizes, remains constant. In her anxiety to inform a young woman that her beau is possibly not marriage material, Marple stumbles and is taken, "[w]ith almost excessive goodwill" (333), into the house of Heather Badcock. Whilst recuperating with a cup of tea, Marple learns of Heather's prior meeting with the actress Marina Gregg and is presented with the key piece of information, which will solve the case of Heather's murder as the novel unfolds. The Development might be new, but Miss Marple realizes that as the people are the same, she can still utilize her detective skills and master the space. Allowing Heather to accept her as a frail old lady in need of help enables Marple to penetrate the inner space of the Development and, eventually, to identify the murderer of one of its inhabitants.

Conclusion

What Auden terms "the ritual of space" (408) in the classic detective story becomes, in Christie's hands, an opportunity for a subtle engagement with how the geographical and psychological landscape of Britain has altered in response to war. Far from representing a semi-repressed desire on the part of the national consciousness to return to a lost Eden, the village space of Christie's Marple novels is a shifting site, which registers the social changes resulting from the two world wars. As Plain comments, detective fiction is "arguably, the most socially responsive of literary genres" and, as such, we should expect to find in Christie's work "significant expression of cultural anxieties" (134). Furthermore, Christie's depiction of the changing nature of village space across the middle years of the twentieth century does not function merely as a suitable backdrop to her plots.

As we have seen, the clear spatial shifts as a consequence of war shape and reshape the detection process of Jane Marple; her psychogeographical methods of detection develop in tandem with the changing nature of space over time. Marple is aware that "St. Mary Mead was not the place it had been [...] nothing was what it had been. You could blame the war" (*Mirror Crack'd* 11), yet she is able to adapt her detective processes to the demands of changing space through her understanding of how that space affects the thoughts and behavior of those with whom she shares her community.

Notes

1 "Panopticon" the prison created by Jeremy Bentham and discussed by Michel Foucault in the following way:

> Like so many cages, so many small theatres, in which each actor is alone, perfectly individualized and constantly visible. The panoptic mechanism arranges spatial unities that make it possible to see constantly and to

recognize immediately. In short, it reverses the principle of the dungeon [...]. Full lighting and the eye of a supervisor capture better than darkness, which ultimately protected. Visibility is a trap. (Foucault 200)

2 *The Mirror Crack'd from Side to Side* was published as *The Mirror Crack'd* in the United States.

3 Information about housing policy in the mid-century and the "New Towns for Old" project can be found in the archive "Housing 1938–1948" in the Mass Observation Archive (www.massobservation.amdigital.co.uk/Documents/Details/TopicCollection-1). Martin and West are grateful for the free trial that MOO provided the University of Chester Library in 2017, which enabled this research to be conducted.

Works Cited

Ackershoek, Mary Anne. "'The Daughters of His Manhood' Christie and the Golden Age of Detective Fiction." *Theory and Practice of Classic Detective Fiction*, edited by Jerome H. Delamater and Ruth Prigozy, Greenwood Press, 1997, pp. 119–28.

Auden, W. H. "The Guilty Vicarage: Notes on the Detective Story, by an Addict". *Harper's Magazine*, May 1948, pp. 406–12.

Balchin, W. "United Kingdom Geographers in the Second World War: A Report." *The Geographical Journal*, vol. 153, no. 2, 1987, pp. 159–80.

Baudrillard, Jean. *Simulacra and Simulation*. The University of Michigan Press, 1994.

Bell, Amy. "Landscapes of Fear: Wartime London, 1939–1945." *Journal of British Studies*, vol. 48, no. 1, 2009, pp. 153–75.

Chasseaud, Peter. *History of the World in Maps*. HarperCollins, 2016.

Christie, Agatha. *The Mirror Crack'd from Side to Side*. 1962. *Miss Marple Omnibus 2*. HarperCollins, 1997.

———. *The Murder at the Vicarage*. 1930. HarperCollins, 2007.

———. *A Murder is Announced*. 1950. HarperCollins, 2002.

Curran, John. *Agatha Christie's Secret Notebooks: Stories and Secrets of Murder in the Making*. 2009. HarperCollins, 2016.

Debord, Guy-Ernest. *A Critique of Urban Geography. Situationalist International Anthology: Revised and Expanded Edition*. Edited by Ken Knabb, Bureau of Public Secrets, 2006.

Foucault, Michel. *Discipline and Punish: The Birth of the Prison*. Translated by Alan Sheridan, Penguin Books, 1991.

———. "Of Other Spaces: Utopias and Heterotopias". *Architecture/Mouvement/Continuité*. Translated by Jay Miskowiec, Oct. 1984, http://web.mit.edu/allanmc/www/foucault1.pdf Accessed 1 Mar. 2019.

Knight, Stephen. *Crime Fiction 1800–2000: Detection, Death, Diversity*. Palgrave Macmillan, 2004.

Lefebvre, Henri. *The Production of Space*. Translated by Donald Nicholson-Smith, Blackwell, 1991.

Light, Alison. *Forever England: Femininity, Literature and Conservatism between the Wars*. Routledge, 1991.

Mezei, Kathy. "Spinsters, Surveillance, and Speech: The Case of Miss Marple, Miss Mole, and Miss Jekyll". *Journal of Modern Literature*, vol. 30, no. 2, 2007, pp. 103–20.

"New Towns for Old" Project. "Housing 1938–1948". Mass Observation Archive www.massobservation.amdigital.co.uk/Documents/Details/TopicCollection-1 Accessed 22 Sep 2019.

Owen, Wilfred. "Anthem for Doomed Youth." 1917. *The War Poets: An Anthology*. Parke Sutton, 2009.

Pâquet, Lili. "Kathy Reichs's Contiki Crime: Investigating Global Feminisms." *CLUES: A Journal of Detection*, vol. 33, no. 1, 2015, pp. 51–61.

Parker, Phillip. *History of the World in Maps*. Harper Collins, 2016.

Plain, Gill. *Literature of the 1940s: War, Post-war and 'Peace'*. Edinburgh University Press, 2013.

Sassoon, Siegfried. "Aftermath." *The War Poets: An Anthology*. Parke Sutton, 2009.

Scaggs, John. *Crime Fiction*. Routledge, 2005.

Tuan, Yi-Fu. *Space and Place: The Perspective of Experience*. University of Minnesota Press, 2001.

Webster, Wendy. *Englishness and Empire 1939–1965*. Oxford University Press, 2007.

2 Christie's Wartime Hero
Peacetime Killer

Paula Bowles

The centenary of the end of the First World War, a conflict that has been scrutinized in many disciplines including history and sociology of war, was commemorated on 11 November 2018.[1] Furthermore, the representation of the conflict in literature, as well as film and television, is widely recognized and extensively explored by scholarly critics and popular commentators. In particular, the war poems of soldiers such as Rupert Brooke, Wilfred Owen, and Siegfried Sassoon, are indissolubly associated with this conflict. Certainly, Alison Light draws on Wilfred Owen's poetry to discuss the absence of explicit violence within Christie's novels (70). While for many today, these poets appear to encapsulate the very essence of the First World War, they were relatively unknown until after the Armistice and therefore form part of a mythologized narrative (Robb 145–51). Indeed, G. D. Sheffield suggests that contemporary views of the First World War identify the conflict "as a uniquely terrible episode in a conflict that achieved nothing' (55).[2] History has a tendency to be male-dominated, particularly within discussions around warfare, but that is not to say that women have made no contribution. Authors such as Edith Abbott, Margaret Mead, Caroline Playne, and Virginia Woolf have all reflected on war and its impact.[3] To this list can be added the work of Agatha Christie, who, through her crime novels, offers an unusual insight into contemporaneous popular understanding of conflict.

A close reading of Christie's crime novels reveals a distinct typology of ex-servicemen, and this will be explored here in more detail. Each of these ideal types, while not all violent, have Christie's frequent disavowal of the hero motif. For Michael Holquist, the popular identification of a hero includes such attributes as "courage", "resourcefulness", and an ability to see beyond institutional and societal frameworks, to do what needs to be done, regardless of personal cost (138). Such identification is not unique; Christopher Prior has alluded to similar themes with his statement that

> Christie's villains do not conform easily to any of the four principal criminal types in post-war mainstream cinema—the spiv, the

delinquent, boy-next-door, the gangster and the maladjusted Second World War veteran—with the partial exception of the last. (10)

Criminology traditionally has had far less to say about war than the other disciplines mentioned above, partly due to its British iteration appearing decades after the First World War.[4] While Garland identifies the intellectual roots of criminology in the late nineteenth century, he suggests that in Britain, the academic discipline, as recognized today, did not exist until 1935 (1). Additionally, as Wayne Morrison has argued, war and conflict have been seen by many within criminology as distinctly removed from the discipline's everyday concerns with exploring crime, justice, and penology (52). As he perceptively notes, "In a [twentieth] century literally awash with human blood and reeking with the stench of corpses, mainstream criminology seemed to inhabit another world" (Morrison 52). However, in recent years, apprehension has been raised about the supposedly disproportionate numbers of ex-servicemen perceived to be serving prison sentences.[5] These concerns have centered on crimes of violence, particularly sexual and domestic, against known women and have led to questions being raised in the media,[6] within criminal justice agencies, and in parliament. Although these organizations and individuals tend toward framing this as a twenty-first century problem, evidence from scholars such as Edith Abbott and bodies such as the Advisory Council on the Treatment of Offenders (ACTO) suggests that this concern can be traced through both world wars and beyond.[7] These texts are generally academic, governmental, or organizational, and there has been no attempt to explore the phenomenon of criminal ex-servicemen in popular culture. This chapter addresses this neglect, by focusing on the recurring figure of the violent criminal ex-serviceman within the crime novels of Agatha Christie.

According to Carolyn Nordstrom, when thinking about violence, researchers need to be critical of assumptions, whether academic or popular (148). Yet, such an approach is not straightforward; Kenneth Morgan warns, in relation to media reports from the Boer War, that such accounts turned from relatively plain descriptions of events to "a jumble of fiction and fact, legend, symbolism, and stereotypes" (16). Elizabeth Burney has identified the importance of nineteenth-century literature to understanding crime and punishment at that time, and it seems plausible that such an approach would also work in relation to twentieth-century writing (160–61). An interdisciplinary approach, such as that taken in this chapter, is not unique in studies of Christie's work; for instance, Herbert Kinnell has forged a similar trajectory, highlighting the reoccurrence and importance of medical doctors in Christie's books. Taking into account the enduring popularity and global reach of Agatha Christie's work, it seems both timely and apposite to explore the phenomenon of criminal ex-servicemen through the lens of her crime literature.

Christie's extensive bibliography incorporates a great many crime novels, short stories, and plays. From Christie's first publication, *The Mysterious Affair at Styles*, the military motif is evident. In this crime novel, unusually for Christie, war forms an explicit and unmistakable backdrop to events. Certainly, *The Mysterious Affair at Styles* diverges from Alison Light's claim that Christie's novels are generally "apparently outside history" (62). Although Christie provides no overt commentary on the war, throughout the text she includes a number of temporal and geographical clues, some ambiguous, others less so, removing any doubt about the timing of events. Undoubtedly, Christie explicitly advises the reader that Hercule Poirot is a refugee fleeing war-torn Belgium, while Arthur Hastings is seeking solace and recuperation from his time on the Western Front. Their meeting, after many years apart, in the incongruous setting of a village post office, involves an elaborate greeting, including the soon-to-be familiar cry of "*Mon ami*, Hastings! [...] It is indeed *mon ami* Hastings!" (23). Thus, the friendship is rekindled, and Hastings provides a detailed description of his good friend Poirot:

> Poirot was an extraordinary-looking little man. He was hardly more than five feet four inches, but carried himself with great dignity. His head was exactly the shape of an egg, and he always perched it on one side. His moustache was very stiff and military. The neatness of his attire was almost incredible; I believe a speck of dust would have caused him more pain than a bullet wound. Yet this quaint dandified little man who, I was sorry to see, now limped badly, had been in his time one of the most celebrated members of the Belgian police. (23)

The description of the man provides military references in relation to his facial hair and attire and thus sets the scene for the novels to come. Alison Light insists that the sheer theatricality of Poirot ensures that he is never mistaken for a "soldier hero" (73). Although there is no suggestion that Poirot is a soldier himself, the military language, selected by Hastings, firmly places both characters in the *milieu* of warfare. Undoubtedly, the characteristics identified by Hastings stress discipline, self-control, and orderliness. Likewise, Poirot's physical impairment, though not explicitly connected to the conflict, supports notions of duty and sacrifice. While not unique to military service, such characteristics could act as a shorthand for positive societal contribution, particularly during and after 1914–18. Such shorthand could not directly answer Savile Lumley's populist poster asking *Daddy, What Did You Do in the Great War?* Nevertheless, such a description indicates an overt veneer of respectability and a clear riposte to any putative concerns around wartime service (Robb 208–25).

Despite Alison Light's argument that Poirot's "refugee status is usefully ambiguous" (74), neither his attire nor manner support the pervasive stereotype of a refugee in terms of narratives around vulnerability. For example, Emma Stewart identifies the struggle many young refugees face noting that "when young people exercised their agency, or did not conform to expectations of vulnerability, they were denied support" (87).[8] Tony Kushner notes that the vast majority of Belgian refugees were professionals, like Poirot, and some of the descriptions of Belgian refugees in the UK were uncannily Poirot-like. Lady Battersea's diary recorded that "Belgians are simple and pleasant like children, rather vain and conceited about their appearance" (qtd. in Kushner 11). A further illustration is provided by the experience of "Lady Rodney" who donated the use of cottages for the benefit of the Belgian refugees (Kushner 9). Both examples are instantly recognizable within *The Mysterious Affair at Styles* published just four years after the Armistice.

Other references to the conflict include two female characters; one is employed in a pharmacy as part of the Voluntary Aid Detachment (VAD) and the other as a Land Girl. Additionally, Mrs. Inglethorp insists that the residents of Styles "are quite a war household", noting that meal times are reduced and nothing is wasted (Christie 13).[9] Similarly, discussions around the availability of petrol to the Styles household implicitly raise the wartime crime of black-marketeering.[10] Finally, Hastings's narrative that he had spent time convalescing from his wounds inflicted at the Somme Offensive, prior to arriving at Styles to continue his recuperation, make the temporal parameters of the novel explicit.

Graham Dawson has identified the hagiographic accounts of military men, such as T. E. Lawrence (of Arabia), as contributing to contemporary understandings of both heroism and masculinity (167–230).[11] Michael Holquist outlined the essential requirement for a hero in much postwar literature, insisting that

> a lone hero can still keep us all from being blown up. At a time when enormous destruction is in the hands of faceless committees, it is reassuring indeed to follow the adventures of a single man who, by exploiting the gifts of courage and resourcefulness which have always characterized the hero, can offset the ineffectiveness of government. (138)

In the twenty-first century, it is commonplace for commentators and academics to position ex-servicemen as heroic and sacrificial. These attempts to homogenize individual military identities and experiences lead to the mythologizing of the "soldier" as heroic, sacrificial, and ultimately, superior to civilians.[12] As Rachel Woodward stresses,

> The warrior hero is physically fit and powerful. He is mentally strong and unemotional. He is capable of both solitary, individual pursuit of his goals and self-denying contribution towards the work of the

team. He's also a bit of a hero with a knack for picking up girls and is resolutely heterosexual. He is brave, adventurous, and prepared to take risks. (643–44)

Christie does not offer this as a contemporary view. Indeed, the only mention of heroism is a vaguely sardonic exclamation from John Cavendish, announcing Hasting's arrival to the house party with the words "Here's our wounded hero" (8). Beyond this comment, Hastings's war experiences appear to be of no interest to the other characters, who are far more interested in civilian affairs, both before and after the murder. This phenomenon has been discussed in detail by Gill Plain in relation to the work of Christie and other crime writers, such as Margery Allingham and Graham Greene. According to Plain, the primacy of one murder renders even world wars temporarily forgettable, if not invisible (105). Thus, Christie does not explain Hastings's role in combat; although she identifies that Hastings was not a regular, professional soldier, but how he came to be a serviceman, whether conscript or volunteer, is not recorded. Hastings's war experience is referenced in later novels—*Murder on the Links* (1923) and *The Big Four* (1927)—where it becomes clear that he served as an officer with the military rank of captain. Although soldiering and war form a distinct part of Hastings's character, they are firmly in the past and appear to have little or no place in his dealings with Poirot beyond the occasional inclusion of his military title. Despite this, Hastings's military service is quietly apparent through textual references to his military bearing, discipline, devotion to duty, and his willingness to observe rank. This can be seen strikingly in Christie's *Peril at End House* (56) whereby Poirot raises concerns around what he describes as Hastings's "prejudices". While Hastings insists that the Royal Naval officer, later exposed as a drug dealer, is "alright [...] I'm sure of that. A real pukka sahib" (56), such a pronouncement only fuels Poirot's suspicions.

William Westley (1966) drew attention to an apparent cultural confusion when it comes to violence, particularly its portrayal in the media and most notably in murder mysteries. He suggested that "While we [the audience] do not glorify violence [...] neither do we abhor it" (125). In Christie's crime novels, murderers and purveyors of violence abound. Equally prevalent, although often less explicit within her writing, is the motif of the former military man. Christie's life span (1890–1976) encompasses much of Albert Camus's "century of fear" (27), and it is therefore perhaps unsurprising that the motifs of war and ex-servicemen run throughout much of her work. Certainly, it would be unfathomable for Christie to be entirely immune from the troubled world that both she and Camus inhabited whilst writing. A number of her recurring characters have military backgrounds—Captain Hastings, Colonel Race, Thomas Beresford—but these positive representations of military men only tell part of the story. Counter to these heroes are the negative portrayals and the absence of hero worship in Christie's critical view of military men, whereby these ex-soldiers are presented variously as tedious, unintelligent, unimaginative, untruthful, physically or mentally damaged, or intrinsically vicious. Alison Light has insisted that Christie "was consistent in her rejection of the heroic" (74). However, Christie's writing goes beyond this, taking full advantage of society's idealized vision of heroism, subverting this supposed excellence, into something far more sinister and ultimately, lethal.

This chapter continues by focusing on those fictional individuals identified as a "Wartime Hero; Peacetime Killer". Crucially, this chapter will contextualize Christie's dangerous ex-servicemen in light of criminological writing. Several criminologists have discussed the impact of war on (ex-)servicemen, and some of this research will be used to examine Christie's identification of the soldier as inherently problematic and, in many cases, dangerous. Certainly, Gimbel and Booth identify an increase in antisocial behavior among veterans and link this to "the military experience", which they claim "socializes soldiers to seek combative solutions to problems or because certain men find violent or combative solutions to problems rewarding" (692).[13]

Type 1: The Dull and Irritable Ex-Servicemen

In Christie's writing, dull and irritable ex-servicemen are generally former officers, often Anglo-Indian, and regularly appear as background characters. For example, in *Dumb Witness* (1937), the late General Arundell has the misfortune to be described as both "boring" and "stupid" (114). The commentator, Miss Peabody, compounds this critique by insisting that "I've always heard that intelligence didn't get you far in the army" (115). Likewise, Colonel Carbury's appearance is dismissed as unmilitary in *Appointment with Death* (1938), while his demeanor is described as almost entirely inert (111). Light has argued convincingly that Christie, as well as other authors, both male and female, "found a kind of modernity in making fun of heroes" (70). Similarly, Christopher Prior has suggested that "Christie was not above poking fun at older imperial characters", identifying "the harrumphing retired colonial military figures" as a "stock recurring stereotype" (8). While this type of old soldier is generally presented as un-heroic, they are not necessarily criminogenic. However, as Christie has convincingly demonstrated, "theoretically nobody was incapable of the ultimate crime" (Prior 8).

Type 2: The Deceitful Ex-Servicemen

Christie's second military type can be described as exaggeration-prone, if not liars, particularly when it comes to their experience of military service. For example, the veracity of both Captain Warburton and

Sir George Stubbs's claims, in relation to their military service, are called into question in *Dead Man's Folly* (1956). The reinterpretation of personal experience is not necessarily suspicious, after all there may be good reasons not to disclose a (potentially dishonorable) discharge from the military.[14] However, in the case of Stubbs, his deliberate lies relate directly to his own military criminality, desertion. Edith Abbott and John Spencer have suggested a continuum of deviance before, during, and after military service. Although there is no final denouement, Stubbs's guilt is made clear in the text, supporting a continuum of criminality extending throughout military and civilian life.

Type 3: The Physically Damaged Ex-Servicemen

A number of characters in Christie's writing were physically injured while undertaking military service and this group makes up the third type of ex-servicemen. For instance, Hastings's injury during the Somme Offensive led to his discharge from the military during the First World War, as we are informed in *Murder on the Links*. Similarly, Major Knighton is injured in the same conflict, but in this instance, Christie utilizes his supposed physical war wounds as a plot device to consolidate his reputable status in *The Mystery of the Blue Train* (1928). In the text, Katherine Grey makes clear the details of his war injuries, noting that he was

> shot in the leg, if I remember rightly—rather a nasty business. I think the doctors messed it up a bit. They said he wouldn't limp or anything, but when he left here he was still completely dot and go one. (127)

Furthermore, the major is keen to reminisce to Poirot about the time he spent convalescing in the Riviera hospital, far away from the mayhem of the First World War. Despite Christie providing a number of further clues, intimating that Knighton's limp was an unexpected surgical outcome of his treatment during the conflict, it is not until the final revelation that the pretense becomes obvious. Here, the supposed respectability of the retired military man, particularly one who has been injured while serving "King and Country", is used as shorthand to divert attention away from the character's guilt.[15] Despite Major Knighton's supposed good character in wartime, he is unmasked as a cold-blooded murderer. Indeed, in his closing statement, Poirot exclaims damningly that the former soldier "is a killer by instinct" (215).

Type 4: The Mentally Damaged Ex-Servicemen

The penultimate type of military criminal observable in Christie's *oeuvre* is that of the mentally damaged ex-servicemen. It is acknowledged that traumatic war experiences are neither confined to combatants nor necessarily causal factors in criminality. This is a point recognized by Hastings when he suggests in relation to Poirot's foibles that perhaps "the war had affected the little man's brain" (*Styles* 38). *The ABC Murders* (1936) provides a striking case study, in which previous debilitating war experiences are almost enough to condemn an innocent man. In this novel, the unfortunate Mr. Cust, is used to misdirect the reader into believing he is a serial murderer. While Mr. Cust insists that he "enjoyed the war" and "felt, for the first time, a man like anybody else" (181), it becomes evident that it is his experiences in the conflict that holds the key to solving the crime. The implied motive is his mental state after military service; the war "unsettled me", he admits, adding "My head's never been right since. It aches" (89). This lingering tension complicates Light's presentation of Christie's interwar writing as the perfect antidote to wartime anxieties, including neurasthenia or shell shock (71).

While incidents of shell shock are well-documented in relation to the First World War, this record was not always sympathetic, and those suffering were liable to be viewed with suspicion.[16] For example, in 1919 both Charles Burtchaell and Douglas McMurtrie were keen to put the blame for shell shock and other neurotic conditions firmly on the individual rather than the military. They both insisted that it was the soldier's inherent weakness rather than war that caused such problems (Burtchaell 527–40; McMurtrie 151–59). With equal cynicism, Grafton Elliott Smith and Tom Pear (1919) intimated that soldiers utilized a diagnosis of shell shock as a mechanism for escaping from the military during the First World War.[17] Such a perspective would seem to negate historian Caroline Playne's (1933) verdict on the First World War[18]; that "all this anarchy is the outcome of *men's* disordered minds", which firmly advocates that any madness lies more in waging war than in individual psychopathology (*Britain* 9, emphasis original). This is a point made more explicit some years later by George Pratt (1944), who stressed that "'shell-shock' is the most natural thing in the world [...] and should never be interpreted as signs of weakness or fragility of the man's personality structure" (55). Thus, the epithet "mad" cannot be applied to those using any means possible to escape from the horrors of industrialized warfare.

A further, more damning dimension was introduced by T. W. Standwell in 1920, when he claimed that the First World War veterans were using a diagnosis of shell-shock as a defense in criminal trials. For Standwell attempts to introduce mental illness as mitigation were seen as "excuses that these present criminals were war heroes, whose exuberances must be forgiven because they had been 'through it'" (62). The use of the word "excuses" challenges more sympathetic and individualistic approaches to criminality. After all, as Clarence Darrow noted, "[n]o one can understand conduct without knowing something of the psychology of human action" (39).[19] Undoubtedly, without Poirot's knowledge of both criminal psychology and Mr. Cust's own personality, it is likely that the story would have had a very different ending.

Although Cust's full appellation "Alexander Bonaparte Cust" is flamboyantly and deliberately suspicious, it is Christie's subtle inclusion of details relating to his military service and subsequent mental health, coupled with the apparent serendipity of events, people, and places, which ensures his place as prime suspect (Christie *ABC*). In essence, Christie's sleight of hand—relying on the reader's conflation of "madness" with "badness"—invites the suspicion of Mr. Cust. As Light makes clear, without recognition of her perceived readership, Christie would have been unable to pull off her startling plot twists. Of course, such a device could only work if the connections between military service, shell shock, and deviance had already been established. With or without a medical diagnosis of mental illness, Willard Waller suggested that

> *The veteran is, and always has been a problematic element in society, an unfortunate misused, and pitiable man, and, like others whom society has mistreated, a threat to existing institutions.* (12–13, emphasis original)

For readers with a similar worldview, Mr. Cust makes the perfect suspect, perhaps a little too perfect, but difficult to resist nonetheless. Fortunately, Poirot is not swayed by such subtle deception, instead recognizing Cust's inherent victimization. Furthermore, Poirot understands that this victimization comes not only from society, but is deliberately driven by the murderer, Franklin Clarke, with Cust implicated every step of the way. Ultimately, without Poirot's sympathy, not to mention the exercise of his "little grey cells", poor Mr. Cust would likely be facing the executioner (7).

Marc Alexander has similarly noted such "scenario-dependence and reader manipulation" (1) in relation to Christie and domestic servitude and stressed the taken-for-granted, unspoken roles of many of her characters. This conflation between military service, mental illness, and criminality is revisited in the later novel *After the Funeral* (1953). On this occasion, a criminal profile suggests that the likely suspect is a "brutal, perhaps slightly half-witted type—a discharged soldier or a gaol bird" (66). Despite advances in science, many of these concerns around the relationship between military service, mental disorder, and criminality remain in the twenty-first century.[20]

Type 5: The Violent Ex-Servicemen

The final group of former military men who crop up with regularity across Christie's novels are the unpredictable men: violent ex-servicemen for whom war has offered a temporary outlet for their supposedly "natural" instincts. In essence, wartime military service offers a unique opportunity and environment for violent men to excel using skills, methods, and techniques, which, in a civilian context, would undoubtedly be deemed criminal. As one of the most important academics in British criminology,[21] Hermann Mannheim, noted in 1941,

> [H]uman beings can, as a rule, endure only limited amounts of any specific sentiment. If they get their necessary quantum of violence by war, no further violence may be needed. To that extent war may act rather as an outlet for men's pugnacious instincts than as a stimulus to them. (127–28)

Certainly, in relation to the character of David Hunter in *Taken at the Flood* (1948), his prior military service, particularly in combat, means that Superintendent Spence is convinced of his guilt. While recognizing Hunter's bravery and heroism as essential to the war effort, Spence is clear that such characteristics do not generally translate well in civilian life. Spence notes that Hunter is the "kind that is likely to win the V. C.—though, mind you, it's often a posthumous one" (127). Spence's recognition that wartime action may not easily translate into peacetime living is supported by Charles Thompson's fervent declaration that:

> We might well keep in mind that society has its own crimes which, however, are not recognized as such because they are committed on so large a scale. Society has its mass-homicides called wars, its mass-robberies called invasions, its wholesale larcenies called empire building. As long as the individual's behavior fits in with the mass-reaction it is considered "good" behavior. As long as he does not question by word or deed the validity of the mass-behavior he may be called a "good citizen." (603)

The inclusion of the Victoria Cross (VC) in relation to David Hunter is thought-provoking. In 1920, King George V's Private Secretary Lord Stamfordham explained that

> [t]he King feels so strongly that, no matter the crime committed by anyone on whom the VC has been conferred, the decoration should not be forfeited. Even were a VC to be sentenced to be hanged for murder, he should be allowed to wear his VC on the scaffold. (qtd. in Smith 108)

It would seem that for Superintendent Spence there was also no incongruity between murder and medals. Furthermore, as Spence notes, the skills appreciated in military service might prove to be equally advantageous in civilian life, such as "Audacity and reckless disregard of personal safety", as well as the type of individual required, who was "The sort that will face any odds" (45). In addition, it is worth noting that Superintendent Spence's confident assertion is supported by experience, essentially, his own policeman's nous, which leads him to insist that "I *know* the type" (127; emphasis original). Despite this professional self-assurance, Poirot does not appear overly convinced, arguing instead that all Spence has achieved is a potential identification of "the *type* of killer" (128; emphasis original). As Willard Waller notes, the (ex-)serviceman "is a very specialized kind of human being, a trained and disciplined killer—indeed a kind of weapon" (21). He stresses that the soldier's "business, of course, is killing, and the army does a good job of conditioning him for it" (44). "But", Poirot argues, "that is all. It takes us no further" (*Taken at the Flood* 128).

Perspectives such as those put forward by the superintendent are not confined to fiction. Academics such as Edith Abbott (1918 "Crime") and Clarence Darrow (1922/2009) linked the release of prisoners in the UK and the United States directly to the military and their later reconviction in civilian life. Likewise, in 1920, the Chief Commissioner of the Metropolitan Police, Sir Nevil Macready, was convinced that violent crimes committed by ex-servicemen had been fueled by their wartime military service (qtd. in the *Manchester Guardian*). He suggested that unemployed young men joined up, "did their bit", and then returned to civilian life, with little regard for their own lives or those of others, as demonstrated by their violent criminality. Such a description would appear to fit the narrative contained within *Taken at the Flood*.

Arguably, Mannheim's research for *War and Crime* (1941) comes closest to supporting the view proposed by Superintendent Spence in *Taken at the Flood*. Writing in relation to the First World War, Hermann Mannheim insists as follows:

> No evidence could be found, for instance, for the belief that the soldier with previous convictions, or even the professional criminal, who turned soldier, behaved worse in any way that the man with a clean sheet. On the contrary, while his share in decorations for bravery exceeded the average, his crime rate was even lower as long as he found himself in the battle front. It was only when coming home on leave or staying in some quiet sport behind the lines that he frequently relapsed. (81–82)

Post–Second World War, the ACTO (1951) offers an official view on the phenomenon fictionally detailed by Superintendent Spence. As in the novel, the ACTO (1951) noted that many of those who served had civilian records of delinquency, if not legally defined criminality, prior to their enlistment. Furthermore, after a spell in the military, they returned to "civvy-street" and recommenced or accelerated their criminal lives. Ultimately, they concluded that "In war the criminal diverges from the ethical to a greater extent than in peace. This fact leads to a lessened respect for the law" (ACTO 113).

Walter Lunden also identified criminality prior to military service, as one of the main causal factors in relation to later offending, suggesting that "Their pattern of conduct had been fixed before they put on the uniform" (768). Additionally, he noted that those with a history of crime both before and after military service were also likely to express these deviant behaviors throughout their period of enlistment. Unfortunately, as John Spencer detailed, such a hypothesis is difficult to test, given the incompatibility of civilian and military records. In particular, during both world wars, Spencer identified the British military's aversion to importing civilian criminal records, preferring to allow men to start their service with a clean sheet (6–7). Nevertheless, John Spencer stressed that there was little evidence to support the argument that military service inculcated a callousness toward others, although he acknowledged that such a view is common (118–19).

Another perspective is offered by Perry Wagley, who drew attention to the perceived elevated status of the military man, suggesting that demobilization may cause a rupture in personal identity. He suggests that "Some of these soldiers will not be willing to accept their relatively insignificant pre-war status and will compensate by engaging in socially disapproved activities" (313). Whether these "socially disapproved activities" extend to murder, as in Christie's novels, for example in *Dead Man's Folly,* is not clear, but Wagley offers an alternative explanation for ex-servicemen's offending.

A similar narrative to that provided in *Taken at the Flood* is also apparent in *Dead Man's Folly,* where again the murderer has a history that encompasses military service. In this case, the elderly boatman, Narracott, gives Poirot his negative view of the (presumed dead) James Folliatt, remarking that

> he were real wild in his temper. Born one of they as can't go straight. But the war suited him, as you might say-give him his chance. Ah! There's many who can't go straight in peace who dies bravely in war. (45)

Clifton Bryant intimated that while military service may not be causally linked to criminality, there is an engrained propensity to recruit those "individuals who are especially prone to unconformity (as opposed to nonconformity) if not antisocial behavior" (38). After all, if an individual is ambivalent or abhors violence, they are unlikely to volunteer for military service, as the behavior and criminalization of conscientious objectors in both world wars demonstrates.[22] Clifton Bryant suggests that the tendency to attract a certain type of man to the military "may indirectly, if not directly, contribute to deviant tendencies" (39). Such a standpoint would appear to offer some support for Narracott's assessment in *Dead Man's Folly*.

While Narracott's view seems to support the idea of military service offering opportunity to the criminogenic individual, it is evident that this need not be accompanied by honorable discharge. Eventually, it becomes clear in this novel that the character has in fact deserted—a military crime. Writing two years earlier, John Spencer (1954) had also discussed deserters, suggesting that these men may "respond to the excitement of the battlefield, but certainly not to the demands of training" (50). In his research on Dartmoor prisoners, John Spencer identified that all had previously gone Absent Without Leave (AWOL), or had deserted while serving in the military. As a result of this, John Spencer connected dereliction of duty, whether temporary or permanent, to offending, before and after military service. In the case of James Folliatt and Sir George Stubbs, Christie makes this connection explicit in *Dead Man's Folly*.

Through her characters, Christie offers a radical interpretation of those usually considered heroes. Rather than a narrative which extols the virtues of those who have served their country, Christie details an alternate view of men who are intrinsically violent, both inside and outside of the military institution. It is clear that Agatha Christie, in her own distinctly English style, challenged, and continues to challenge, the archetypal representation of the soldier as a hero. Certainly, it is evident that for Christie, military service in wartime was not a signifier of intrinsic respectability but enough to make a man a credible murder suspect, if not a murderer.

Notes

1 See, for example, Hans Joas's *War and Modernity* (2003) and Siniša Malešević's *The Sociology of War and Violence* (2010).
2 This perspective is also iterated by Robb, who identifies the role of poetry and other literature in shaping "the public's concept of the war as a futile slaughter and a monstrous injustice" (220).
3 Robb identifies that for some commentators, women were seen as a causal or motivational factor for men's engagement in the First World War (48–50).
4 For further exploration of the history of British criminology see Mike Levi's "Emerged from the American Shadows? Reflections on the Growth of Criminology in the UK" (2017).
5 These concerns have been raised by organisations such as Napo (The Trade Union, Professional Association and Campaigning Organisation for Probation and Family Court Staff) in documents such as "Ex-Armed Forces Personnel and the Criminal Justice System" (2008) and "Armed Forces and the Criminal Justice System" (2009), and the Howard League for Penal Reform in *Report of the Inquiry into Former Armed Services Personnel in Prison* (2011), as well as Stephen Phillips's review *Former Members of the Armed Forces and the Criminal Justice System: A Review on Behalf of the Secretary of State for Justice* (2014).

6 See, for example, Ed Caesar's "From Hero to Zero" in *The Sunday Times* (2010).
7 For more on this theme, see Clarence Darrow, Milton Erickson, Hermann Mannheim, John Spencer, and Willard Waller. Details in the reference list.
8 For more on stereotyping around refugees, see Aoife O'Higgins.
9 Although outside of the purview of this chapter, it is remarkable that in this novel it is the women of Styles who are employed in war work and not the men (J. C. Bernthal, Gillian Gill).
10 For further discussion around black-marketeering see Clifton Bryant and Hermann Mannheim.
11 Likewise, Sheffield and Robb have explored the representation of the military hero in popular culture.
12 Examples of this valorisation of military men as heroes can be seen in literature from the HLPR, Helen McCartney, Emma Murray, Stephen Phillips.
13 For more discussion around problematic and often criminal ex-servicemen see Edith Abbott "Crime", ACTO, Hermann Mannheim, Edward Smithies, John Spencer.
14 For more discussion in this area, see Edith Abbott, Joanna Bourke.
15 This can similarly be observed in Christie's *Peril at End House*. On this occasion, Hastings professes the excellence of Commander George Challenger, failing to recognize that his hearty *bonhomie* obscures his cocaine dealing.
16 For greater focus on shell-shock see Joanna Bourke, *Dismembering*, "Effeminacy", Peter Leese.
17 The introduction of conscription in 1916 made such dereliction of duty a criminal offence (*cf.* Military Service Act 1916).
18 According to Sybil Oldfield (2004), "Caroline Playne analysed not just the popular press but also the drama, fiction, history writing, popular science, and political speeches of pre-war Europe" (12).
19 This can be seen in the deliberations involved in the successful appeal of "Marine A" (Morris).
20 For evidence of this relationship, see HLPR, Maleševic, McCartney, Murray Napo, and Phillips.
21 Levi (2017) identifies Hermann Mannheim alongside "Norbert Elias, Max Grünhut […] and Sir Leon Radzinowicz" as the founding fathers of British criminology (4).
22 For further discussion around conscientious objection see Brock and Vellacott.

Works Cited

Abbott, Edith. "Crime and the War." *Journal of the American Institute of Criminal Law and Criminology*, vol. 9, no. 1, 1918, pp. 32–45.

Advisory Council on the Treatment of Offenders (ACTO). "The War and Criminality in England and Wales." *The Effects of the War on Criminality*, edited by the International Penal and Penitentiary Commission, Stæmpfli and Cie., 1951, pp. 85–123.

Alexander, Marc. "The Lobster and the Maid: Scenario-Dependence and Reader Manipulation in Agatha Christie." *Annual Conference of the Poetics and Linguistics Association (PALA)*, 23–26 Jul., Sheffield, UK, 2008, pp. 1–9.

Bernthal, J. C., *Queering Agatha Christie: Revisiting the Golden Age of Detective Fiction*. Palgrave Macmillan, 2016.

Bourke, Joanne. *Dismembering the Male: Men's Bodies, Britain and the Great War.* Reaktion Press, 1996.

———. "Effeminacy, Ethnicity and the End of Trauma: The Sufferings of 'Shell-Shocked' Men in Great Britain and Ireland, 1914–1939." *Journal of Contemporary History*, vol. 35, no. 1, 2000, pp. 57–69.

Brock, Peter. *Against the Draft: Essays on Conscientious Objection from the Radical Reformation to the Second World War.* University of Toronto Press, 2006.

Bryant, Clifton D. *Khaki-Collar Crime: Deviant Behavior in the Military Context.* The Free Press, 1979.

Burney, Elizabeth. "Crime and Criminology in the Eye of the Novelist: Trends in Nineteenth Century Literature." *The Howard Journal*, vol. 51, no. 2, 2012, pp. 160–72.

Burtchaell, Charles. "Disease as Affecting Success in the War." *Transactions of the Royal Academy of Medicine in Ireland*, vol. 37, 1919, pp. 527–40.

Caesar, Ed. "From Hero to Zero." *The Sunday Times*, 4 Apr. 2010. www.timesonline.co.uk/tol/news/uk/article7084032.ece Accessed 8 May 2010.

Camus, Albert. *Neither Victims nor Executioners: An Ethic Superior to Murder.* 1946. Translated by Dwight Macdonald, Wipf and Stock Publishers, 2007.

Christie, Agatha. *The ABC Murders.* 1936. Pan Books Ltd, 1958.

———. *After the Funeral.* 1953. HarperCollins, 2014.

———. *Appointment with Death.* 1938. HarperCollins, 2016.

———. *The Big Four.* 1927. HarperCollins, 2016.

———. *Dead Man's Folly.* 1956. Collins, 1979.

———. *Dumb Witness.* 1937. HarperCollins, 2015.

———. *Murder on the Links.* 1923. Granada, 1978.

———. *Murder on the Orient Express.* 1934. Collins, 1978.

———. *The Mysterious Affair at Styles.* 1920. Collins, 1988.

———. *The Mystery of the Blue Train.* 1928. Pan Books Ltd, 1954.

———. *Peril at End House.* 1932. Collins, 1973.

———. *Taken at the Flood.* 1948. Collins, 1985.

Darrow, Clarence. *Crime: Its Causes and Treatment.* 1922. Caplan Publishing, 2009.

Dawson, Graham. *Soldier Heroes: British Adventure, Empire and the Imagining of Masculinities.* Routledge, 1994.

Elliott Smith, Grafton and Pear, Tom Hatherley. *Shell-Shock and its Lessons.* 2nd ed. The University Press, 1919.

Erickson, Milton Hyland. "Study of the Relationship between Intelligence and Crime: A." *Journal of Criminal Law and Criminology*, vol. 19, no. 4, 1929, pp. 592–635.

Garland, David. "British Criminology before 1935." *British Journal of Criminology*, vol. 28, no. 2, 1988, pp. 1–17.

Gill, Gillian. *Agatha Christie: The Woman and Her Mysteries.* Free Press, 1990.

Gimbel, Cynthia and Booth, Alan. "Why Does Military Combat Experience Adversely Affect Marital Relations?" *Journal of Marriage and Family*, vol. 56, no. 3, 1994, pp. 691–703.

Holquist, Michael. "Whodunit and Other Questions: Metaphysical Detective Stories in Post-War Fiction." *New Literary History, Modernism and Postmodernism: Inquiries*, vol. 3, no. 1, 1971, pp. 135–56.

Howard League for Penal Reform [HLPR]. *Report of the Inquiry into Former Armed Services Personnel in Prison*. Howard League for Penal Reform, 2011.

Hynes, H. Patricia. "On the Battlefield of Women's Bodies: An Overview of the Harm of War to Women." *Women's Studies International Forum*, vol. 27, no. 5–6, 2004, pp. 431–45.

Hynes, Samuel. *A War Imagined: The First World War and English Culture*. Pimlico, 1992.

Joas, Hans. *War and Modernity*. Polity, 2003.

Kinnell, Herbert. "Agatha Christie's Doctors." *BMJ: British Medical Journal*, vol. 341, no. 7786, 2010, pp. 1324–25.

Kushner, Tony. "Local heroes: Belgian Refugees in Britain during the First World War." *Immigrants & Minorities*, vol. 18, no. 1, 1999, pp. 1–28.

Leese, Peter. *Shell Shock: Traumatic Neurosis and the British Soldiers of the First World War*. Palgrave Macmillan, 2002.

Levi, Mike. "Emerged from the American Shadows? Reflections on the Growth of Criminology in the UK." *Newsletter of the European Society of Criminology: Criminology in Europe*, vol. 2, no. 16, 2017, pp. 4–8.

Light, Alison. *Forever England: Femininity, Literature, and Conservatism between the Wars*. Routledge, 1991.

Lumley, Savile. *Daddy, What Did You Do in the Great War?* 1915. Parliamentary Recruiting Committee. Imperial War Museum, London. www.iwm.org.uk/collections/item/object/17053 Accessed 2 Apr. 2018.

Lunden, Walter A. "Military Service and Criminality." *Journal of Criminal Law, and Criminology*, vol. 42, no. 6, 1952, pp. 766–73.

Maleševic, Siniša. *The Sociology of War and Violence*. Cambridge University Press, 2010.

Manchester Guardian. "From the Guardian Archive, 24 January 1920: Is There a Crime Wave in the Country?" 1920. *The Guardian*, 24 Jan. 2012. www.guardian.co.uk/theguardian/2012/jan/24/crime-wave-uk-1920 Accessed 2 Aug. 2012.

Mannheim, Hermann. *War and Crime*. Watts and Co., 1941.

McCartney, Helen, "Hero, Victim or Villain? The Public Image of the British Soldier and Its Implications for Defense Policy." *Defense & Security Analysis*, vol. 27, no. 1. 2011, pp. 43–54.

McMurtrie, Douglas C. *The Disabled Soldier*. The Macmillan Company, 1919.

Mead, Margaret. "The Women in the War." *While You Were Gone: A Report on Wartime Life in the United States*, edited by Jack Goodman, Da Capo Press, 1946, pp. 274–89.

Military Service Act. London, HMSO, 1916.

Morgan, Kenneth O. "The Boer War and the Media (1899–1902)." *Twentieth Century British History*, vol. 13, no. 1, 2002, pp. 1–16.

Morris, Steven. "Marine A, Who Killed Wounded Taliban Fighter, Released from Prison." *The Guardian*, 28 Apr. 2017. www.theguardian.com/uk-news/2017/apr/28/marine-a-alexander-blackman-released-from-prison Accessed 28 Apr. 2017.

Morrison, Wayne. *Criminology, Civilisation and the New World Order.* Routledge-Cavendish, 2006.

Murray, Emma. "Post-Army Trouble: Veterans in the Criminal Justice System." *Criminal Justice Matters,* vol. 94, no. 1, 2013, pp. 20–21.

Napo. "Armed Forces and the Criminal Justice System." 2009 *Napo,* www.lifechangeuk.com/_webedit/uploaded-files/All%20Files/Veterans%20Case%20Studies%202009%20(2).pdf Accessed 8 May 2010.

———. [The Trade Union, Professional Association and Campaigning Organisation for Probation and Family Court Staff]. "Ex-Armed Forces Personnel and the Criminal Justice System." 2008. *Napo,* www.napo.org.uk/publications/Briefings.cfm Accessed 8 May 2010.

Nordstrom, Carolyn. "Deadly Myths of Aggression". *Aggressive Behavior,* vol. 24, no. 2, 1998, pp. 147–59.

O'Higgins, Aoife. "Vulnerability and Agency: Beyond an Irreconcilable Dichotomy for Social Service Providers Working with Young Refugees in the UK." *New Directions of Child and Adolescent Development,* vol. 2012, no. 136, 2012, pp. 79–91.

Oldfield, Sybil. "Playne, Caroline Elizabeth (1857–1948)." 2004–2012, *Oxford Dictionary of National Biography.* www.oxforddnb.com/view/article/38530 Accessed 30 Mar. 2018.

Phillips, Stephen. *Former Members of the Armed Forces and the Criminal Justice System: A Review on Behalf of the Secretary of State for Justice.* Ministry of Justice, 2014.

Plain, Gill. "'A Stiff is Still a Stiff in this Country': The Problem of Murder in Wartime." *Conflict, Nationhood and Corporeality in Modern Literature: Bodies-at-War,* edited by Petra Rau, Palgrave Macmillan, 2010, pp. 104–23.

Playne, Caroline E. *Britain Holds On, 1917–1918.* George Allen and Unwin, 1933.

Pratt, George K. *Soldier to Civilian: Problems of Readjustment.* McGraw Hill, 1944.

Prior, Christopher, "An Empire Gone Bad: Agatha Christie, Anglocentrism and Decolonization." *Cultural and Social History: The Journal of the Social History Society,* doi: 10.1080/14780038.2018.1427354, 2018, pp. 1–18.

Robb, George. *British Culture and the First World War.* Palgrave Macmillan, 2002.

Sheffield, G. D. "'Oh! What a Futile War'; Representations of the Western Front in Modern British Media and Popular Culture." *War, Culture and the Media: Representations of the Military in 20th Century Britain,* edited by Ian Stewart and Susan L. Carruthers, Flicks Books, 1996, pp. 54–74.

Smith, Melvin Charles. *Awarded for Valour: A History of the Victoria Cross and the Evolution of British Heroism.* Palgrave MacMillan, 2008.

Smithies, Edward. *Crime in Wartime: A Social History of Crime in World War II.* George Allen and Unwin, 1982.

Spencer, John Carrington. *Crime and the Services.* Routledge and Paul, 1954.

Standwell, T. W. "Are You a Potential Post-War Criminal?" *Health and Strength,* 24 January 1920, p. 62.

Stewart, Emma. "Exploring the Vulnerability of Asylum Seekers in the UK." *Population, Space and Place,* vol. 11, no. 6, 2005, pp. 499–512.

Thompson, Charles B. "A Psychiatric Study of Recidivists." *The American Journal of Psychiatry*, vol. 94, no. 3, 1937, pp. 591–604.

Vellacott, Jo. *Bertrand Russell and the Pacifists in the First World War*. The Harvester Press, 1980.

Wagley, Perry V. "Some Criminologic Implications of the Returning Soldier." *Journal of Criminal Law and Criminology*, vol. 34, no. 5, 1944, pp. 311–14.

Waller, Willard Walter. *The Veteran Comes Back*. The Dryden Press, 1944.

Westley, William A. "The Escalation of Violence through Legitimation." *Annals of the American Academy of Political and Social Science*, vol. 364, Patterns of Violence, 1966, pp. 120–26.

Woodward, Rachel. "Warrior Heroes and Little Green Men: Soldiers, Military Training, and the Construction of Military Masculinities." *Rural Sociology*, vol. 65, no. 4, 2000, pp. 640–57.

Woolf, Virginia. *A Room of One's Own* and *Three Guineas*. 1938. Oxford University Press, 2008.

3 Writing through War
Narrative Structure and Authority in Christie's Second World War Novels

Brittain Bright

The Second World War marked an extraordinarily productive and experimental period of Agatha Christie's career. While her work of the 1920s was marked by its novelty, and ranged from masterpieces to damp squibs, she achieved a formal perfection in the 1930s, producing such classics as *Death on the Nile* (1937) and *Murder at the Vicarage* (1930). Following that period of accomplished consistency, the instability of Christie's writing during the war years is particularly notable. The novels that bookend the war years constitute some notable exceptions to Christie's oeuvre, including her only novel set outside of the twentieth century, and her only novel in which everyone dies. More significantly, though, several of these novels demonstrate a profound destabilization of narrative perspective, and in some cases a radical departure from the patterns of work produced before and after. Their forms pose questions to the structural, temporal, and focal restrictions of detective fiction, and their concerns range from explorations of insanity and power to expressions of despair and exhaustion. Throughout, Christie examines her genre, deconstructing and reconstructing it, and proposing new solutions that ally the detective process, not only with freedom and justice, but with British democracy itself. From the prewar, fear-fueled *And Then There Were None* (1939) to the restoration of the detective, in the form of an international alliance, in *Sparkling Cyanide* (1945), the trajectory of Christie's war novels, particularly those outside her major series, reflects an engagement with form that enacts concerns reaching far beyond fiction.

It could be argued that of course Christie was experimental, particularly at the height of the war, during which she lived and worked in London: she was literally writing for her life, or at least her afterlife. She actually sped up her already rapid pace of production; whether that factor made her less meticulous, or more creative, the destabilization of the war years affected her style. The prewar *And Then There Were None* bespeaks a sense of menace that haunted the nation even before the horrors of war took hold, but the less-noted *Sad Cypress* (1940), *Towards Zero* (1944) and *Sparkling Cyanide* (1945) also feature unconventional structures and narrative strategies. The deconstruction of

Towards Zero and the multiple narration of *Sparkling Cyanide* are less noticeably radical than the threatening *And Then There Were None*: though the later two novels also bespeak a potential lack of faith in the system upon which so much detective fiction is built, they, unlike the first, work toward the restoration of that system, and express ultimate faith in its function, if not its sometimes-imperfect processes.

The generally accepted narratological analysis of detective fiction is that proposed by Tzvetan Todorov in his 1977 essay, "The Typology of Detective Fiction": its "purely geometric architecture" consists primarily of its inversion of the *syuzhet* (the events of the story) and the *fabula* (the narration of those events) (45). To this "whodunit" formula, Todorov attributes the success of novels like Christie's, because "the masterpiece [...] is precisely the book which best fits its genre" (43–44). However, he concludes this essay by acknowledging the breakdown of the "traditional" categories of detective fiction and considering how to contextualize "marginal" and "intermediary forms". Although he references authors like Patricia Highsmith, that breakdown is equally in evidence in the supposedly canonical work of Agatha Christie. Todorov continues, "the new genre is not necessarily constituted by the negation of the main feature of the old, but from a different complex of properties" (55) and during the Second World War, Christie queried many of these traditional properties, using them to reconstruct the "traditional" form anew.

Throughout the 1930s, Christie had been shifting the narration of her novels from an overt narration, in which the narrator is a visible character, to covert narration, in which the "narrator" is an invisible presence. Her work of the 1920s is typified by an overt narrator, Captain Hastings, who is the "Watson" figure of the Hercule Poirot novels. Though not a major character in the Poirot series as a whole, Hastings, because of his Holmesian heritage and his presence in the earliest novels and stories, figures prominently popular stereotype of Christie's works, as well as in many adaptations. However, Hastings had all but disappeared by the mid-1930s, as the last novel in which he features, excepting *Curtain* [1975], is *Dumb Witness* (1937). As she erased her "Watson", Christie adopted a largely impersonal tone, even in such emotionally charged works as *Death on the Nile*. Readers rarely have any access into characters' minds and thus are only able to interpret from external cues and speech. Seymour Chatman situates narration on a sliding scale between the narrator who is present in the text ("overt narration"), to the narrator who is behind the scenes ("covert narration"), to the narrator who is apparently not present ("nonnarration"), by their "degrees of audibility" (196). Several notable novels of the 1930s, including *Death on the Nile* and *Murder on the Orient Express* (1934), are written so that the "narrator" virtually disappears: they are, as close as it can possibly be expressed, "pure" mysteries, ideal whodunits, in which the setting, characters, and narrative structures all exist to serve the plot. Their extraneous flourishes cut away, these novels follow the dramatic principle of Chekhov's gun: "If in the first act you have hung a pistol on the wall, then in the following one it should be fired. Otherwise don't put it there".[1] The covert narration (bordering on nonnarration) of many of the 1930s novels has a veneer of precision, exactitude, and coolness that has given credence to the idea that such works are "mechanical". While the narration reports that "Poirot thought", or even "Poirot felt", that narration is never at any time focalized through Poirot. These novels, so exemplary of the detective tradition, forbid the reader from seeing from the detective's perspective. The precision of these works, then, in many ways, is their most notable aspect.

However, it is important to note that there *is* still a narrator, no matter how covert, and more importantly that that narrator is one who the reader recognizes as "Agatha Christie". According to Chatman,

> In covert narration we hear a voice speaking of events, characters, and setting, but its owner remains hidden in the discursive shadows. Unlike the "nonnarrated" story, the covertly narrated one can express a character's speech or thoughts in indirect form. [...] Some interpreting person must be converting the characters' thoughts into indirect expression, and we cannot tell whether his own slant does not lurk behind the words. (197)

There is a supreme authority to this narration, an authority that exists outside the text, and which can be tied to the notion of the author as "interpreter". As Susan Sniader Lanser points out, "since authorial narrators exist outside [the narrative], they conventionally carry an authority superior to that conferred on characters, even on narrating characters" (16). By adopting the term "authorial", I do not mean to echo, as Lanser does, F. K. Stanzel's "authorial mode", which is his term for the "personalized narrator" in the nineteenth-century novel (187). Instead, I use the term to correlate with "authority" and to indicate the certainty inherent in the structure of the detective novel. The "authority" expected of Agatha Christie is certainly a product of her identity as "author".[2] Despite Todorov's contention that "the author cannot, by definition, be omniscient as he was in the classical novel" (46), this superior authority is certainly characteristic of much of Christie's narration. Readers are accustomed to feeling the author's sure hand gliding over the plot and leading them inexorably toward a seamless conclusion.

That narrator is such a dependable entity that when it is covered over by other narrative voices, the condition of the story is profoundly affected. The novels of the 1930s, dominated by the orderly Poirot and controlled by the authorial Christie, give way abruptly at the outset of the war to other protagonists and other voices. Of the twelve novels she published between 1939 and 1945, only four feature Hercule Poirot. Miss Marple and Tommy and Tuppence returned to novel form for the first time in a decade, but, more significantly, five of these wartime novels feature non-series protagonists (as opposed to four of twenty-four in the years from 1920 to 1938).[3] Even the Poirot novels of this period, particularly *Sad Cypress* and *Five Little Pigs* (1942), are markedly different: the detective plays a relatively small role, and the narratives thematize memory and point of view, often focalizing large parts of the story through suspects or investigators other than the detective.

According to Gérard Genette's theory of focalization, the narrative "regulate[s] the information it delivers [...] according to the capacities of knowledge of one or another participant in the story" (162). This technique is of particular use, of course, in detective fiction, because it enables the narration to omit information, but it also creates a web of potential perceptions, through which the reader has to maneuver, rather than a straight path behind a single detective. As Todorov notes, "no observation exists without an observer" (46), and, when focalization becomes a factor in the narrative (as it was at times in Christie's 1920s work, though much less in the 1930s), it can become a tool for deception. In this mode, the reader knows what a character knows, and no more—but, of course, in the case of the detective novel, probably *not everything* he or she knows. Genette's definition not only refines the concept of "point of view", but also encompasses a directionality of understanding, almost a motive in itself. The uncertainty that this mode may thus generate is certainly useful for the author of detective novels, but creates a very different situation for the reader than that of authorial superiority.

Changes in narrative voice and focalization in Christie's work do not begin, magically, to appear at the onset of instability in Europe. There are "previews" of it, most notably in *Death in the Clouds* (1935) and *Appointment with Death* (1938). However, these earlier novels feature a "shifting limited" narration, in which, according to Chatman, "a narrator may shift his mental entry from one character to another and still remain relatively covert" (215). The brief views into various characters' heads that appear, for instance, when the passengers take their airplane seats in *Death in the Clouds* do not form the structural principle of the work. The "authorial" Christie remains firmly in place for most of the novel. The technique that Christie uses in that scene, however, later becomes key to *And Then There Were None*. When Norman Gale, in the earlier novel, thinks, "Damn it, I feel quite excited. Steady, my boy ..." (*Death in the Clouds* 16), as he is distracted by an attractive woman while he prepares to commit murder, it primes the reader for the later, "They're going mad ... they'll all go mad ... Afraid of death ... we're all afraid of death ... *I'm* afraid of death ... Yes, but that doesn't stop death coming ..." (*And Then There Were None* 136).

After seven years spent almost exclusively on Poirot novels, Christie produced *Murder Is Easy* and the astonishing *And Then There Were None* in 1938 (Morgan 220). While the former has notable aspects, it is in many ways a typical Christie in its inversion of expectations and its "least-likely" culprit. The latter, however, was a bombshell. It was as these novels went into production, in 1939, that the author and her family moved into Greenway, her Devon home. While she recalled the time as idyllic, she and her peers would certainly have been aware of the foreboding international news, as well as the divisions of British public opinion on German aggression after the invasion of Czechoslovakia in the autumn of 1938 and British Prime Minister Neville Chamberlain's subsequent "appeasement" treaty. It is not surprising, then, that *And Then There Were None* develops a sense of growing inevitability. The countdown motif, based in a nursery rhyme, quickly takes on an identity as a death sentence, and the narrative mercilessly propels the characters onward.

The radical lack of visible narrative authority in *And Then There Were None* is perhaps the most alarming thing about the novel: the sleight-of-hand solution is actually far less destabilizing than that of *The Murder of Roger Ackroyd* (1926), and its cast of "murderers who got away with it" is only an extension of that employed in *Cards on the Table* (1936). Indeed, in many ways, the novel is a quintessential Christie: while the conclusion, in which everyone dies, is unique, readers actually already expect everyone to be lying, or everyone to be guilty (of something). As Heta Pyrhönen points out, there is a standard presumption in Christie's work that "everyone is guilty, which casts a strong doubt on whether anyone is what he claims to be" (192). Christie, who felt that "writing plays is much more fun than writing books, because you haven't got to bother about long descriptions of places and people" (BBC Radio 1955), suited herself by constructing virtually the whole novel in dialogue or internal monologue. This technique may be theatrical, or Modernist, but it is, emphatically, distant from the authorial certainty of a detective-led novel.

Starting in a reflective mode, *And Then There Were None* gives each character a short introduction from his or her own perspective, in a mixture of direct and indirect thought report. Then, upon the characters' arrival on the island, the focus begins to jump from one character to another, the change often indicated with a brevity close to that of a stage direction: "Philip Lombard said sharply", "Fred Narracott said cheerfully", "Vera thought" (direct thought report), "General Macarthur said" (19). These dialogue-heavy sequences lack interiority, with a narration so covert as to frequently give the impression that there is no narrator. It might be thought that such a sequence would mark a return to the authorial Christie as the narrator, but she refrains almost entirely from narrative comment and, keeping the sense of authorial control out of the novel, acts as a reporter. As Stanzel observes, novels that are heavy in dialogue often restrict the narrator, and ostensibly remove the personality of that narrator, creating a situation of "non-identity" in the novel (56). In *And Then There Were None*, the narration retains a subtle sense of identity, but is so far ranged toward the "covert" that her brief appearances are surprising, and disconcerting.

The quick shifts between characters, as well as between internal and external speech, only accelerate, like a snowball rolling downhill, until the loss of control seems to extend into the narration itself:

> Breakfast was a curious meal. Every one was very polite. ... "May I get you some more coffee, Miss Brent?" ... "Miss Claythorne, more ham?" ... "Another piece of bacon?" ... Six people, all outwardly self-possessed and normal.
>
> And within? Thoughts that ran round in a circle like squirrels in a cage. ... "*What next? What next? Who? Which?*" ... "*Would it work? I wonder. It's worth trying. If there's time. My God, if there's time....*" "*Religious mania, that's the ticket ... Looking at her, though, you can hardly believe it.... Suppose I'm wrong....*" "*It's crazy—everything's crazy. I'm going crazy. Wool disappearing—red silk curtains—it doesn't make sense. I can't get the hang of it.....*" "*The damned fool, he believed every word I said to him. It was easy ... I must be careful, though, very careful.*" "*Six of those little china figures ... only six—how many will there be by to-night?*"
>
> "Who'll have the last egg?"
>
> "Marmalade?"
>
> "Thanks, can I give you some ham?"
>
> Six people, behaving normally at breakfast ... (121–22)

This singular passage moves inward from the narrator, whose authorial voice satirically remarks the "polite" "normal[ity]" of the guests/murderers/victims, through the outward voices of those people, and into their thoughts. The rare appearance of the authorial voice illustrates how far distant this text is from a standard detective story, with the *fabula* firmly established over the *syuzhet*, and a detective at the center of the narrative. It acts as a frame for thoughts that not only "run round" inside each head, but run between them, linked by ellipses. The use of the ellipsis here fills several functions. The ellipses within the speech examples of the first paragraph mark the incidental remarks therein as representative samples, but the ellipses following the narrator's comments pointedly leave her statements open to comment, and doubt. The ellipses of the externally focalized scene-setting, though, also call attention to the ellipses between, and within, the characters' thoughts; Rick Altman observes that this kind of ellipsis can emphasize potential absence, or omission, of information (262). Genette refers to such an omission as a "paralipsis", which he defines as a "lateral ellipsis", which "side-steps a given element" (52). He defines these paralipses as characteristic of the "classical detective story", in which case the detective conceals information from the reader (197); such omissions, of course, are not meant to be noted by that reader. In this case, however, the paralipses are made visible as punctuated ellipses, and act to draw attention to the omissions. The slippage of the internal focalization between characters masks the lack of attributions within the sequence, but "he believed every word I said to him" subtly alerts the reader to the missing, vital, information.

More than any of her other novels, perhaps, this one exemplifies Nicholas and Margaret Boe Birns's contention that Christie "allows us momentary empathy with the actions of her plots without ever permitting us to forget that these actions are embedded in a linguistic field" (133). Two points in this analysis are essential to understanding the narrative of *And Then There Were None*. First, the "linguistic field": by drawing attention to the patterns of conversation as much as to the words themselves, and by contrasting these apparently stable external patterns to the disintegration of rational thought, Christie keeps the reader off-balance and fuels the momentum of the countdown to *None*. The second, and complementary point, is that of "momentary empathy": the reader moves through this multiple-focus text with such speed, as illustrated above, that firm identification with any character is unlikely. Also, the interiority of the novel allows the reader to know, rather than suspect, that all of the characters are, to varying degrees, guilty of murder. Thus, either everyone must be exonerated, or no one, and, very quickly, it is clear that it is to be no one. Thus, any identification with the characters will be short-lived on two counts: they are guilty and they are doomed. If, as Slavoj Žižek proposes, "the role of the detective is [...] to dissolve the impasse of this localized, free-floating guilt by localizing it in a single subject and thus exculpating all others" (57), *And Then There Were None* is even more emphatically detective-less.

Though Christie alerts her reader to the disintegration of the detective structure, she imposes a strict structure nonetheless, that of the countdown. As Alison Light comments, Christie's frequent use of nursery-rhyme references is also disquieting: "the mounting excitement of their repetition depends on the unsteady boundary between the homely and the malevolent" (88). The "Ten Little Indians" rhyme upon which the murders are modeled is quickly established as the pattern of the novel, and the pressure that it exerts on the characters even drives the last surviving ones to fulfil its requirements. The novel is not about war, then, but fear: fear of what one might do, be compelled to do, or even want to do. One of the reasons that no one can survive the island is because no one is worthy; in an almost quasi-religious way, everyone hopes for salvation from the mainland, but knows, in the end, that it will not come. Such a plot device seems prescient, given the British isolation of 1939–40. Of course, Christie could not have foreseen the desperate need for the United States to enter the war; however, as a witness of the First World War, she dreaded another. The anticipation of war, however, proved, at least in her writing, worse than reality.

The disconnection from the expected form and the lack of stable identification make a significant impact on the narrative. Though "we must follow individual characters", as Altman writes, "we always do so with a certain degree of indifference, knowing that none of them individually represents the text's object. Instead, we find ourselves tracing our own paths through the text" (286). The reader may be at sea without the authority of the known narrator in this widely focalized text, but that reader ultimately gains narrative power in the process, enacting Todorov's "homology [that] must be observed: 'author : reader :: criminal : detective'" (49). There is little satisfaction in this position, however, because, as Altman also notes, the discomfort induced by multiple-focus texts emphasizes the reader's "inability to control the narrative" (285). He observes that these narratives "set familiar pieces into unexpected patterns, calling into question the comfortable habits of readers" (262). While there is little that is familiar about the setup of *And Then There Were None*, the jarring multiplicity of its narration makes it feel more unknowable. Not only does the reader *know* that one of the focalizers must be the murderer, but the reassuring authorial voice momentarily reappears at rare intervals, as if pointing out its own absence.

The nihilism of *And Then There Were None* stands out, not only because everyone dies, but because the crime is unsolved. The letter that concludes the novel is profoundly unsatisfying, not least because it undermines the reader's faith in the detective form. Never again would Christie allow such a destructive degree of narrative instability—in fact, several of her later war novels engage the reader in reasserting the detective structure, and the later multiple-focus novel *Sparkling Cyanide* features not just one, but three detectives. Before she returned to the experiment of true multiple-focus, though, Christie pursued an examination, and even a reconstruction, of the narrative structure of the detective novel through several texts, beginning with *Sad Cypress*.

Sad Cypress, the last book Christie finished before the war began (Thompson 316; Morgan 224), is, in theory, a Poirot novel, but it picks up several significant threads that join Christie's wartime novels. The power of the detective, as well as that of the authorial narrator, recedes; much of the narration is concerned with memory and perspective; and its structure is self-aware and foregrounded in the story. The novel is also the beginning of Christie's reframing of the detective's role and process. It begins not with the great detective himself, but with the mechanics of a trial, an official legal process that deprives Poirot of his private starring role in presenting the solution. Right away, then, the Christie reader sees that this is a profound re-figuring of the detective novel in general, and of the Poirot novel in particular. If nothing else, it deprives the detective of his place at center stage. It also removes virtually all of the humor typical of a Poirot novel, again indicating its lack of concern with the personality of the detective. The author indicated that she regretted putting Poirot into the novel at all (Christie quoted in Wyndham 25); however, as will become evident, his presence is not immaterial, but rather essential to Christie's reconfiguration of narrative, and the reassertion of detective and democratic values.

As do the later novels *Towards Zero* and *Sparkling Cyanide*, *Sad Cypress* manipulates the typological structure of the detective novel. The story of the investigation runs parallel with that of the trial (which is supposed to be the result of that investigation). The beginning of the story, in terms of the *syuzhet*, takes place far later in the narrative structure: the focalizer, the detective, and the reader are all looking back. The focalizer, who might usually be assumed to be the protagonist, is presented as, at least potentially, the criminal. Of course, after *And Then There Were None*, no reader could be deceived by a sympathetic focalizing character; however, the structure that generates empathy, the sustained focalization through the character on trial, indicates a significant change of perspective on the detective process itself. If, indeed, the wrong person has been arrested, the process of detection is fallible. Thus, in *Sad Cypress*, Christie asks, can it be saved? Is it worth saving?

The commencement of the novel, then, is failure. Elinor, like Audrey Strange in *Towards Zero*, feels completely disconnected from the process of investigation, saying, in almost the same words, that she is "very tired" and "glad [...] it is—over" (133).[4] Though the reader's perspective on these two protagonists is utterly different—the narration of *Towards Zero* pointedly excludes any focalization through Audrey—both seem to have given up on detection. Though characters in detective fiction, Christie's among them, frequently express their dissatisfaction with the detective's methods, the *despair* of these two women is unusual. Could their lack of faith in the traditional assumptions of detective fiction be read as a similar expression of doubt about familiar societal structures in the age of total war? Certainly, Christie was not a defeatist. As Light and her successors have observed, the Modernist element of Christie's fiction often serves a purpose contrary to its outward appearance: in citing "traditional" values, she often mocks or casts doubt upon them. So, though the looming threat of being hanged, of death in the Blitz, of fascism itself, may make an individual want to despair, the structures of these novels right themselves in the end. Surely, in fact, the reader is expected to argue on behalf of detection and solution. This, then, may be the true explanation for Poirot's appearance in *Sad Cypress*: in this case, he functions as a symbol more than a character. After the nihilistic

And Then There Were None, Christie needed him to reassert a contract of "fair play" with the reader, and to give that reader a way to resist, even reproach, Elinor's despair and fatigue.

In the period following *Sad Cypress*, Christie wrote two novels with war-related themes (oblique in *One, Two, Buckle My Shoe* [1940] and explicit in *N or M?* [1941]), as well as one that returned to the "perfect puzzle" form (*Evil Under the Sun* [1941]), but it is with *Towards Zero* that she once again took up her own battle with the narrative, and took up (rather a different) Battle again. Written in 1941 (Thompson 344), just after the height of the Blitz, the novel makes no outward acknowledgment of the war; indeed, it seems to be set firmly in the 1930s, and its mentions of French sports fixtures and Norwegian yacht cruises were pointedly nostalgic at a time when both France and Norway were occupied countries. However, the narrative is no throwback to times past. Instead, the structure of the novel is a radical interrogation of the detective form itself; not only does it highlight the haphazard and flawed nature of the detective process, but its disruption of usual formal relationships is a very pointed consideration of the traditional detective novel, as considered in Todorov's Formalist analysis.

In the prologue, the elderly solicitor Mr. Treves propounds the structural problem of the detective novel that it does not begin at the beginning:

> "I like a good detective story," he said. "But, you know, they begin in the wrong place! They begin with the murder. But the murder is the *end*. The story begins long before that—years before sometimes—with all the causes and events that bring certain people to a certain place at a certain time on a certain day.
>
> [...] All converging towards a given spot ... And then, when the time comes—over the top! *Zero Hour.*" (12–13)

The martial idiom of this theory ("over the top" suggests the trench warfare of the First World War) is particularly interesting when considering the parallels between Christie's narrative battle and the war during which she fought it. The characters are all, briefly, cast as soldiers, who are giving their fictive lives for the cause of the detective story. In terms of narration, this section of the novel performs a very peculiar trick: it begins outside the story, but ends inside it, in a self-conscious gesture that creates a situation that is simultaneously *fabula* and *syuzhet*. Despite the fact that Lanser declares, "in the 'figural' mode [when] all narration is focalized through the perspectives of characters, [...] no reference to the narrator or the narrative situation is feasible" (16) Christie has a character, who will appear in the story, articulate the structure of the novel and then place himself inside it. The prologue concludes with Mr. Treves, having returned home, musing to himself, "If I were to write one of these entertaining stories of blood and crime, I should begin now, with an elderly gentleman sitting in front of the fire opening his letters—going, unbeknownst to himself—towards zero ..." (14). At this point, he reads a letter that changes his plans for the following summer and is precipitated into the action of the story. Thus, the theory that frames the novel, to the extent of dictating its title, exists both intra-textually and extra-textually.

Taking Treves's statement above as a guide, the reader should realize that this novel reconceives the traditional *fabula/syuzhet* opposition of the detective plot. Indeed, the final section is titled "Zero Hour", and the prologue states "the murder is the *end*", so the murder committed in the middle of the book is explicitly not *the* murder. When Superintendent Battle takes on the traditional detective's role of explaining the plot to the suspects in the conclusion, he explains the mechanics and motive of a murder that has not happened: "Lady Tressilian's death was only incidental to the main object of the murderer. The murder I am talking of is *the murder of Audrey Strange*" (229; emphasis original). From a narrative perspective, this particular summing-up is unique. Battle prefaces his explanation with almost exactly the same words as Mr. Treves uses in the prologue, words that, in the story, he has not heard. Though the repetition is explained with perfectly Christie-an logic when Battle says, "What I'm going to say is not original—actually I overheard young Mr. Daniels, the KC, say something of the kind, and I wouldn't be surprised if *he'd* got it from someone else" (223); his repetition of Treves's theory completes the story's narrative frame. This doubling of explanations in prologue and conclusion emphasizes a profound shift in narrative expectation, inserting the *fabula* inside the *syuzhet* rather than layering one over the other: the story of the investigation has, in this case, taken place at the same time as the story of the murder, and is, in fact, the same story.

Genette insists that interchange between diegetic levels "produces an effect of strangeness that is either comical [...] or fantastic" (325), but in this case it is, instead, critical. The novel is full of such reflections, each emphasizing its construction. Treves's theoretical utterances explicitly define the action from the beginning. However, lest the reader miss the import of the prologue, it is reinforced in the words of the nurse who tends Angus MacWhirter in the first chapter, who argues that his life may have value by, "just being at a certain place at a certain time" (23). Furthermore, the second chapter, which features a sexless, anonymous "figure" writing a "carefully detailed project for murder" (24), stages both the concepts of planning and participation. The latter scene, though, is deceptive: the story has been framed, so the figure is not actually planning, but participating. That "figure", for it is never further identified, is itself connected by the use of the awkward pronoun "it" to the child in the story that Mr. Treves tells at dinner, and its writing of the plan is later echoed in Battle's recall of the phrase "a fine Italian hand" (193). The plan for the murder, though, is subsidiary to the plan for the novel.

Towards Zero, in all its consciousness of form, does not mark the detective's triumphal return, for the simple reason that Battle does not, quite, reach the correct solution. Introduced in *The Secret of Chimneys* as "squarely-built [...] with a face so singularly devoid of expression as to be quite remarkable" who is "a damned good man at [his] job" (212), he is more human, and more fallible, in his last appearance. He also intuits the solution before he reaches it, a very un-procedural method; the formerly "wooden" Battle has a personal motivation and level of comprehension, in *Towards Zero*. In other novels he exists purely as a professional figure, with no internality or focal narrative power; he exists, largely, to confound the expectations of characters and readers by being an intelligent and perceptive policeman. Here, however, he has a family, a personal life that takes him to the scene of the crime, and particularly a daughter who happens to be "a very unusual type of liar" (32). However, despite his heightened powers of perception, he needs the help of an outsider to solve the case. MacWhirter might be cast as a volunteer, a layman who enters the professional world for a specific cause: in this case, he is the recipient of a clue that allows him to make what Pyrhönen calls a "creative abduction", a logical leap of intertextual association (86). MacWhirter's nonexperience, in this case, is an asset: he does not know enough about the investigation to be convinced by the manufactured evidence. So, expertise may have more limits than it previously did, but added to it is the power of originality. The breaking down of old structures, then, is not in vain: they are being rebuilt in new and creative ways, and acknowledging the value of these.

A further salient, and peculiar, feature of the war novels is the emergence of insanity as a motive. Insanity, in these cases, is not that of a "passing tramp" (a convenient solution proffered at the start of many of Christie's novels in order to avoid confronting violence within the community or family): criminality still comes from within rather than from without. More threateningly, it is a methodical, *logical* insanity, in which the crimes seem perfectly justified by a specific, extreme, rationale. While plenty of Christie's wartime murderers are still motivated by avarice or fear, the criminals of *Murder Is Easy*, *And Then There Were None*, *Towards Zero*, and *Death Comes as the End* are all actually insane, as, arguably, are those of *One, Two, Buckle my Shoe* and *The Hollow*. The murderous madness, in each case, is prompted by an event that serves as adequate "motive", but in each case, the criminal is someone who has, knowingly or not, nurtured a seed of insanity since youth. Could the creation of Miss Wainwright, Justice Wargrave, Nevile Strange, and Yahmose, who all feel that they have a "right" to their desires, be directly related to the evident monomania of Hitler, and of Nazi policies of "entitlement" such as Lebensraum? To reinforce the point, Christie even creates a leader, Alistair Blunt, who insists, "I don't want to tyrannize" (*One, Two, Buckle My Shoe* 234) but who is also undeniably monomaniacal. If such ideas can motivate a nation to militarism and genocide, suggests Christie, surely they could motivate individuals to multiple murder.

In the case of *And Then There Were None*, such madness uncontained, and even victorious, was too nihilistic, or perhaps too realistic. Hence reason returns to prominence in *Towards Zero*: despite the careful planning of the criminal, who actually lays a flawless trap, he is defeated by the intuition of the stolid, procedural detective and the intervention of the unknown factor in the person of MacWhirter. Again, the detective plays his role, but the new man facilitates its completion, a pattern that recurs in *Sparkling Cyanide*. One of Christie's last books to be published in the war years, *Sparkling Cyanide* reflects one of the earliest, *And Then There Were None*, with its multiple-focus narration. Like *Towards Zero*, though, it interrogates and re-writes patterns of detection.

Given the appearance of Colonel Race in *Sparkling Cyanide* and of Superintendent Battle in *Towards Zero*, both novels could be putatively situated in the Poirot universe: Battle even mentions Poirot during his investigation. These two characters are also tied to each other, having both appeared, with Poirot and Ariadne Oliver, in *Cards on the Table* (indeed, *Sparkling Cyanide* almost repeats this working relationship, except that Battle is replaced by his protégée and near-facsimile, Chief Inspector Kemp). More saliently for this analysis, though, both detectives have their background in Christie's early work, when she was "trying things, as one does" Thompson 130): Race's first appearance was in *The Man in the Brown Suit* (1924), and Battle's in *The Secret of Chimneys*. Both potentially represent a need for the author to return to a pre-formula type of writing, to free herself from the need to be "Agatha Christie" in all works.

Conversely, both Battle and Race represent institutions, or institutional wisdom: Battle is a high-ranking police officer, and Race a former intelligence operative and head of the Counter Espionage Department (*Sparkling Cyanide* 136). Both are products, to some degree, of the First World War and represent the postwar strength of the nation (and Race, of the Empire), but nonetheless, in *Towards Zero* and *Sparkling Cyanide*, both need supported from new entrants to the field: MacWhirter and, in the later novel, Anthony Browne are the characters who make the intellectual leaps required to solve the case.

In the last portion of *Sparkling Cyanide*, Browne is revealed to have semiofficial standing, but as a secret agent, and an American, he remains the outsider despite his specialized knowledge. However, he is a necessary outsider, whose nationality seems far less coincidental given that Christie wrote the novel in the middle of the war, after the United States joined the Allies. While *Sparkling Cyanide* does not mention the war, the questions that surround Browne's assumed persona of suspected saboteur assume underlying national concerns about militarism and secrecy. His addition means that, effectively, there are three detectives—the institutional detective Kemp, the military detective Race, and the undercover detective Browne—and solving the case, which can be considered a "domestic" version of Fifth Column infiltration, is a necessarily a joint effort.

The whole structure of the book is a sort of collaboration. Less conversational than most Christie novels, *Sparkling Cyanide* is multi-focus, but not in the floating-focalization style of *And Then There Were None*. Instead, it layers individual characters' narratives, building each one upon the other to construct a complete picture. No single narrator, authorial or otherwise, is as visible as the narrators in *Towards Zero*, or as distant as the authorial narrator in *And Then There Were None*. Altman asserts that this multiplicity necessarily involves the reader in "a process of rewriting":

> The reader begins by following each character in turn, identifying with some more than others, fitting each piece into an overall outline [...] As the text advances, the reader re-orders the narrative material according to an increasing number of thematic intersections, suggested by metaphoric ties, conceptual parallelism, or narratorial intervention. (286)

The reader is privy to the thoughts of the characters, but the "fitting together" of information is still a process vital to the completion of the story. Structurally, the reader is still aware that the traditional closed circle of suspects still prevails, so one of the focalizers must be a murderer: the layering process only emphasizes the limited pool of suspects, and glancing references to espionage complicate the process of investigation. The fact that each character acts as a focalizer in turn, in effect bidding for narrative priority, hints that no access is enough, that every person remains unknowable.

As previously indicated, the novel relies upon, but questions the value of, memory. The first book of *Sparkling Cyanide* is explicitly introduced as "remembrance": "Six people were thinking of Rosemary Barton who had died nearly a year ago..." (7). As Chatman puts it, "thinking is itself the 'plot'" (216). The American title of the novel, *Remembered Death*, was actually Christie's preferred one, which was changed because of concerns that it would seem to recall war losses: this original title, like *Towards Zero*, is as much about the structure of the novel as its topic. Each chapter is titled with the name of a character and begins by defining the relationship of that character with the dead woman, and the events around Rosemary's death are focalized through that character.

Running in parallel, the six chapters move back and forth in time, and, though the authorial narrator is present, the interpolated narration creates what Genette calls a "subtle effect of friction" through the focalizing character's own reflections upon the "past" (217); that past, for some characters, goes back as far as childhood, but is always refracted through the idea that each is "thinking of Rosemary". The focalizer, as Genette remarks, "is at one and the same time still the hero and already someone else" (218), because the character must necessarily be narrating in retrospect. Christie specifically points to this friction, and the evolution of character, in nearly every chapter: Stephen Farraday thinks, "What a fool—what an incredible fool he had been!" (51), and Iris Marle (Rosemary's sister) "pondered over the picture of herself. What had she been like?" (10). These multiple narrations and multiple focalizations allow Christie to imply a motive for each character, and they allow each character to reflect upon the others. Narratively, they permit the reader to build a complete picture, but one which must have gaps, and in this instance the narrative omissions are emphasized rather than elided. Ellipses in punctuation are not as prominent in this section as they are throughout *And Then There Were None*, although there are seven ellipses in the last three pages of Ruth Lessing's "memory" chapter (42–45) but the narration draws attention to its moments of paralipsis: "The Ruth who came back to the office was not quite the same Ruth who had left it" (43).

In these moments, Christie emphasizes the directionality of focalization. As Burkhard Niederhoff points out,

> Genette consistently writes "focalization *sur*" in French: while a story is told *from* a particular point of view, a narrative focuses *on* something. This preposition indicates the selection of, or restriction to, amounts or kinds of information that are accessible under the norms of a particular focalization. (116)

As in *And Then There Were None*, the multiple-focus narration indicates absences, but in *Sparkling Cyanide*, it gestures toward these instances of selection and restriction. Ruth thinks, "Why did you send me to see him? Didn't you know what he might do to me?" (44). By stressing these narrative gaps, Christie again casts the reader as an investigator; in this case, though, unlike that of the earlier novel, that reader acts alongside the detectives. However, more detectives does not necessarily mean more definition: their efforts to control the troubling multiplicity of the narrative complicate things by having three "authoritative" possibilities.

Not coincidentally, the novel's solution lies in language: "A waiter could have poisoned the champagne, but *the* waiter didn't. Nobody touched George's glass, but George was poisoned" (222). The narrative focus on memory and repetition vanishes in a stroke as the very swift resolution of the plot appears, and the focus shifts from Rosemary, who represents memory, to Iris, who represents vision, not only in her name but in the references to her "clear eyes" that are scattered throughout the narrative. The message is clear: looking back too much is not only unwise, it is dangerous: only by focusing on the present is it possible to find a solution.

In bringing her reader resolutely back to the present—present values as well as present danger—Christie resolves, for a time, her testing of the narrative. In calling the reader to defend, and participate in, the detective process during the Second World War, she interrogated both detection and those readers. After a relatively static period of nominal peace, followed by one of impending threat, war, when it came, was not crushing, but rather liberating for the writer. Through a process of questioning and re-envisioning, she ultimately returned detection to the hands of the reader, thus expressing an essential faith in the individual, and in the principles, rights, freedoms, responsibilities, and failures inherent in a democratic system. The new participants in detection do not "tear down the old order", as some of Christie's more idealistic young characters want to do; instead, they work within old institutions, providing fresh ideas that reinvigorate them and re-fit them for the present world, and eventually for the postwar era.

Notes

1 Anton Chekhov, Bartlett's quotations.
2 When this article discusses that authorial narrator, I have used the feminine pronoun, as it is, in my mind, so explicitly tied to Christie's identity as an author.
3 Though Colonel Race and Superintendent Battle are recurring characters in the 1920s and 1930s, neither dominates any novel, including those discussed here, to the extent that they should be considered series heroes.
4 Audrey says, "I'm glad it's—over! [...] I'm so tired" (*Towards Zero* 270–71).

Works Cited

Altman, Rick. *A Theory of Narrative*. Columbia University Press, 2008.
Birns, Nicholas and Margaret Boe Birns. "Agatha Christie: Modern and Modernist". *The Cunning Craft*, edited by Ronald G. Walker and June M. Frazer, Western Illinois University, 1990, pp. 120–34.
Chatman, Seymour. *Coming to Terms: The Rhetoric of Narrative in Fiction and Film*. Cornell University Press, 1990.
Christie, Agatha. *And Then There Were None*. 1939. Pocket Books, 1944.
———. *Death in the Clouds*. 1935. Collins, 1990.
———. *One, Two, Buckle my Shoe*. 1940. HarperCollins, 2016.
———. *Sad Cypress*. 1940. Fontana, 1975.
———. *The Secret of Chimneys*. 1925. Triad, 1978.
———. *Sparkling Cyanide*. 1945. Fontana, 1960.

———. *Towards Zero*. 1944. HarperCollins, 2002.
Genette, Gérard. *Narrative Discourse: An Essay in Method*. Translated by Jane E. Lewin. Cornell University Press, 1980.
Lanser, Susan Sniader. *Fictions of Authority: Women Writers and the Narrative Voice*. Cornell University Press, 1992.
Light, Alison. *Forever England: Femininity, Literature, and Conservatism between the Wars*. Routledge, 1991.
Morgan, Janet. *Agatha Christie: A Biography*. HarperCollins, 1997.
Pyrhönen, Heta. *Murder and Mayhem: Narrative and Moral Problems in the Detective Story*. University of Toronto, 1999.
Stanzel, Franz Karl. *A Theory of Narrative*. Translated by Charlotte Goedsche. Cambridge University Press, 1986.
Thompson, Laura. *Agatha Christie: An English Mystery*. London: Headline, 2007.
Todorov, Tzvetan. *The Poetics of Prose*. Cornell University Press, 1977.
Žižek, Slavoj. *Looking Awry: An Introduction to Jacques Lacan through Popular Culture*. MIT Press, 1992.

4 Taking on Hitler
Agatha Christie's Wartime Thrillers

Merja Makinen

In her autobiography, published in 1977, Christie recalls her disbelief as the cultured, gentleman she and her husband, Max, were visiting in Baghdad in 1932 was transformed by his anti-Semitism, rabidly insisting on Jewish extermination as the only solution. She writes:

> On that day as we sat in Dr Jordan's sitting-room and he played the piano, I saw my first Nazi—and I discovered later that his wife was an even fiercer Nazi than he was [...]. There are things in life that make one truly sad when one can make oneself believe them. (482)

The *Autobiography* does not dwell on the encounter, but her thrillers are in many ways haunted by the figure of Hitler and how his evil oratory can persuade particularly the young to an orgy of destruction. Christie's later (spy) thrillers always focus on a powerful organization manipulating naïve trade unions or idealistic youth for social unrest and ultimately for world domination. The originator of the clandestine movement to overthrow society is sometimes motivated by ideology, such as handsome Edward Goring in *They Came to Baghdad* (1951), at other times by avarice, like the wizened financier Aristides in *Destination Unknown* (1954), hiding behind ideological justifications. However, after 1940 Christie's thrillers contain at least one youthful character whose blond, Aryan beauty is directly linked to Milton's fallen angel, Lucifer, from *Paradise Lost,* to evoke the misguided destruction of the Hitler Youth, a reference finally made overt in the 1970 *Passenger to Frankfurt.*

Christie made an initial attempt to engage her readers with her views on Hitler during the Phoney War[1] and Prime Minister Chamberlain's belief in appeasement with "The Capture of Cerberus", one of twelve Poirot short stories based on the labors of Hercules. This was repressed by her literary agent, Edmund Cork, who advised her that *The Strand* magazine, publishing them from 1939, would not publish this final one (Curran 426–27). War was declared on Germany in September 1939, and in November 1940, she wrote to the magazine requesting the return of the unpublished "Cerberus". A later version of the story was composed for the collection of the stories published in book form after the war in 1947, with a different character "returned from the dead". This literary suppression because of political currency, the very thing the fiction wished to address, was also attempted by Cork for the thriller *N or M?* (1941) during the Blitz because the United States had not yet entered the war and he feared the American publishers, with their eye on their audiences, would reject it (mainstream US opinion opposed military intervention during 1940–41). This time Christie prevailed and it was published in 1941 in both the UK and the United States. In December 1941, Japan attacked Pearl Harbor and the United States entered the war. It is the role of literary agents and publishers to be concerned about audience reception and sales, but the very immediacy that Christie was endeavoring to harness was discouraged during the Second World War. Twenty-five years after the end of the hostilities, Christie published her final direct meditation on Hitler and Nazism, and while *Passenger to Frankfurt* (1970) was once again disliked by her agent and publishers, it proved an immense success with at least seventy thousand hardback copies sold during the first year (Thompson 468).

In the late 1930s, Christie advanced her first representation of Hitler in a version of "The Capture of Cerberus", which was not published until 2009 in John Curran's *Agatha Christie's Secret Notebooks* (433–51). While a Poirot case, and hence technically a detective story, the detective is uncharacteristically athletic and daring in his rescue, allowing a generic nod toward the thriller: "It was not Hercule Poirot's custom to indulge in activities in his proper person, but for once he broke through his rule" (445). As a spy master, he engages a psychologist and a number of competent young men for "a special mission" (442), and then travels to Alsace with a middle-aged dog-stealer and a young cat-burglar. Scaling a high perimeter wall, he dares the baying hound to enter the area of danger and meet the escapee at the bottom of the ladder. The rescued character is recognizably Hitler, being a "short man with a bullet head and a little dark moustache" (446). He is described as the

> [D]ictator of dictators [...] able to set huge crowds rocking with frenzied enthusiasm. His high, strangely tuned voice had a power all its own [who] at judicious intervals [...] added various territories to the Central Empires. (438–39)

Called "August Hertzlein", his initials match Hitler's,[2] and, as Curran points out, there is a direct reference to the Nazis in the story and Hitler is named in the notes planning it (Curran, 452, 31). The setting is just before the outbreak of war; Poirot reflects that wars settle nothing and wishes for a positive to Hitler's negative:

> If only a man could arise who would set enthusiasm for peace flaming through the world—as men have aroused enthusiasm for victory and conquest by force. (433)

In 1939, this focus on great leaders and orators with a talent for arousing violence elides Churchill's rousing speeches of the day,[3] while censuring the characterization and simultaneously robbing Hitler of his authority by casting Hertzlein as a popular figurehead, an unintelligent but thrilling, intoxicating voice, manipulated by a shadowy, larger organization familiar from her earlier thrillers such as *The Secret Adversary* (1922) and *The Secret of Chimneys* (1925). During 1939, the popular animus focused on the individual figure of Hitler as the focus of blame, rather than Nazism or Germany, as documented by diarists for Mass Observation on the declaration of war in September 1939:

> A few of the expressions which I put down almost immediately were: "We've got to stop him now", "Bloody well stop him". My mother and another woman said together. "Put him on an island like the Kaiser" [...] "He's started it then," "Blooming devil, we can't let him do that, can we?" (Qtd. in Sheridan 46)

Christie's focus on the individual man is culturally acute, but she also indicates that the Nazi organization is the larger threat:

> People in the know explained learnedly how Hertzlein was not really the supreme in the Central Empires. They mentioned other names—Golstamm, Von Emmen. These, they said, were the executive brains [...]. Nevertheless it was Hertzlein who loomed in the public eye. ("Cerberus" in Curran 438)

Despite the deeper grasp of Nazism, it is the individual figure of the dictator who both drives the threat of war and, once the Nazi organization has been confounded, leads the shift toward peace. The powerful individual is, then, both undercut and reinforced in the text's grasp of historical forces.

Contemporary optimism that war could be averted, during the time of Britain's Phoney War is ridiculed as immature—like hopes that Hertzlein/Hitler has developed incurable cancer or a heart disease, or fallen in love with "a Russian Jewess"—since Nazism is more than just one demagogue. This is reiterated when the man is apparently assassinated and turned into a martyr for the cause, even more powerful a figurehead than when alive. Christie's construction of the Nazi regime is conventional: it is efficient, with perfect organization, and it preys on the naïveté of the young—"the Brothers of Youth" in mass rallies—by claiming that totalitarians deserve to dominate because democracies were cowardly. Extolling the "glorious forces of the Youth", the speeches promise them that through their violent sacrifice they will "inherit the earth" (439). The impetus for Poirot's investigation is to save a young man's reputation, since Lutz's father insists that his son worshipped Hertzlein too much to assassinate him. However, Poirot enlists British youth in his successful counterattack, so this is not a simple dichotomy of youth pitted against experience; the Nazi youth are emotionally swayed while the British youth are "competent". Both are recruited by men of experience: Hertzlein and Poirot.

Incredibly, the tale allows for a resolution of the threat to democracy. Hertzlein's assassination has been feigned and the man incarcerated in an insane asylum when his conversion to Catholicism threatened Nazi power over the German public. The text invokes the meekness of Christianity as its counter to destructive and dominating impulses of violent political rule. The dictator becomes the figurehead Poirot wished for, of sorts: "*I* am the means appointed by God to give peace to the world!" (448), Hertzlein declares, having himself been converted to Catholicism through the fervency of a preacher. Poirot flatters Hertzlein as a "man of ideals, a visionary" but, problematically, the dictator's egotism still dominates despite his conversion. The dichotomy of man's overweening pride versus Christian meekness is as important here as it is in many of Christie's moral judgments on her murderers, indicating a flawed and untrustworthy sense of self. The one "sane" Hertzlein had been effectively hidden in the asylum, among numerous paranoiacs, also claiming to be "the dictator of dictators" (438), until discovered by Poirot, so that insanity is implicated in the delusional voicing of self-importance. Nazi politics is being placed in the hands of deluded self-obsessed megalomaniacs, the only ones wrong enough to position themselves as Nietzschean Supermen and to strive for world domination. Hertzlein's Damascene conversion is asserted but unexplained, as he inspires the Hitler youth toward "Peace... Love... Brotherhood" (450). The individual un-problematically vanquishes the "executive brains" of the Nazi organization and sweeps the German youth toward pacifism in a rushed denouement. This textual hiatus ostensibly leaves the saving of the Western world to God and the short, mustachioed Belgian, himself not averse to taking pride in his own capabilities. Despite the topic, and the telling seriousness of its context, the tone is light as befits a piece of wish fulfilment, an "if only" as war is declared in Britain. Both Curran (427–30) and Thompson (468) cite the 1970 comment by Christie, that she was not interested in politics to define her oeuvre, but publication of "Cerberus" in 1939 would certainly have shifted this dominant judgment of Christie as a writer who is uninterested in politics, since the story is a direct textual intervention engaging with the outbreak of the Second World War.

Successfully published three years later, most critics agree that *N or M?* engages directly with the war and the political unease about a traitorous Fifth Column within Britain. Christie's husband Max Mallowan called it "an anti-Nazi book" (Morgan 230). The novel continues the traditional stereotyping of Nazi Germany as the epitome of efficiency and organization, cold and inhuman in contrast the "good-hearted, muddle-headed" British democracy. Here there is an even more detailed evaluation of British optimism and "wishful thinking" that war could be avoided, which prevented effective preparations. This clearly levels a criticism at appeasement, a criticism softened by delineating it as part of the nature of democracy: "Muddled, easy-going liberty" (*N or M?* 7). Tuppence and Miss Minton voice the same hopeful beliefs that Hitler has a fatal disease, that the Blitzkrieg is the final gasp of a collapsing German industry, initially aired in the first "Cerberus", and that it will all be over within two months, only to be challenged by a much more percipient Mr. Cayley who insists "it will be at least another six years" (34). In reality, it would take another five.

Contemporary references to the Blitzkrieg, gassing, food rationing, and the fall of France and Dunkirk make this novel timely for its first readership, ending as it does just before the Battle of Britain, with Tommy and Tuppence successfully protecting the British South Coast from invasion. However, the site of the Beresfords' success embodies the war's emotional displacement, as a temporal uneasy transition between the past and a hoped for future peace. The Beresfords are turned out of their safe home surroundings to spy at a seaside resort, residing in a boarding house, ordinarily a place of dislocation and, under these circumstances of searching for the "enemy within", one of psychological unease and distrust. Rebecca Mills has argued that the village settings in her post–Second World War detective fiction, "Christie invokes the claustrophobia of people knowing too much about each other, and the anxiety of not knowing quite enough" (Mills 37). In the Leahampton boarding house, no-one is known, the protagonists are in free-fall, creating an agoraphobia where everyone is suspect and almost everyone is lying about their identity; Haydock, Mrs. Sprott, Mrs. and Sheila Perenna, Carl von Deinem, Anthony Marsden, and, of course, the Beresfords themselves as Mr. Meadowes and Mrs. Blenkinsop. As Tommy Beresford reflects on the unsettling anxiety of the temporary home, the "depression engendered by the harmless and futile atmosphere of Sans Souci disappeared. Innocent as it seemed, that innocence was no more than skin deep" (72). The critical reception correctly positions the novel as war-time propaganda and Plain accurately identifies that "the body under threat [...] is the vulnerable body of the nation itself" (137) since, as Plain indicates, the spread of Fifth Columnists questions Churchill's ideal of a people's war uniting the country.

In her autobiography, Christie states that at the beginning of the war, Graham Greene invited her to "do propaganda work", which she declined because

> I lacked the single-mindedness to see only one side of the case. Nothing could be more ineffectual than a lukewarm propagandist. You want to be able to say "X is black as night" and *feel* it. (523, emphasis original)

This 1977 statement seems disingenuous in the light of the 1939–41 original "Cerberus" and *N or M?* texts. Critics have rightly called the novel patriotic propaganda, but it is not necessarily as Stephen Knight (91) terms it, "jingoistic", since it does not claim Nazism is "black as night" and so perhaps escapes Christie's own interpretation of the term "propaganda". The text interrogates the term patriotism in a number of ways. The famous statement of Nurse Cavell, who could be positioned as either a spy or a hero, that "[p]atriotism is not enough [...] I must have no hatred in my heart" (56) tempers any rabid "black as night" belief. Sheila Perenna reveals herself to be the daughter of an IRA activist shot by the British as a traitor, and this complicates the notion of fighting for one's country, as the orphaned daughter denounces patriotism, arguing that people matter more than ideologies. Tuppence explores how she is torn between her affection and respect for the German refugee, Carl, and the need to fight him as the enemy. He too voices his conflicted predicament, working in a chemical factory to help defeat the Germans, when he is himself a German—but Tuppence counsels him that he is working for humanity, before going on to denounce jingoistic knee-jerk patriotism and acknowledging a complicated fluidity in her own behavior, separating Nazi ideology from the actual people in Germany:

> "The Germans" I say and feel waves of loathing. But when I think of individual Germans [...] I feel quite different. I know then that they are just human beings and that we all feeling alike. That's the real thing. The other is just the War mask that you put on. It's a part of War, probably a necessary part—but it is ephemeral.(88)

The novel may well be an anti-Nazi text, but it is clearly not unthinkingly anti-German and contemplates the cultural masquerade that war enforces upon its participants, creating conflicted selves and allegiances even in the effective spy, Tuppence/ Mrs. Blenkinsop. Spying as a profession is also interrogated. Tommy feels ashamed of using his real sympathy for Sheila to get information out of her, and everything is thereby "cock-eyed" (89). There is a complexity being voiced about the reputed enemy. Haydock, the jingoistic war-monger, cannot be trusted as a voice in the text because he is a Prussian and one of the Nazi Fifth Column leaders. M, the female spymaster, is masquerading as a mother called Mrs. Sprott, having adopted little Betty as her cover, knowing that a young English mother will prove invisible to suspicion, and coolly shooting the birth-mother who might give her away. A final mother arrives with the German Anna, whose hatred against the English who killed her son in the previous war makes her both implacable as an opponent, and empathetic because of her loss.

What might be missed by the modern reader, in this discourse around femininity and motherhood, is the Nazi propaganda of the time that valorized the domestic mother staying at home to raise the next generation of Nazi youth, and sacrificing her own drives for the Fatherland. Sprott's distorted maternal cover, willing to sacrifice children to the cause, speaks to how such a political message belies the monstrous behind its serene façade, while Tuppence's ingenuity and brains and courage demonstrate the full breadth available to the democratic British mother (sensibly worried about her children fighting in the war), uncircumscribed by such dogmatic ideologies. The emotional anxieties about an infiltrated Britain are in this novel mitigated by the Beresfords' secure reliance upon each other, the resonance of anxiety surfacing textually only with Tuppence's brief but aching concern for the safety of her children, judiciously controlled to allow her to save the coast from invasion. Motherhood, then, becomes a site for the writing of politics, of Nazism and democracy as it affects the personal spheres of women during the war.

The novel, both part of the war effort and yet not single-mindedly jingoistic, directly represents both Hitler and Nazism in the novel. How does Christie "take on" Hitler in this ostensible war novel? In contrast to the short story, the most obvious shift is to Nazism, rather than the individual figurehead, as the opponent, although there is an amount of slippage between Nazism, Germans, and Hitler. The specific references to Hitler are erroneous British hopes that he is fatally ill or raving mad. In contrast, the main focus becomes the Nazi-led planning of the internal Fifth Column and on the external planning of the conquering of Europe, the "efficiency of the enemy" and the "co-ordination of his well-planned war machine" (7). The Fifth Column traitors are attracted by "the Nazi aims and the Nazi creed and desiring to substitute that sternly efficient creed for the muddled, easy-going liberty of our democratic institutions" (8). Sometimes the British muddle is held up as a humane ideal; at others it is the deliberate misdirection of the Fifth Columnists, as the text attempts to "explain" Britain's poor performance to date. As *N or M?* comments, "The worst of that is over. We've corrected our mistakes. We are slowly getting the right men in the right places" (8). In contrast, the Fifth Column is one of "brains, organization, a wholly carefully thought-out plan" (124). Tommy is fleetingly moved to a "flash of genuine admiration" (143) at the perfection of the plans from the methodical enemy. As Grant insists, in another complication of patriotism, "It's not the skunks and the rats of the land who volunteer to go to the enemy's country. It's the brave men" (132). Haydock is uncovered as a Prussian bully, "with the Junker's true insolence" (142) but the real opprobrium is reserved for Mrs. Sprott "bad through and through", (211) because she is an English traitor.

Haydock's appeal to the Beresfords delineates the appeal of Nazism to the internal traitors, with the focus on Aryan class supremacy. The Nazi aim is to create a "new Britain" devoid of muddle, corruption, and "inefficiency" to be ruled by a chosen English, equally Aryan, elite: "the best *type* of Englishmen—Englishmen with brains, breeding and courage. A *brave new world*" (200). The Beresfords' spy master Grant evaluates this appeal psychoanalytically as "a lust for power", a "megalomaniacal pride", and starts the disparaging biblical reference that will reoccur in Christie's later thrillers: "In every land it has been the same. It is the Cult of Lucifer—Lucifer, Son of the Morning. Pride and a desire for *personal glory!*" (212)

Despite the fact that both Haydock and Mrs. Sprott are at either ends of middle age, Tuppence reiterates, "The Nazi creed was a youth creed" (80). But in fact, so is the British armed response. The Beresfords' daughter is involved in code-breaking and their son is in the Air Force. Both children patronize their parents as past it, and the book opens with Tommy and Tuppence's frustration at not having their experience used in the war effort. "They don't want people of my age for nursing [...] They'd rather have a fluffy chit who's never seen a wound or sterilized a dressing" (2). The jaunty humor of the novel (itself part of the war effort in keeping up morale) functions around the middle-aged couple successfully protecting Britain from invasion, a brave, intelligent agency, which they hide from their condescending young.

The novel, written during the course of the war, on the topic of fighting Germany, has strikingly few representations or denunciations of either the Nazis or Hitler. Hitler hardly makes an appearance and the German Nazis are afforded the trait of heroism alongside the stereotypes for superb planning and technical efficiency. The real emotional concentration of the novel is upon the usefulness of the middle-aged, the opprobrium toward the dangerous "Wooden Horse" of British traitors, and an exploration of an inhabitable British patriotism that challenges the cultural racial hatred at the time. While the issue of how far it can be defined as "propaganda" is open to debate, the novel can clearly be seen as part of the war effort.

This challenge of finding the usefulness of middle-aged experience had a personal element. At the outbreak of the war, Christie attended Torquay Hospital to update her professional expertise, and in London worked in the University College Hospital dispensary. Her husband, Max, like Tommy, was initially unable to find useful war work until his

Arabic expertise had him sent to work first in the Air Ministry, then in February 1942 in the Middle East. Christie's attempts to join Max were blocked by the War Office. Christie's correspondence to her literary agent, Cork, sketches thwarted attempts to be sent out as a correspondent to join Max during this period (Morgan 244, Thompson 249). Ironically, given *N or M?*'s focus on the dangers of internal traitors, the accidental naming of Major Bletchley, alongside the mention of code-breaking, had MI5 suspecting Christie of herself being a Fifth Columnist, pinpointing the place of their most secret intelligence, Bletchley Park in Buckinghamshire. Their suspicions were reinforced when her London house was bombed and she moved into her friend Stephen Glanville's Hampstead block, the Isokon building, known to house a number of Russian spies (Warren).

The thriller *They Came to Baghdad* (1951) links *N or M?* to *Passenger to Frankfurt* (1970) through two quotations: "Lucifer, Son of the Morning" and "The Young Siegfried". The major part of the thriller focuses on the settings in Baghdad and a lively adventure plot of murders and kidnappings, with a secret, worldwide "Fifth Column" setting Russian communism against American capitalism, planning to create a "New Heaven and a new Earth" by a "small chosen band of higher beings" (316), which the text names, without any further explanation, "[T]he young Siegfrieds of the New World. All young, all believing in their destiny as Supermen" (316). The details of the organization are left hazy as the text focuses on a biblical condemnation, via the fallen angel theme, of Edward Goring, who is plotting world domination while masquerading as a peace activist. Edward's youth links to his beauty, cruelty, and glamor; "*Lucifer, Son of the Morning, how art thou fallen?*" (314). This fallen angel's megalomania becomes associated with insanity through the same biblical focus; "You get mad, perhaps, if you try and act the part of God" (324). In opposition, Christie again situates Christian "humility and brotherhood" (176). Conspicuously in this novel the young fill both the evil and the good roles: Victoria, Anna, Richard, and Carmichael between them thwart the attempted apocalypse.

Destination Unknown (1954)[4] briefly contains a reference to a charismatic, charlatan Director, ostensibly in charge of a secret pool of young scientists, spouting "heady intoxicating stuff" (*Destination Unknown* 235), which the more cynical inmate, Andy Peters dismisses as "Clouds of glory" (236). The protagonist Hilary Craven aligns her own involvement in the Director's audience to a woman acquaintance's anecdote of being at a Hitler rally and, although swept up in the moment, finding nothing memorable in hindsight (234). Peters has a further throwaway comment, that female members' adoration of the Director contains a "hint of the Heil Hitler attitude" (231). A German woman scientist believes herself part of the "super-race" (221), but her Fascist ideology is undercut by others who believe they work for the greater good of

Communism, or for capitalist wealth. The text tells us that the German is not overly "intelligent" (221), but Hilary's own mystification by the Director's speech is also challenged on gender grounds, by Peters: "Snap out of it... Be a woman! Down to earth and basic realities!" (236). There is a textual conflict here between a general feminine gullibility associated with fandom, and one courageous woman who is "well-balanced, sane and intelligent" (271), and Christie never quite resolves it. This time the shadowy secret organization plotting in the desert is motivated at its core by pure greed, further minimizing ideology as having agency. Aristides laughs at the idea of world domination, because he does not "want to be God" (263), simply to exercise immense financial power. The mature, experienced, world-weary characters thwart the plot, with the final confrontation being between two ancients, one the clear-minded British former Lord Justice, the other the fabulously rich, powerful Aristides.

Interestingly, the "small, yellow, wrinkled, old" (258) master-villain, Aristides, defines "youth" in relation to scientific work as not above forty-five, bringing a whole new complication to Christie's definitions of youth and of maturity. In this novel the references to Hitler or the Nazis are textually slight and carry little conviction, functioning as an authorial shorthand on auto-pilot as Christie develops the villainy. It will take another sixteen years, spurred on by a time of youthful rebellion, for Christie to return more seriously to these themes and to link the beautiful, young anarchic Siegfrieds to Nazism and Hitler directly. Then, as in both *N or M?* and *Destination Unknown*, it is only the mature and the elderly who are trusted to combat the youthful threat.

Christie returned dramatically to the historical character of Hitler, in *Passenger to Frankfurt*, creating a Nazi legacy passed on to the Fuhrer's "son", titled, "Young Siegfried" (to link him to Lucifer), and the worldwide rise of anarchic, destructive troops of the young hell-bent on a Third World War. Christie's uncharacteristic "Introduction" to the novel makes a bid for cultural relevancy for her "extravaganza" based on "actual *facts*" (9, emphasis original). The novel is positioned as holding "up a mirror to 1970 in England" (8), to reflect "worship of destruction, pleasure in cruelty" (9). The themes of youth and of Nazi sadism continue, with the wise and well-connected Aunt Matilda justifying revisiting the past to explain the present, with a conservative finality akin to Miss Marple's, because life consists of sixty-five knitting patterns: "[T]here aren't so many patterns in life, you know. One recognizes patterns as they come up" (55). She notes later, "Youth chanting slogans, slogans that sound exciting [...] You rebel, you pull down, you want the world to be different from what it is" (57). Matilda's preface with her use of the inclusive "you" appears sympathetic, but the insistence that the young are blindly being manipulated removes their agency and her historical example shifts the textual evaluation:

> That's what people said about Hitler. Hitler and the Hitler Youth [...] It was a fifth column being planted in different countries all ready for the supermen. The supermen were to be the flower of the German nation. That's what they thought and believed in passionately. Somebody else is perhaps believing something like that now. (57)

The level of anxiety expressed in this novel is extreme; R. A. York calls it "partially hysterical" (82) in its bid for currency and social comment. In contrast to *N or M?*, equally current in its depiction of Nazism but lacking such nervous apprehension, *Passenger to Frankfurt* shares the fear of trauma that Jessica Gildersleeve identifies in the late Poirot novels *Hallowe'en Party* (1969) and *Elephants Can Remember* (1972),

> which emphasizes the past as an essential source of knowledge for understanding the past and protecting the future. This privileging of memory [...] in Christie's late Poirot novels figure an anxious desire to protect against the possibility of traumatic return, a gothic plot in which the terrible secrets and crimes of the past return to haunt the present. (97)

Aunt Matilda, like Ariadne Oliver in *Elephants Can Remember*, voices the terror that the present "nowadays" will refuse to acknowledge the valency of old people's memories in protecting the young from a dangerous future.

The year 1968 was famously a moment of youthful left-wing rebellion and challenges to the establishment, and the text makes mention of a wide range of these to anchor the fantasy in "actual facts". Dismissing the Chinese as too wrapped up in Mao, and the Russians as mired in the ramifications of Communism, the novel points to Europe, the United States, and South America for the major sites of unrest, the manipulation of political idealism to infect young people with the desire for destruction. The aftermath of the 1968 anti-Vietnam demonstration where thousands of British youth marched is mentioned with the comment that Grosvenor Square is now quiet, as the protagonist Stafford Nye leaves the American Embassy after a dinner, with broken glass on the pavement and arrested youth in Bow Street police station. But the major points of interest are in South America, California, and Baltimore ("Universities? [...] One gets very tired of universities"; *Passenger to Frankfurt* 113). Asia, Italy, Portugal, Spain, and "Paris of course" are all indicted in this "student indignation" (83) alongside South America. In May 1968, students occupied the Sorbonne in France and joined with the workers' series of general strikes to create a brief but powerful civil unrest. The 1960s Berkeley "free speech" movements at the University of California, and the US-wide 1969 "Moratorium" march involving millions are also being referenced. 1968 also saw the "Prague Spring" bid for liberalization in Czechoslovakia, and student antigovernment marches in Mexico. The iconic Che Guevara left Cuba in 1965 to fight in Bolivia and was shot in 1967. Matilda reads up on the inspiring philosophers, who are being funded by the manipulators, "Marcuse, Guevara, Lévi-Strauss, Fanon" (135). As York comments succinctly, "the heterogeneity of the list shows the limits of the author's understanding" (82). Where many of us involved in those heady days saw it as a time of social revolution, a challenge to hidebound imperialism, racism, and sexism,[5] the elderly Christie positioned the spirit as something manipulated by a neo-Fascist lust for destruction and sadism. Her insistent refrain, as unrest moves into full-scale world war, is that once having experienced the thrill of destruction, the young are corrupted to "anarchy".

In the novel, the great English statesman Lord Altman reiterates that the idealistic desire to destroy "injustice and crass-materialism" and the "desire to destroy what is evil, sometimes leads to a love of destruction for its own sake. It can lead to a pleasure in violence and in the infliction of pain" (174). This refrain, echoed by Matilda, Altman, Mr. Robinson, Renata, and the narrator, is stressed for a reason that the older of Christie's readership would recognize and locates the novel's urgency to the trauma of historical return. Such slogans were used during the Second World War to describe the fascist enemy. The BBC, reporting the "wanton destruction" of the bombing of Coventry in 1940, described the Luftwaffe using exactly the same tropes: "Nazi disciples of slaughter who kill mostly for the joy of killing and destroy mostly for the joy of destroying" (from the 1940 "Martyred City of Coventry" reproduced in "Jeremy Vine" 20:09+). Christie's novel elides left-wing enthusiasm and idealism to position the Third World War at the feet of Hitler, reviving the experiences of her mature readers.

In a similar plot to the Cerberus short story, a double is placed in the bunker to be killed, and Hitler is spirited away to Latin America, a continent where indeed numbers of escaped Nazis fled at the close of the war, along the Odessa ratlines. At the embassy party, a woman guest describes having heard Hitler speak in terms identical to those in *N or M?* and *Destination Unknown*, but in this novel the experience is recounted by the individual present, rather than as hearsay, a more dynamic representation: "[H]is ideas were wonderful [...] They inflamed you. The things he said. I mean you just felt there *was* no other way of thinking" (79, emphasis original) but once she reviews the speech written down, she again discovers that the words were empty and "meaningless". Lord Altman extrapolates the power that such orators have to communicate "a wild enthusiasm" through their personal magnetism, a power shared by both great religious teachers and individuals bent on evil. Renata returns to this dualism and to Hitler as the great orator moving a country to evil as she and Stafford Nye voyage to Bavaria, to the lair of the monstrous Charlotte von Waldsausen. Again an unknown woman's report is quoted, raising the question of why it is being gendered (and the hope that feminine foolishness is not being inscribed) placing Nazism as the enemy of Christian morality:

> 'We Germans have no need of a Jesus Christ! We have our Adolf Hitler here with us" [...] Hitler was a spell-binder. He spoke and they listened—and accepted the sadism, the gas chambers, the tortures of the Gestapo. (93)

In this 1970 novel, Hitler's oratory is not turned to world peace as in 1939; instead his "son", Franz Joseph, the designated Young Siegfried with clear links to Edward's fallen Lucifer in *They Came to Baghdad*, has an equally powerful rhetoric that enables him to lead the youth of the world into a destructive war. Britain can only counter this by the use of a chemical weapon, Benvo, which instills involuntary and permanent benevolence. The rallies of Young Siegfried, the beautiful golden-haired hero, are given contemporary currency as his followers' fervor, especially the young women, copy the Beatlemania of the 1960s: "His voice rings like a bell and women cry and scream and faint away when he addresses them" (108). A little contradictorily, Christie continues the religion–evil dualism by also allying the event to one of Billy Graham's Madison Garden rallies, while simultaneously stressing the empty meaning of Siegfried's words that fuel the fans" ecstasy: "His voice, rising, falling, with its curious exciting quality, its emotional appeal, had held sway over that groaning, almost moaning crowd of young women and young men" (110). The mature Stafford Nye is, as Hilary before him, also "roused to enthusiasm" at the time but can recall none of the promises after the event, and rejects the focus on feeling and the emotions, putting the more old-fashioned "discipline" and "restraint" in their place. His comment on the event is "Pasteboard" (110), signifying the false manufactured performance and undercutting the mystification as did Peters" "Clouds of Glory" in *Destination Unknown*.

The character of Charlotte von Waldsausen, a phenomenally rich German fanatic who bankrolls the organization and the purchase of armaments and drugs to progress the cause, is extreme. A female version of Aristides, the depiction focuses on her gross materiality, her huge size, "a wallowing whale" (137) with her appetite for the best paintings, jewels, and antiques as adjuncts for her own sense of her inflated importance. The representation insists on the beautiful blond guards clashing their swords in a theatrical comedy. Christie's thrillers have always distrusted money and have insisted on financial power's supremacy in the execution of evil. By gendering the monstrous evil, linked to a Bavarian castle eyrie with a manufactured aristocratic claim, the figure is pushed into a comic caricature that the other characters have to counter with their insistence on her invincibility, despite the "nonsense" of her justifications. Positioning herself as the "mother" (191) of the young golden boys she gathers around her again introduces the trope of the false, sinisterly maternal into the Nazi representation. Her balefulness is allied to the "Old Man of the Assassins" (106) and invokes the SS's "Order of the Death's Head" (140), as she strives to reproduce the Nazi regime of a super race of young men worldwide. Where the unnamed women praising Hitler are constructed as vapid and unthinking, Charlotte is both considered, financially acute and, behind the mountebank trappings, given immense power and near success. Like Mrs. Sprott of *N or M?* she is a dangerous adversary, and again raises the question of Nazism's allure for deviant femininity more seriously.

Christie's depiction of Hitler is again ambivalent and contradictory. He is in control (Himmler needs his permission to create the "SS executive instrument", 140), yet also a "man of no importance in himself, but [...] undoubtedly [with] the power of leadership" (139). The plot has a twist on the Cerberus story, when one character brings Hitler to view the twenty-four "Adolf Hitlers" in an insane asylum, and leaves with a substitute whose body is found in the bunker. Two days later, the patient's "family" removes the actual Hitler from the asylum and spirit him to Argentina. There his relationship with a beautiful Aryan woman bears a son whose foot is branded with a swastika. Hitler dies insane, raving at his lack of power, and the boy is "prepared, as the Dalai Lama might have been prepared, for his great destiny" (152). While the text undercuts the authenticity of Franz Josef's blood as he is not Hitler's son but another imposter groomed by the real villains, Christie's apparently preposterous narrative, which her publishers insisted she subtitle "An Extravaganza", hit a cultural nerve and was the first in in a spate of novels and high-budget films. In the midst of the paranoid thrillers of the 1970s, such as *The Conversation* (1974), *3 Days of the Condor* (1975), and *The China Syndrome* (1979), with their shadowy, secret rogue groups, exist three films from contemporary novels, which also featured returning Nazi groups. Ronald Neame's *The Odessa File* (1974) from the 1972 novel by Frederick Forsyth, has John Voight as a young German reporter uncovering the organization of SS veterans sending biochemical warheads to Egypt to use against Israel. John Schlesinger's *Marathon Man* (1976), from William Goldman's 1974 thriller starring Dustin Hoffman and Laurence Olivier has a Nazi war criminal returning from South America to claim his loot of diamonds. Two years later, John Schlesinger's *Boys from Brazil* (1978) from the 1976 Ira Levin novel, has an even more preposterous plot as Gregory Peck, playing an aged Josef Mengele, clones nearly a hundred Hitlers in South America, bringing the boys up to be the leadership of a putative Fourth Reich. Peck's audacious plan is foiled by Laurence Olivier, playing an elderly Nazi hunter who was based on Simon Wiesenthal (also portrayed in *The Odessa File*). Wiesenthal was instrumental in the capture of Adolf Eichmann from Argentina in 1962, whose trial and execution kept Nazi war crimes in the news in the early 1960s, and Janet Morgan asserts that Christie began thinking about her plot in 1963 (362).[6]

In this cultural context, the success of Christie's Nazi-themed *Passenger to Frankfurt* in 1970 is less surprising than it might first appear and supremely prescient, giving credence to her introduction's bid for relevancy. Unsurprisingly, given the success of these "Nazi war criminal" movies, Christie was pursued by Hollywood in the early 1970s to have her novel filmed but, disillusioned with adaptations of her novels, she refused (Aldridge 123–25). At a time of cultural revolution and governments in crisis, Christie was not the only one to cast her eyes backward to the uncomplicated simplicity of old enemies and villains to explain and explore the current situation. Phyllis Lassner sees the novel as a speculative political fantasy whose plot's

> reassessments of the Allies victory in World War II [...] question the lasting possibilities for peace and stability by dramatizing anxieties about the reemergence of Fascist principles ring the Cold War and its proxy the Vietnam War. (228)

While her political acumen might be challenged in *Passenger to Frankfurt*, returning to take on Hitler one more time allows Christie to urgently recall what she saw as the very prescient dangers of overweening pride and arrogance, and a creed of "cruelty and torture and violence and death" (153) twenty-five years after the Second World War ended. The faults of the novel are not so much with its fantastic conception, a conceit that chimed with contemporary times, but with the lack of action or suspense. Despite its spectacular opening of espionage in a Frankfurt airport waiting lounge, too much of the novel's events are reported narrative, with the dramatic depictions staged in rooms where a varying group of static characters discuss the events in a repetitive insistence on the cruelty of the young, joyful in destruction, the masterminds behind the scenes, of money, science, and armaments, and the worldwide spread and danger of the "Militant Youth". Thompson positions the novel as one of the elderly Christie's "fear of the youth cult" (468), quoting the author's explanation: "My interest was aroused by the youth attitude of rebellion and anarchy, chronicled in news all over the world" (468–69). The characters who challenge and vanquish the threat are the middle-aged Stafford Nye and Renata, plus the elderly aunt Matilda and Lord Altman. Allying itself with *Destination Unknown,* and unlike "The Capture of Cerberus" and *They Came to Baghdad*, the young can no longer be relied upon in *Passenger to Frankfurt*.

After 1939, when Agatha Christie targeted specific cultural relevancy in her thrillers she selected a Hitler figure and Nazi superiority to depict villainy. An unsurprising choice at the start of the Second World War, the more immediate representation is unexpectedly lighter in tone, carrying with it a positive wish fulfillment that the enemy could be vanquished, while still voicing the dislocation and anxieties of combat. This belief in the future is signified by a trust in the young. The enemy is accorded bravery and their own patriotism in a receptive representation that challenges the extremity of enforced xenophobic masquerade in relation to effective agency. This confident openness slowly erodes up to 1970. The more desperate repetitive insistence on worldwide trauma, and the threat linked clearly to wayward, sadistic youth, comes when Christie was eighty, and textually demonstrates a less secure hold on the future, and hence a despair in the young. The depiction of Hitler remains static; a great orator linked in some form to madness, with an insane asylum locating the megalomania within mental ill-health. Hitler's self-agency is minimized as the Nazi headquarters, the brilliant brains behind the scenes, manipulate his self-grandeur to harness the mesmerizing oratory. Christie targets the Nazi philosophy of racial elitism, of Aryan supremacy, as the real evil, connecting it with Milton's Lucifer, a fallen angel who knew the right alternative but chose evil to fulfill his false self-pride: "Better to reign in Hell than serve in Heaven" (Milton 362). The religious arrogance, the deliberate choice of evil and cruelty, is a much less forgivable crime than psychosis. Youth, health, and beauty become more closely associated with the sadism and egotism and in all the novels can only be challenged by a self-humility and a recognition of equality and brotherhood, situated finally in Christian doctrine. Rather than any powerful rebuttals, the texts deliberately rely on a humane muddling-through that only just vanquishes the robotic efficiency of the villains. Taking on Hitler from 1939 to 1970, Christie relies on, and utilizes, cultural opprobrium for the historical figure to comment specifically upon on her current political situations. The positive, secure textual voice of the 1940s, the accepting explorations of patriotism, the tug of relevancy between youth and maturity, the issue of gender and motherhood in relation to ideology and agency, all work toward supporting the war effort without, in Christie's terms, becoming blinkered propaganda. The more desperate anxiety of the octogenarian author, afraid that she may not be listened to as she revisits history to try to prevent the present from traumatically embracing destruction, is textually betrayed by the strident and obsessive repetitiveness of the narrative, circling back on itself in ever-decreasing circles. Where *N or M?* and *They Came to Baghdad* enjoy their sense of place and detailed minor characterization, *Destination Unknown* and *Passenger to Frankfurt* do not, eschewing such depths of texture and becoming thinner novels because of it, as their narratives depict a textual lack of curiosity and openness. Christie's reviving of Hitler in the 1970s belies an embracing of narrow stereotypes but in this she was not alone. Once again she accurately identified the cultural moment, for many audiences, proving the enduring contemporary relevance of her lesser-known thrillers.

Notes

1. The Phoney War is the period of between the expiry of Britain's ultimatum to Germany on 3 September 1939 and the evacuation of Allied forces from Dunkirk (26 May–4 Jun. 1940).
2. I would like to thank Rebecca Mills for pointing this out in correspondence.
3. Churchill's "Disaster of the First Magnitude" and "The Lights Are Going Out" speeches, for example, were given in 1938, before he became Prime Minister.
4. I would like to thank Rebecca Mills for reminding me to include this thriller, in a personal discussion.
5. I began attending CND anti-Vietnam marches to Grosvenor Square in 1964 as an adolescent.
6. Christie met Wagner's grand-daughter in Bayreuth and heard anecdotes about the composer and Hitler.

Works Cited

Aldridge, Mark. *Agatha Christie on Screen*. Palgrave, 2017.
Christie, Agatha. *An Autobiography*. Collins, 1977.
———. *Destination Unknown*. 1954. HarperCollins, 2003.
———. *N or M?* 1941. Signet, 2000.
———. *Passenger to Frankfurt*. 1970. Fontana, 1973.
———. *They Came to Baghdad*. 1951. HarperCollins, 2003.
Curran, John. *Agatha Christie's Secret Notebooks*. HarperCollins, 2009.
Gildersleeve, Jessica. "Nowadays: Trauma and Modernity in Agatha Christie's Late Poirot Novels." *Clues: A Journal of Detection*, vol. 34, no. 1, 2016, pp. 96–104.
"Jeremy Vine: Live from Coventry." *BBC Radio 2*, 8 Nov. 2017.
Knight, Stephen. *Crime Fiction since 1800: Detection, Death, Diversity*. Palgrave, 2010.
Lassner, Phyllis. "Double Trouble: Helen MacInnes and Agatha Christie's Speculative Spy Thrillers." *The History of British Women's Writing, 1945–1975*, edited by C. Hanson and S. Watkins, Palgrave, 2017, pp. 227–41.
Mills, Rebecca. "England's Pockets: Objects of Anxiety in Christie's Postwar Novels." *The Ageless Agatha Christie: Essays on the Mysteries and the Legacy*, edited by J.C. Bernthal, McFarland & Co., 2016, pp. 29–44.
Milton, John. *Paradise Lost. The Major Works*. Edited by Stephen Orgel and Jonathan Goldberg. Oxford University Press, 2003, pp. 355–618.
Morgan, Janet. *Agatha Christie: A Biography*. HarperCollins, 1997.
Plane, Gill. *Twentieth Century Crime Fiction: Gender, Sexuality and the Body*. Edinburgh University Press, 2001.
Sheridan, Dorothy, ed. *Wartime Women: An Anthology of Women's Wartime Writing for Mass Observation, 1937–45*. Heinemann, 1990.

Thompson, Laura. *Agatha Christie: An English Mystery*. Headline, 2007.
Warren, Jane. "The Strange Case of the Thriller Writer and the Soviet Spies." *The Express*, 17 Mar. 2014.
York, R. A. *Agatha Christie: Power and Illusion*. Palgrave Macmillan, 2007.

5 "When She Eats She Will Die"
Informal Meals and Social Change in *Sad Cypress* and "And Then There Were None"

J.C. Bernthal

During and in the wake of the Second World War, the most popular author writing in English was Agatha Christie. Despite crime fiction having exited its golden age, Christie's books and plays remained strong commercial successes. In this chapter, in common with most contributors to *Agatha Christie Goes to War*, I contend that part of Christie's sustained appeal during the Second World War lay in her engagement with contemporary issues. A motif running through Christie's output in this period is the informal meal; the social gathering where friends or misfits eat around a table; diners are often waited upon, but they eat tinned goods or fish-paste sandwiches. Sometimes, but not always, a person dies. This chapter situates these meals within their temporal and national contexts: they represent continuity in the wake of great social upheaval but are also frequently the locus of a violent renegotiation of tradition. Here, I focus on two texts: the novel *Sad Cypress* (1940) and the play "And Then There Were None" (1943).

Despite increasing scholarly attention being paid to Christie, little work has been done on her presentation of food. Silvia Baučeková's *Dining Room Detectives: Analysing Food in the Novels of Agatha Christie* (2015) provides a welcome remedy to this vacuum, exploring the parallels between preparing ingredients for a dish and preparing clues for the solution to a crime. However, Baučeková's valuable work is not contextualized, and therefore this chapter develops the focus further to look at food and its presentation in Christie within a specific temporal context. In life as in art, Christie had a passion for food: "I never saw a woman eat more", her chief theatrical producer recalled, "nor enjoy it more" (Gregg 34). Food is a constant presence in her work, and a superficial Internet search reveals hosts of blogs and magazines offering recipes inspired by the books. Some of these recipes' titles alone—"Pistachio and Rose Cake" (Grimshaw), "Little Belgian Truffles" (Alison's Wonderland Recipes), "Fig and Orange Scones with Devonshire Cream" (Paperandsalt), "Delicious Death: Super Fudgy Chocolate Cake!" (Alison's Wonderland Recipes)[1]—indicate the twin concepts of comfort and decadence that characterize a certain way of reading Christie. She is, according to this reading, a purveyor of "comfort" and "indulgence", an author who has always been read to distract from the harsh realities of the day (B. Wilson). There is, though, more to Christie than cream teas and luxury dinners: in her texts, meals are strategically placed at moments of heightened tension, where the act of collective eating is a social ritual amidst the disorder of death, violence, and uncertainty.

The two texts considered here are uniquely stamped by the Second World War and, in them, mealtimes have very different social significances. *Sad Cypress* was written and published in the war's early stages, and in it the characters cling to eating rituals, with rationed bread and sandwich paste forming uneasy substitutes for the old extravagances. The ritual of afternoon tea—which requires extra trips to the town to prepare—turns sour when a member of the party dies, and everyone suspects that the homogenous, modern sandwich paste has been poisoned. However, it turns out that the poison was not in the paste but in an emblem of imperialism and British tradition: the tea.

Toward the end of the war, Christie adapted her 1939 novel *And Then There Were None* for the stage, as a thriller in which ten people with clear roles in the prewar world are isolated on an island, being punished with death for past misdemeanors. The characters have no way to stave off their impending deaths, and all they can do is structure their days around meals, in a hollow simulation of the order and certainty they experienced before traveling to the island. Formal mealtimes are soon abandoned for makeshift meals, eaten in a huddle and straight from the tin. Tins here are no longer items to be regarded with suspicion, but lifelines, because preserved food is less likely than fresh food to have been poisoned. Formal mealtimes are soon abandoned for makeshift meals, eaten in a huddle and straight from the tin. At the start of the war, then, Christie presents a society suspicious of tins and rationing, but which needs them in order to maintain old traditions. Toward the end, the community she depicts needs preserved foods in order to survive, and, even then, this exercise of preservation is futile. The rituals of eating must be fundamentally reconsidered because the interwar world and worldview they belong to are already gone.

"Delicious Death"

It is a truism that eating structures social routines; "three principal daily eating events" form a recognized staple of day-to-day Western life (Yatesa and Warde 299). According to Julia Kristeva, social interactions and relationships are fundamentally based in eating. Most children grow and develop by feeding from their mothers, so that their first human relationships are predicated on the passage of food from body to body. This early "dependency" creates a ritual, which, for Kristeva ("Credit-Credence" 24–25), structures all future interactions. Here, her thinking has its roots in Freudian and Kleinian psychoanalysis, but she develops it into a theory of abjection, which has proved useful in considering the relevance of food and the corpse in crime fiction, and to which I will return in due course. For now, Kristeva helps us to appreciate a fundamental link in twentieth-century thought and culture between eating and social structure.

During times of national instability—war, terror alerts, recession—regular meals have remained, historically, in place across Britain (Myrdal and Klein 36; Yates and Warde). The nature of these meals has adapted over time, with social hierarchies, work dynamics, normalized family structures, and the roles of women shifting dramatically. However, meals remain a general point of structure and continuity even at times when little else can be certain. The Second World War remains the major destabilizing event in living British history. An uncanny historical period in which death was a daily reality reported in rhetoric that emphasized the nation's life and future, the war ushered in a crisis of direction. British citizens were routinely told that destroying the German enemy was the only way to preserve a traditional, peaceful national identity: one propaganda poster, for example, illustrates a cozy-looking house and car torn apart by explosives, with the slogan "IT CAN HAPPEN HERE—UNLESS WE KEEP 'EM FIRING!" However, the reality was one not of continuity but of fundamental change on social, educational, and economic levels. The "Dig for Victory" campaign of 1941 successfully fostered an impression of national unity, as citizens were encouraged to grow their own food and save or donate their scraps instead of relying on imports. However, as Clare Griffiths comments, the campaign also fostered a widespread "mood [of] frustration with limitations on quantity and variety" (Griffiths 216)—and who could grow what and when was never equal. There was little to unite those who lived through the war but a "sense of being witness to momentous times", while attempts to create a spirit of "national unity" through advertising campaigns and propaganda appeared increasingly futile (Rose 2).

Following the declaration of war in 1939, the Ministry of Food was established, to promote new, cheap foodstuffs as part of a modern shared identity. Food rationing was imposed in 1940 to divided public opinion on the measures. Initially, bacon, butter, and sugar were rationed, eventually followed by milk, dairy produce, bread, tea, and some fruits and vegetables. In early 1940, *Farmer's Weekly* declared: "Food is news to-day. Every man and woman in Britain is interested in it" (25). For many, food became a focus for discussions around social class and injustice. The economic conditions of the 1930s meant that most people had already gotten used to cheap, mass-produced food in tins, jars, and packets, but others noticed a dramatic change in the quantity and quality of food. While some newspapers lamented that upper and middle-class individuals had been reduced to eating "cheap meals" from "feeding center[s]", others reported on the "luxury feeding" practices of the very wealthy who were able to "dodge meat rationing" at secret restaurants (quoted in Rose 35). The overwhelming impression in the press, however, was of a diverse nation united in embracing and working with the necessary sacrifices over food. The *Sketch*, a conservative newspaper, for instance, emphasized the "equality of sacrifice" that rationing entailed (ibid). In a similar spirit, an early popular celebrity cookbook was produced in 1940: *A Kitchen Goes to War: Famous People Contribute 150 Recipes to a Ration-Time Cookery Book*. Contributors included John Gielgud, Jack Warner, and Agatha Christie.[2] This idea of everybody pitching in creatively assumes that, however scarce resources have become, people require more than regular nourishment; they require regular socialized eating routines.

The Second World War was also marked by nostalgia, and while "making do" with rations, many wistfully recalled an age of plenty, which for most people had never existed. Faced with the fear that children would grow up "unfamiliar with what we reckon to be 'a good square meal'" (*Famer's Weekly*, quoted in Rose 208), powerful fantasies of excess centered on the dining table. Several novelists in the war years—including Nancy Mitford, Elizabeth Bowen, and Diana Tutton—wrote about lavish dinners, sprawling across tables and afternoons with the attendant ritual and convention of vanished times (Humble 135–44). The escapism of popular literature, then, found partial expression in nostalgic presentations of social eating. In a society with an uncertain sense of future, the one remnant of continuity and structure, allowing for nostalgic embellishments, is the fact of regular meals.

In the more Spartan environs of a nation at war, indulgences could be found in literature, but crime fiction specifically was perceived as offering a kind of creature comfort in its promise of a resolution. Critics such as Edmund Wilson and W. H. Auden described reading detective fiction as "a vice" or "an addiction" akin to smoking, drinking, or exceeding one's rations. Christie's work often engaged with its contemporary reputation: for example, in *A Murder Is Announced* (1950), set firmly in the postwar world of rationing and recycling, much is made of a sickly chocolate cake dubbed "Delicious Death" and miraculously concocted from limited, imported resources. As Sarah Martin and Sally West point out in their contribution to the present volume, the cake is prepared by a maid who has no access to the extensive black-market network and who concocts this treat the hard way. It is one example among many of Christie directly reflecting her own reputation for escapist indulgence and indicates an underlying awareness that "Delicious Death" is itself a technically challenging, scarcely credible feat. However, unlike many of her contemporaries, Christie presented some meals realistically, as sparse and hurried affairs—and their frequent proximity to death in her fiction means that even a basic daily routine becomes insecure in a period affected by war.

"A Nice Cup of Tea"

Sad Cypress, a mystery set in 1939, was published on the eve of war. The novel displays a self-conscious connection with questions of heritage and continuity. The victim in *Sad Cypress* is a naïve twenty-one year-old, Mary, who is the illegitimate daughter of Laura Welman, although she is unaware of this. When Laura Welman dies intestate, her money goes to Mary, although Mary is killed before she becomes aware of her inheritance. At the same time, she has attracted the attention of her cousin Elinor's fiancé, inspiring intense melancholy in Elinor, which turns to envy, hatred, and self-pity. The crime in the novel revolves around an informal lunch scene, which appears exactly halfway through the text: it is at the emotional and physical center of the book. This is both a climax—the end of Part One—and a beginning—the start of a murder investigation. The prologue presents Elinor's trial for murder, after which the text flashes back to its origins, with Part One building up to this casual meal by increasingly spotlighting the food or drink that might carry poison.

Mary is to join Elinor one afternoon at Laura Welman's empty home, to sort through the deceased's personal effects. They will be accompanied by a nurse, Jessie Hopkins. Elinor spends the morning in a bad temper, wandering around shops in an attempt to take her mind off her romantic and financial problems. Thoughts festering, she enters a dairy, a bakery, and a grocer's shop to buy ingredients for sandwiches. The grocer suggests several pots of paste—"Salmon and shrimp? Turkey and tongue? Salmon and sardine? Ham and tongue?"—but Elinor reflects that all potted paste "taste[s] much alike" (*Sad Cypress* 89). She asks if pastes might lead to food poisoning, but the grocer assures her that he only stocks "an excellent brand" and she leaves with two pots (89). With words from the prologue—"Sandwiches … Fish paste … Empty house …" (8)—evoked, and the knowledge that Elinor will be charged with Mary's murder, readers are directed to mistrust the bland sameness of branded products.

At the house, Elinor unpacks her shopping in the pantry and wonders what would happen if Mary were to die (93). Then she finds Mary, who is with Hopkins, and suggests that the three of them should eat sandwiches together. "It's just on one o'clock", she explains, "and it's such a bother to have to go home for lunch" (97). This is "a picnic lunch"—a far cry from the leisurely and waited lunches that most prewar Christie characters enjoy, for example in *Lord Edgware Dies* (1933), in which a dinner table is so vast that a woman is able to send a doppelganger without fear of anyone examining her face too closely. In another of Christie's war novels, *The Hollow*, one character is so heartbroken at seeing a woman reduced to lunching on sandwiches in a "snack bar" rather than being served a home-cooked meal in her own house that he proposes marriage (*The Hollow* 153). The characters of *Sad Cypress*, too, are not used to impromptu meals: in fact, moments of heightened emotion in Part One of the book—such as Elinor realizing that her engagement cannot last—are cut off by announcements that lunch or dinner is served (41, 45). Over sandwiches, however, Elinor's hatred of Mary mounts despite her attempts to follow a social formula, and the result is sterile conversation (98–101). Other lunches in the novel consist not of fish paste, which is regarded with suspicion because it "stays on [shop] shelves for months" (139), but "remarkably fresh" fish, caught the same morning—these meals take place in large, formal "pleasant" rooms (185). The "picnic lunch" as a convenience, then, where "no one stands on ceremony" (111) and the nurse is included, is a sign of changing times and eroded hierarchies; the suspicious mass-produced paste is consumed in an atmosphere described as "queer", "cold", "cool", "frozen", and tense (99, 98, 101, 102).

While Elinor talks to Mary about family history, internally wishing that she could "go back" to a time before Mary arrived, Nurse Hopkins leaves the room to make a pot of tea (98–101). Ostensibly, Elinor is trying to bond with her new relative and move forward after a family death, but her feelings suggest the opposite, and the tea that Hopkins will bring links the past and the present with a symbol of continuity. Although every other element of the lunch has been bought for purpose, it is taken for granted that even an empty house will hold a canister of tea. Tea traditionally suggests hospitality but throughout the twentieth century, with the rise of tea shops, it has also represented a commercial attempt to *evoke* domesticity as a received tradition serving capitalist developments (Jolliffe 4–5). Hopkins insists on making tea herself on the stove: loose leaf, of course, and not tea bags imported from New York. Making the tea herself, she insists, is "old-fashioned" (20), but really it reflects a modern lack of servants. Hopkins herself is somewhat more modern than she seems: described as "homely-looking" and apparently deeply invested in how the household is run (20), she is in fact a "District Nurse" who visits several clients a week (19). Rather than being a fixed part of any one household, a companion as in some of Christie's other novels, she represents an external, paid-for presence.

From her first appearance, Hopkins is connected with tea. One of her first pieces of dialogue is, "I can *always* do with a cup of tea. I always say there's nothing like a nice cup of tea—a strong cup!" (19). Hopkins is always accompanied by tea or its paraphernalia: if not directly "hospitable with the teapot", she is sitting in a café, or munching a Bath bun (19–22, 93–105, 125–32, 171, 196). The word most often used of Hopkins is "homely", although, it will emerge, she is a con-artist from New Zealand who uses her teapot to lull people into sharing gossip that she can use for blackmail (248). When Hopkins announces "Here's the tea!" at the casual lunch, she seems "unaware of the anti-climax" (100).

Elinor has been watching Mary bite into the sandwiches, working hard on hiding her "desperate" emotions with a polite "mask" (101), but she has been imagining the fish paste as poison and, watching Mary eat, has been fantasizing about contamination (241). Hopkins pours some tea for herself and Mary, drains her cup, and disappears to switch off the kettle.

When Elinor steps back into the pantry, Hopkins is standing over the sink, "wiping her face with a handkerchief" and washing up (102). The two women wash up the tea things, with special attention to the paste pots, and eventually step out, to find Mary dying among the sandwiches. Hopkins "glare[s] at Elinor", "eyes hard with suspicion" (105). Elinor is later arrested for murder, and an investigation follows, as her defense team tries to find out who else could have laced the sandwiches, or even the sandwich paste, with morphine. Nobody considers the tea, ostensibly because the nurse also drank it (110), but also because of a much-repeated distrust of mass-produced sandwich fillings (89, 139, 219) and sandwiches left uncovered on a counter (189, 195, 221)—tea is unconsciously considered safe. Eventually, we learn that Hopkins poisoned the tea and injected herself with an emetic so that she would regurgitate the morphine into the pantry sink. It is not the dubious modern foodstuff that has carried poison, but the meal's one element of continuity: the tea.

Hopkins killed Mary because she wanted her money. She had previously killed Mary's mother, who was about to make a will favoring Elinor, so that she would die intestate and everything would go to Mary. Then she had encouraged Mary to make a will leaving everything to her adoptive aunt in New Zealand whom Mary then believed to be her only surviving blood relative. Hopkins later turns out to be the aunt in disguise. Her murders are based on exploiting legal and social conventions that see blood as the most binding tie. By cutting off the old woman's life before she could express her wishes about her estate, Hopkins has ensured that the money has only one place to go—to Mary—and by priming Mary with the maxim that money should stay in the family, she has secured it for herself. But for her scheme to work, and for suspicion to fall on the more modern-minded woman with her modern-minded sandwiches, Hopkins has to take poison.

In vomiting, she abjects the poison; that is to say, she expels what would otherwise kill her. Kristeva describes abjection as

> an extremely strong feeling which is at once somatic and symbolic, and which is above all a revolt of the person against an external menace from which one wants to keep oneself at a distance, but of which one has the impression that it is not only an external menace but that it may menace us from inside. ("Julia Kristeva" 136)

The cause of abjection is "not lack of cleanliness or health [...] but what disturbs identity, system, order. What does not respect borders, positions, rules. The in-between, the ambiguous, the composite" (Kristeva, *Powers of Horror* 4). Hopkins, the district nurse who wants to inherit another family's money, remains poisoned and poisonous. She watches the girl die; she continues to gossip over tea; she tries to make off with the money. In vomiting the tea, she maintains its innocence: "Nurse drank the tea", says the doctor. "Couldn't have been anything in there" (*Sad Cypress* 110). Sweet, innocent Mary must have been killed by Elinor, the modern hedonist who spends other people's money on cinema tickets and trendy hats. In fact, the story of continuity in Mary's money does not add up: if blood ties matter, her money should go to Elinor, not to an aunt-by-adoption. For Nurse Hopkins there is no problem that cannot be solved with a cup of tea, the stronger the better. Mary is the biggest problem, so the tea is stronger than usual. But Hopkins, like the homeliness of her teapot, is bogus.

Elinor does not get hot and bothered like Hopkins—she is always "cold". She gets Mary, the unexpected obstacle, out of her system in a less visceral way: by imagining to herself that the sandwiches are poisoned. At the end of the book, Elinor says:

> It seems so queer now ... like a kind of possession. That day I bought the paste and cut the sandwiches I was pretending to myself, I was thinking: "I've mixed poison with this and when she eats she will die—and then Roddy will come back to me." (240)

The doctor assures her that this is good and healthy, because "thinking murder [is not] the same thing as *planning* murder" (241, emphasis original). In the act of make-believe, Elinor has acknowledged change but maintained a sense of self by physically and spiritually internalizing both paste and poison. She has not made it a material obstacle outside herself but an alternative reality. In the world of 1939, this means accepting change and adapting with it.

When Elinor and Hopkins discover Mary close to death, the nurse glares at the prime suspect, suspicious and afraid. Readers are supposed to assume that she believes Elinor guilty of murder, but in truth it must be that she fears her plan could go wrong. Mary is as good as dead, and now Elinor is the problem: what does she know? What can she change? Hopkins is afraid that the simple traditions she stands for will fall apart under scrutiny because they are messy, incompatible, and much more dangerous in the changing world than fish paste.

"Have a Guzzle by Yourself"

For Kristeva (*Powers of Horror* 178–80), images that repulse and terrify also affirm life within the subject viewing them. To this extent, war is the ultimate expression of the abject. It is a state of affairs in which violent death is a daily reality, routinely and self-consciously sanitized. British citizens during the Second World War were frequently reminded of soldiers dying for them, of the enemy being killed for them; of death happening in the tidiest possible way, with national heritage taking the place of the corpse as its consequence. Corpses, for Kristeva, are striking because they "show me what I thrust aside in order to live" (3); in seeing a dead body an individual affirms its otherness and therefore their own vitality. As Gill Plain has discussed in relation to crime fiction, Kristeva helps us understand the ways in which the genre's "narrative catharsis" enables the reader's "fascination with death to be contained and indulged" (10). Quoting Kristeva, Plain suggests that crime fiction, as a literature of abjection, has the power "to transform [the] death drive into the start of life" (28). Despite the everyday fact of death during the war, and the military corpses built up in rhetoric, few people had actual access to the bodies of those killed in battle. Meat—carefully rationed and increasingly processed—was for many the only contact they had with physical corpses. It is, then, significant that one of Christie's most popular wartime thrillers, in which nearly all the characters die, makes extensive use of a tin of tongue.

Christie adapted *And Then There Were None* (1939) for the stage in 1943. Like *Sad Cypress*, both versions are explicitly set before the Second World War, although the huge changes and reevaluations wrought by war are reflected in the texts.[3] In fact, "And Then There Were None" had to switch theaters because its original venue was bombed mid-run (*An Autobiography* 497). The plot concerns eight motley houseguests and two hired servants, lured to an ultramodern mansion on an island for a weekend party. A gramophone record accuses each of them in turn of having killed people in ways that the law cannot touch. Over the weekend, they die one by one, following the pattern of a counting song. There is nobody else on the island so they soon realize that the murderer is one of them. A weekend house party is structured around meals, and as characters become more desperate for help to arrive, increasingly unable to leave the clockless room or even step onto the terrace for fear of assassination, their only indication of the time of day is the number of hours since they last ate. Meals in "And Then There Were None" have an all-or-nothing quality to them: once the butler has died there is no one to ring the gong and introduce a formal affair, and the survivors simply stop bothering. However, the absence of a meal is always noticed, with increasing anxiety as, watching each other die, the characters grow more barbaric.

Adapting the novel, Christie made several changes, presumably for dramatic impact, not least of which was having two characters survive. Another big change was in the presentation of meals: in the original, Christie uses breakfast, lunch, or dinner as a chance to ramp up tension, contrasting polite formulaic dialogue with inner monologues:

"What next? What next? Who? Which?"
[...] "Thanks, can I cut you some bread?"
Six people, behaving normally at breakfast... (*And Then There Were None* 120–21, emphasis original)

Without the possibility of inner monologues, and with set restrictions limiting action to one scene, a living room, Christie removed nearly all the meals from the play. However, there are artistic as well as practical justifications for this.

In the technically prewar novel, characters maintain structure until the end. After the butler's wife dies, the butler serves a late breakfast and cold meats for lunch; after he dies, the women do the cooking, and when there is only one woman left the survivors dine in the kitchen: resorting to professional and gendered hierarchies, they maintain the basic routine of three meals a day despite knowing that they are all going to die on the island. In the play, the first death occurs before dinner, and the next two mean that breakfast never happens. In Act Two, the butler worries about lunch, because he is not as good a cook as his dead wife and the boat with provisions has not arrived. He asks if "cold tongue and gelatine [would] be satisfactory", with "tinned fruit and cheese and biscuits" ("And Then There Were None" 41). As in the novel, the meal is a sign of social structure persisting despite the lack of fresh food or skill to prepare it: despite it being a lunch of reserves, it is still served formally and announced with a gong. In the next scene, characters agree that "going to lunch" was "right": as one guest, a judge, puts it, "The Court always adjourns for lunch" (51).

Then the butler dies and there are no more meals. Staged in 1943–44, amidst continuous bomb threats, "And Then There Were None" reflects a complete break from the structures of normality as the characters become corpses before each other's and the audience's eyes, and the survivors become increasingly animalistic. Finally, the heroine announces: "We're [in a] zoo. Last night we were barely human any more" (69). "We can't go on like this", says a doctor. "[W]e shall need food—sleep" (61), but nobody can prepare food because they cannot be trusted unsupervised: "it might be inadvisable to eat or drink something you had prepared out of our sight", says the judge (62). The one character who keeps reiterating his hunger is Inspector Blore, a policeman whose crime was getting an innocent man convicted of theft and killed in prison. Time and again, Blore insists, "What about something to eat?" (62), "What about the food idea?" (63), and "Starving won't do us any good" (65). "Do stop thinking about your stomach, Blore", says the hero of the piece. "This craving for food and drink will be your undoing" (73).

When dinner is skipped on the second day, Blore can stand it no longer. "Go and have a guzzle by yourself", says the young hero (63). Blore finds a tin of biscuits and "wolf[s] the lot" because nobody else is hungry (65). The animal language is emphasized in both stage directions and dialogue.

Eating biscuits in front of the others, Blore demonstrates that he is unable to live without the structure of three meals a day, but he abandons their "square" aspect and their social side. In the microcosm of the Island, civilization has collapsed and Blore, trying to recreate the old structures for himself alone rather than as a communal act, is the butt of a joke.

By the end of the scene, five guests have become three. The final scene takes place the next morning, and opens with a makeshift meal that is neither breakfast nor lunch. The three survivors are hunched around a table, eating tongue from a tin. They are laughing hysterically, exchanging jokes about their imminent deaths (68). They think they have identified the murderer—another guest who has disappeared: "I feel a new man", says one; "everything seems different", says another (68). Having decided that they know what is happening, they feel finally ready to have another go at meals. However, as any audience member aware that there is half an hour of drama left will realize, this is a false resolution. Meals might suggest continuity and, after their absence, a restoration of order, but there has been no real resolution to the puzzle; an absent man has been named as the criminal for an easy fix. The falseness of this resolution is indicated by the characters' knowledge that they are still in danger of death, and the hysteria with which they eat in a parody of formal dining, not even decanting their food from its airtight container.

In 1943, tinned food was not unusual: as a method of preservation, canning had been around for well over a century, and tins had been common in pantries for decades (Jango-Cohen 6–13). However, tinned meat only really gained popularity during the Second World War, when a shortage of fresh meat, raised prices due partly to difficulties around importing and exporting, and changes in consumption habits, saw the rise of Spam and other products. A meal based around tinned tongue, let alone one consisting solely of it, is a dramatic signifier in a building where the previous meal was announced with a gong. Tongue is a significant meat product here: eating it, the characters are finally speaking to one another, wagging their own tongues. It is also an uncanny thing to eat for survival: a tongue, severed, pealed, canned, and sliced, then rolled over one's own tongue to take one's mind off violence. By eating preserved food, the characters face their own need for self-preservation: a tin of tongue, when they return to the routine of eating, is a final, processed attempt to trust established methods of preservation.

Christie also made repeated use of tinned tongue in the novel, as the meals get cruder: "If I even see [another] tinned tongue, I shall be sick!" (*And Then There Were None* 157). The language suggests violent rejection not just of the grotesque, un-lavish meals, but also of external preservation. Canned meat, after all, was usually imported. The equivalent line in the play is: "I must say I was hungry. But all the same I don't think I shall ever fancy tinned tongue again" ("And Then There Were None" 68). It is much more refined language, suggesting a return—or an attempt to return—to the polite and ordered world the characters left for the island. Desperation is betrayed by the manic laugh with which the actor is instructed to deliver the line, and the fact that in the next few minutes, someone will die.

Blore cannot control his venal appetites. Having enjoyed the meal, he says he is still hungry; this is when the hero tells him to stop thinking with his stomach. As he makes his way to the kitchen, Blore hears a motor horn and rushes out, convinced that salvation has arrived from the mainland. There, he trips over a wire and is killed by a falling object, off-stage (73). Blore has always been the fool, the corrupt police officer, the character who thinks only of feeding, and the stress of the weekend has brought this out in his selfish "guzzle". As soon as he has gone back to meals he has become an anomaly, not fit for social rituals, and he must be expunged. His death, away from the scene, leaves the two survivors who have bonded over tongue. The rest of the action happens quickly: they go wild with suspicion, the heroine tries to kill herself, the true culprit appears and conveniently dies, and the young couple kisses over his corpse: "We got married, and then there were none!" the hero announces, as he joins his beloved in a noose and they kiss. From the distance, a motorboat approaches (78).

Hunching madly around a tin of tongue has rehabilitated the two survivors, now ready to return to the world: not just to the routine of days structured around meals, but to the ultimate regulation of marriage. Unlike Blore, they have not given in to their carnality but preserved themselves as best they could, like meat in a tin. They know no other way to live. It is an unsatisfying ending, and some productions of the play have changed the script, inserting the novel's ending, in which all the characters die (Harmston). However, as we have seen, Christie changed more than the body-count when she adapted a verge-of-war novel into a wartime play. She changed the group of strangers trying desperately to cling to social rituals into a social group that has lost all control and can only try to recreate what it knows if it is to survive. Yet, it is survival in a noose. The man who wolfs the biscuits is guilty of carnal excess, unstructured and independent, and he is abject.

Conclusion

What lies behind abjection? According to Kristeva ("Julia Kristeva"), "it is a desire for separation, for becoming autonomous, and also the feeling of an impossibility of doing so" (136). In war, the horror of violence is commoditized, processed for entertainment and instruction. If somebody is changed by war they cannot live in peace; in an Agatha Christie, if somebody is changed by food they cannot be social. They must be sick, or they must die. Fish paste, mass-produced and mysterious, is a red herring. Safe, homely tea is poison. Fragile social rituals are preserved in tins, imported and unknown, but the only safe thing in a home away from home.

In the fiction of Agatha Christie, informal meals provide textual spaces for attitudes to social change to reach a point of passionate crisis, where social coding is at its frailest because it no longer promises routine and certainty, and has come to exist as a gesture. Christie's writing has long been understood as the exemplar of conservatism, as a body of work in which order is always restored—but she reflects a society that needs to change and does not know how because it cannot let go of the past. This is most pronounced in texts written in the context of overwhelming national crisis, where informal meals present a moribund social order in microcosm. The whodunit format—the inevitability of death and blame—lends these scenes political power.

Notes

1 See also Young's "Crystalized Ginger" (2015) and "Ice-Cream Floats" (2017), and Laing's "An Agatha Christie Birthday Cake to Die For" (2010).
2 Christie's recipe for "Mystery Potatoes" involves serving mashed anchovies and margarine in baked potato skins (Ross 100).
3 In the received tradition, and for clarity, the novel will be referred to in italics as *And Then There Were None*, and the stage version within quotes as "And Then There Were None".

Works Cited

Alison's Wonderland Recipes. "Delicious Death: Super Fudgy Chocolate Cake!" *Alison's Wonderland*, 22 Oct. 2015, wonderlandrecipes.com/2015/10/22/delicious-death-super-fudgy-chocolate-cake-dark-chocolate-frosting-and-easy-halloween-toppers Accessed 4 Mar. 2018.

———. "Little Belgian Truffles." *Alison's Wonderland*, 29 Oct. 2015, wonderlandrecipes.com/2015/10/29/little-belgian-truffles Accessed 4 Mar. 2018.

Auden, W. H. "The Guilty Vicarage." *Harpers*, May 1948, pp. 406–12.

Baučeková, Silvia. *Dining Room Detectives: Analysing Food in the Novels of Agatha Christie*. Cambridge Scholars Publishing, 2015.

Christie, Agatha. *An Autobiography*. 1977. Harper, 2011.

———. *And Then There Were None*. 1939. Planet Three Publishing, 2002.

———. "And Then There Were None".1943. *The Mousetrap and Other Plays*. Harper, 2011, pp. 1–78.

———. *The Hollow*.1946. Fontana, 1971.

———. *Sad Cypress*. 1940. Collins, 1951.

Gregg, Hubert. *Agatha Christie and All That Mousetrap*. William Kimber, 1980.

Griffiths, Clare. "Heroes of the Reconstruction? Images of British Farmers in War and Peace." *War, Agriculture, and Food: Rural Europe from the 1930s to the 1950s*, edited by Paul Brassley, Yves Segers and Leen Van Molle, Routledge, 2012, pp. 195–208.

Grimshaw, Vicki. "Taste the Food from your Favourite Books with These Novel Recipes." *Daily Mirror*, 17 Jun. 2017, www.mirror.co.uk/news/uk-news/taste-food-your-favourite-books-10639174 Accessed 4 Mar. 2018.

Harmston, Joe (dir.). *And Then There Were None*. Touring Theatrical Production. Bill Kenwright Limited. First performance 20 Jul. 2015.

Humble, Nicola. *The Feminine Middlebrow Novel, 1920s to 1950s: Class, Domesticity, and Bohemianism*. Oxford University Press, 2001.

Jango-Cohen, Judith. *The History of Food*. Lerner Books, 2009.

Jolliffe, Lee. "Introduction: Connecting Tea and Tourism." *Tea and Tourism: Tourists, Traditions, Transformations*, edited by Lee Jolliffe, Channel View Publications, 2007, pp. 3–33.

Kristeva, Julia. "Credence-Credit." *In the Beginning was Love: Psychoanalysis and Faith*, translated by Arthur Goldhammer. Columbia University Press, 1987, pp. 23–29.

———. "Julia Kristeva." *Women Analyze Women: In France, England, and the United States*, edited by Elaine Hoffman Baruch and Lucienne J. Serrano, New York University Press, 1988, pp. 129–48.

———. *Powers of Horror: An Essay on Abjection*. Translated by Leon S. Roudiez. Columbia University Press, 1982.

Laing, Jemima. "An Agatha Christie Birthday Cake to Die For". *BBC Devon*, 10 Sep. 2010, news.bbc.co.uk/local/devon/hi/people_and_places/history/newsid_8988000/8988240.stm Accessed 4 Mar. 2018.

Myrdal, Alva and Viola Klein. *Women's Two Roles: Home and Work*. 1956. Routledge, 2001.

Paperandsalt. "Agatha Christie: Fig and Orange Scones with Devonshire Cream." *Paper and Salt*, 1 Oct. 2012, paperandsalt.org/2012/10/01/agatha-christie-fig-and-orange-scones-with-devonshire-cream Accessed 4 Mar. 2018.

Plain, Gill. *Twentieth Century Crime Fiction: Gender, Sexuality and the Body*. Edinburgh University Press, 2001.

Rose, Sonya O. *Which People's War? National Identity and Citizenship in Wartime Britain, 1939–1945*. 2003. Oxford University Press, 2008.

Ross, Peter. *The Curious Cookbook*. British Library, 2012.

Wilson, Bee. "Why We Should Eat Like Hercule Poirot at Christmas", *Daily Telegraph*, 19 Dec. 2014, www.telegraph.co.uk/foodanddrink/11288310/Why-we-should-all-eat-like-Hercule-Poirot-at-Christmas.html Accessed 4 Mar. 2018.

Wilson, Edmund. "Who Cares Who Killed Roger Ackroyd".1944. *The Art of the Mystery Story: A Collection of Critical Essays*, edited by Howard Haycraft, Simon & Schuster, 1947, pp. 390–97.

Yates, Luke and Warde, Alan. "The Evolving Content of Meals in Great Britain: Results of a Survey in 2012 in Comparison with the 1950s." *Appetite* 84, 2015, pp. 299–308.

Young, Kate. "Food in Books: Crystallised Ginger from *The Adventure of the Christmas Pudding* by Agatha Christie." *The Guardian*, 24 Dec. 2015, www.theguardian.com/books/little-library-cafe/2015/dec/24/food-in-books-crystallised-ginger-from-the-adventure-of-the-christmas-pudding-by-agatha-christie Accessed 4 Mar. 2018.

———. "Novel Recipes: Ice-Cream Floats from Agatha Christie's *Crooked House*." *The Guardian*, 18 Aug. 2017, www.theguardian.com/books/little-library-cafe/2017/aug/18/novel-recipes-ice-cream-floats-from-agatha-christies-crooked-house Accessed 4 Mar. 2018.

6 "A Worrying, Nerve-Wracked World"

Agatha Christie's Emergence as a Playwright during and after the Second World War

Julius Green

Histories of British theater tell us that the 1950s belonged to Samuel Beckett, John Osborne, and Shelagh Delaney but, arguably, it was Agatha Christie who was the most successful playwright of the decade, becoming, in 1953, the only woman ever to have had three of her plays presented in the West End simultaneously—a record, which she holds to this day.

Her most productive decade as a novelist was the 1930s; but for Agatha Christie, playwright, this was a period of frustration and disappointment. By the outbreak of the Second World War, despite having penned seven full-length plays on a variety of subjects, she had so far only seen one of them performed (a brief run of her only Poirot play, *Black Coffee*, in 1930–31). Frustratingly for her, there had been successful adaptations of her work for the stage by other writers; but it was not until toward the end of the war, when she was in her mid-fifties, that Christie would establish herself as a celebrated West End and Broadway playwright in her own right.

Alison Light's definitive study of the significance of Agatha Christie's contribution to popular fiction between the wars has led to this facet of her work, and the middle-class "conservative modernity", which Light identifies as characterizing it (61–112), being regular starting points for academic appraisals of both Christie's literary contribution and her role as a social commentator engaging (albeit indirectly) with such issues as class identity and the role of women. This focus on the interwar novels inevitably anchors appraisals of Christie's frame of reference in the resonances and sociopolitical outcomes of the First World War, and a mythology has consequently evolved regarding the extent and significance of her engagement with the conflict. We increasingly hear statements to the effect that "Agatha Christie, both as a person and as a novelist, was forged in the fires of the First World War" (Weinberg), but it is important to put her much-reported wartime work as a Voluntary Aid Detachment nurse at the Red Cross hospital in Torquay's town hall into perspective.

It is apparent from her own account that Christie's experiences at the town hall were very different from the frontline horrors of the war's field hospitals. She notes that "half our patients seemed to be trench feet cases" (*An Autobiography* 239), and writes entertainingly about hospital staff politics, acting as a "human towel rail" (230) for surgeons performing operations and composing love letters for convalescing soldiers to their sometimes numerous girlfriends (239–40). Like many before and since, she fainted at her first sight of blood in the operating theater, but her approach to nursing—including clearing up after operations and disposing of amputated limbs—appears to have been mature, calm, and practical, and something for which she had a natural aptitude: "From the beginning, I enjoyed nursing. I took to it easily, and found it, and always have found it, one of the most rewarding professions that anyone can follow" (230). She writes with sadness of the death of friends and of "the background of life being altered" but notes that her own experiences in the war were very different from that of her new husband, Archibald, whose overseas postings with the Royal Flying Corps put him "in the middle of death, defeat, retreat, fear" (233).

Like many who lived through both world wars on the home front, Agatha Christie was notably more directly affected by the Second than the First. Attacks on London and some coastal towns by Zeppelins and Gotha G.IV bombers, as well as a number of German naval raids, accounted for 1,413 civilian deaths in the First World War; but 60,595 would perish as a result of enemy action in the Second (Jones), conclusively bringing to an end the British civilian population's long-enjoyed geographical isolation from the ravages of European conflict. Rebecca Mills is one of the few academics to analyze Christie's post-1939 novels in this context, but as a result of excluding Christie's work for the stage she finds herself in agreement with Stephen Knight's argument that Christie's wartime work is characterized by an "Austenesque pattern of radical displacement" (30) and concludes that in Christie's canon "the full effect of wartime and its tensions and deprivations are delayed as well as displaced" (30). Virginia Woolf famously argued that Jane Austen and other writers of the romantic era enjoyed an "immunity" from the wars raging in Europe at the time (quoted in Favret 46), and the nature of Austen's engagement with the subject has since been much debated (see Favret). While there is a strong case that Christie, as a civilian during the pre-radio news First World War was, to an extent, similarly "immune", the same can certainly not be said for her engagement with the Second.[1]

The whole of the British south coast was technically a front line throughout most of the Second World War, and more than 130 people were killed in over a dozen bombing raids on Torquay alone between 1940 and 1944 (Brine); but it was still relatively safe compared to London. Christie's decision to leave her Devon home and join her second husband Max Mallowan (who was working for Royal Airforce Intelligence) in the capital at the height of the Blitz, remaining there even once Max had been posted to Cairo, thus meant that she had effectively elected to "go to war" and place herself in the midst of "death (and) fear". Her work as a dispenser at University College Hospital did not involve treating casualties from the front line, but the war itself was considerably more immediate than it would have been had she remained in Torquay. In her autobiography, Christie notes,

> It had become natural to expect that you yourself might be killed soon, that the people you loved best might be killed, that you would hear of deaths of friends. Broken windows, bombs, land-mines, and in due course flying-bombs and rockets—all these things would go on, not as something extraordinary, but as perfectly natural. (489)

She slept with a pillow over her head to avoid flying glass: "I myself never went down to any shelter during the war. I always had a horror of being trapped underground" (486).[2]

Christie and Mallowan lived in a number of rented London flats in the early part of the war, with "noisy sessions of bombs going off all round us" (485), as well as briefly at their own house in Sheffield Terrace, Holland Park. In September 1940 the office of Christie's agent Edmund Cork suffered bomb damage and the following month Sheffield Terrace was hit (in its owners' absence). In March 1941, Mallowan's friend and archaeologist colleague Stephen Glanville introduced the couple to the stylishly modernist Lawn Road Flats in Belsize Park. Here they took up residence alongside a colorful group of emigres, artists, and Soviet spies (see Burke), whose intellectually stimulating company undoubtedly broadened Christie's creative, social, and political frame of reference and helped to inform her characterizations and plots in what was to be a particularly productive period of writing. In her thoughtful and challenging 1958 domestic drama *Verdict*, which she probably started work on at around this time, The Lawn Road milieu is reflected in her portrayal of East European academics living in a London flat. Notable among them is the idealist Professor Karl Hendryk who, having fled persecution in his own country, encounters his nemesis in the form of the fascistic eugenicist Helen Rollander, who states that "[p]eople who are sick and worn out and useless should be removed so as to leave room for the ones who matter" (*Verdict* 596).

By way of light relief, Christie spent occasional weekends at the Haslemere house of her friend the actor Francis Sullivan (the first stage Poirot) and his wife, the set designer Danae Gaylen. "I always find it restful to stay with actors in wartime", she notes in her autobiography, "their entire talk was of theatrical people, theatrical things, what was going on in the theatrical world, who was going into E.N.S.A.

[Entertainments National Service Association]—it was wonderfully refreshing" (*Autobiography* 489–90). Her lifelong fascination with theater is also evident in her letters to Mallowan during the war, which are full of well-observed critiques of the major Shakespearian productions of the day (Correspondence). Agatha Christie, whose imaginary world has offered a welcome escape to so many, found her own escape in the world of theater, and specifically an escape from the stresses of being a civilian in wartime London.

Before the war, Christie had written a number of plays, some of them quite remarkable works, outside of the thriller genre. In 1937, she sent her epic history of the pharaoh Akhnaton to John Gielgud, whom she greatly admired, but he politely rejected it on the grounds that its multiple settings and enormous *dramatis personae* would make it impractical to stage. It is likely that Gielgud may also have been reluctant to attach himself to a project that explored the catastrophic consequences of a policy of appeasement at a time when the British government was pursuing such a policy with Germany; one of the requirements of the Lord Chamberlain's Office play licensing department was that plays must not be "calculated to impair friendly relations with any foreign Power" (Johnson).

Christie had more luck with her passionate, witty, and cleverly constructed domestic drama, *A Daughter's a Daughter*. Compared by surprised critics to the work of Terence Rattigan at its eventual West End premiere in 2009, it was to have been produced by Basil Dean, the man who launched the playwriting careers of Clemence Dane and Margaret Kennedy, and in mid-August 1939 preparations were being made for a production potentially starring Gertrude Lawrence, one of the most popular actresses of the day. Within a few weeks, though, Britain had declared war on Germany; production plans were abandoned, and Dean's energies were diverted to his work as co-founder of the ENSA, providing wartime entertainment to the troops.[3]

Shortly after war broke out, Christie was approached by Graham Greene, who was working for the Secret Intelligence Service, with a suggestion that she undertake propaganda work for the government. Despite being a great admirer of Greene, she declined: "I did not think that I was the kind of writer who would be any good at propaganda, because I lacked the single-mindedness to see only one side of the case" (*An Autobiography* 505). What Greene did not know was that Christie was at the time working on a stage version of the novel that was to become her most enduringly popular, *And Then There Were None*.[4] This dramatization would prove to be Christie's first West End and Broadway success as a playwright and was set to become a wartime morale booster every bit as effective as Laurence Olivier's more calculated 1944 film version of Shakespeare's *Henry V*.

The conceit of Christie's thriller, published by Collins in November 1939, is that ten strangers are lured to the only house on an island, where they discover that they are all the intended victims of a killer who is committed to executing each of them in a manner inspired by a then-popular children's counting song. The eight guests and two domestic staff are alleged by the killer to have escaped justice for previous misdemeanors, so that their deaths represent a form of retribution. A masterpiece of dramatic construction, it inevitably did not take long for playwrights to show an interest in adapting the novel for the stage. Christie, however, was determined to dramatize it herself, and it seems that she completed the first draft of the script within months of the book's publication. Her producers, however, asked that she change the ending for the stage version: "Their suggestions were for once sensible and in fact an improvement", she wrote to Edmund Cork, "the alternative 'happy ending' 'He got married and then there were none', I have always contemplated as a possibility if I can do it my own way, which is agreed" (letter dated 4 Nov. 1942. Correspondence).

Christie here refers to two alternative final lines that were used for the counting song. The one in which the final character "went and hanged himself, and then there were none" leads to the novel's bleak and mystifying outcome, where all ten of the visitors to the island are found dead. The other, where the final character "got married, and then there were none" offers the possibility of a "happy" ending, which was the version used in a gaudily illustrated children's book of the time.[5]

The play eventually opened at the Wimbledon Theatre in September 1943 and received its West End premiere at St. James's Theatre two months later. Although the prewar West End puts the current one to shame with regard to its promotion of work by female playwrights, the absence at war of a generation of men, as with so many other industries, helped to further consolidate women's position in the theater. As well as Christie, the many women who saw their work premiered in the West End during the war included Enid Bagnold, Esther McCracken, Daphne Du Maurier, Rose Franken, Margaret Mayo, and Lillian Hellman (see Gale). The production was directed by Irene Hentschel, the first woman to direct Shakespeare at Stratford, and Christie was full of admiration for the skill with which Hentschel crafted its thrills and atmospherics (*An Autobiography* 472).

The wartime conditions that prevailed throughout the play's first West End run are evident from an announcement in the St. James' Theatre program:

> Warning of an AIR RAID will be given by a RED electrical sign above the orchestra pit. ALL CLEAR will similarly be shown in GREEN. Patrons are advised to remain in the Theatre, but those wishing to leave will be directed to the nearest official air-raid shelter, after which the performance will be continued for so long as is practicable. (St James' Theatre)

Fortunately, a performance was not in progress when the St. James' suffered bomb damage at the end of February 1944 and the production was forced to relocate to another theater for several weeks.

It may seem surprising that Christie's first theatrical success was staged in these adverse circumstances, but there was clearly an intrinsic quality to the piece that struck a chord with wartime theatergoers. On one level, the play explores the familiar Christie themes of guilt and the nature of justice, and employs her tried and tested device of bringing together a group of strangers in an isolated location. But all of these ideas are here developed to an extreme, enhanced by the claustrophobia of the setting. Unlike other adapters of the novel for stage and screen, Christie skillfully sets her own dramatization in only one room, so that the characters believe themselves to be risking death if they step outside of it. As tension builds in the face of the inexorable progress of a bloodthirsty unseen adversary, they thus find themselves in a not dissimilar predicament to the occupants of an air raid shelter, reflecting Christie's own fear of being trapped in such a scenario. It does not take a huge leap of imagination to see how this scenario might have resonated with the vulnerable inhabitants of an island state at war with a powerful enemy and where, as the program's notes on evacuation procedures make clear, everyone is a potential victim.[6]

Christie's plot, like William Golding's *Lord of the Flies* (1954), examines the disintegration of social order in a group marooned on a small island. In her original play script, though not in the published edition, the character Vera makes the point that, after the horrors of the night, "we are the 'zoo'".[7] During the war many of the established niceties theatergoing were abandoned; travel to and from theaters was a challenge (as it is to and from the island in the play) and, because the majority of performances were matinees, evening dress and post-show restaurant dining became things of the past. At the outset of the play, in the host's absence, dressing for dinner is "optional", and the image of the potential victims running short of food, fuel, and even cigarettes would have had a particular resonance. The disembodied, threatening pronouncements of the killer, played to the assembled guests on a record, are likely to have resonated with audiences who, for the first time, were able to hear the speeches of their own enemy in their homes on radio news.

Christie's novel is a prewar work, but the final script of the play was not completed until the autumn of 1942, by which time London had experienced the Blitz. Despite the *dramatis personae* including a retired First World War general and an army captain who has served in East Africa, there is no direct reference to the country being at war either currently or imminently. Nonetheless, without deliberately creating wartime or a military piece, Christie had exactly tapped into the contemporary zeitgeist, and her crafting of the new, upbeat ending undoubtedly sealed the play's success in this context. In the play the two surviving characters are shown to be innocent of the "crimes", which the murderer believes them to have committed, and one of them is even revealed to have been a war hero. Their ultimate vindication, defeat of their persecutor, and escape from the island thus inadvertently turned the play into a morale booster as well as a thriller; such was its appeal that Field Marshal Montgomery attended a special performance for the troops, and it would later become a staple of the ENSA repertoire. Christie herself was invited to join an ENSA tour toward the end of the war, but the sudden return of Max from Cairo necessitated a change of plan.

As well as its revised ending, one of the reasons for the wartime success of Christie's play was undoubtedly the involvement in its production of the People's Entertainment Society (PES). This extraordinary organization, founded in 1942 at the height of the war, was the brainchild of the East End Member of Parliament Alfred John Barnes, later Minister of Transport in the postwar Attlee government. Conceived as the theatrical production wing of the co-operative movement, the PES's proud aim was to

> foster and further the art of the drama in accordance with the principle that true art, by effectively presenting and truthfully interpreting life as experienced by the majority of the people, can move the people to work for the betterment of society. ("Rules of the People's Entertainment Society")

The PES's support not only involved direct financial input, but also constant publicity for the production among its members, including the promotion of group bookings.

Successful touring and Broadway presentations followed the London premiere, but the circumstances of war were less kind to three other plays penned by Christie, all of which their producers hoped would capitalize on her sudden breakthrough as a dramatist. *Appointment with Death*, radically adapted by Christie from her 1938 novel, closed after forty-two performances on 5 May 1945, five days after Hitler's suicide and three days before the end of the war in Europe; not surprisingly, the public were glued to their radios during these momentous events, and theatrical entertainment was not a priority. Ironically, just over three months later it would be the boom in theater attendances caused by demobbed soldiers celebrating the end of the war that Edmund Cork would blame for the failure of *Hidden Horizon* (adapted by Christie from her 1937 novel *Death on The Nile*) to find a West End home following its national tour. On 23 August 1945 he wrote to Christie, "Such business as is being done today has never been known among London theaters, and there is not a single show that need come off" (Quoted in Green 218). Meanwhile, in America, the try-out at Martha's Vineyard Playhouse of Christie's extraordinary 1945 adaptation of her 1944 novel *Towards Zero* was comprehensively upstaged by the surrender of Japan two days previously, following the bombing of Hiroshima and Nagasaki; a mooted Broadway transfer was abandoned, and the play was never heard of again.[8]

After the war, Christie continued to work on ideas and scripts for plays, but none would actually reach the stage again until 1951, by which time, in her notably Poirotless adaptation of her 1946 Poirot novel *The Hollow*, it was very clearly a postwar world that she was portraying. *The Hollow* may be set at a country house party (which is by no means typical of a Christie play), but it revels in questioning the precepts of that setting and, importantly, places the inhabitants of the house concerned very precisely in a postwar milieu. The play's portrayal of a crumbling aristocracy in a time of rapid social change seems almost to take its cue from Chekhov, and among the many challenges to the established order of things faced by the play's central Angkatell family is one from within, as young Midge opts to go and work in a shop, declaring to a would-be suitor: "Your world and mine are far apart. I'm only half an Angkatell. The other half's just plain business girl, with unemployment always lurking around the corner in spite of the politicians' brave words" (208). Meanwhile, the butler Gudgeon attempts to train a young maid whose father is a Labor voter: "You can't help your parents, Doris" (190).

1952s *The Mousetrap* again demonstrates Christie's ability as a playwright to capture the spirit of the age. In this case, we have moved on a stage from the disintegrating rural idyll of *The Hollow*, as a modern young middle-class couple struggle to convert an inherited manor house into a hotel in the era of ration book austerity. "There are one or two rather incongruous bits of Victorian furniture", say Christie's stage directions "and the house looks not so much a period piece, but a house which has been lived in by generations of the same family with dwindling resources" (287). Judging from contemporary photographs, Roger Furse's original set design probably fulfilled this brief more successfully than subsequent re-workings ("The Mousetrap Designers").[9] By 1954's comedy-thriller *Spider's Web*, the couple at the center of events are tenants (rather than owners) of a large country house, having been offered it at a knockdown rate, thus completing a triptych of plays (*The Hollow*, *The Mousetrap*, and *Spider's Web*), which effectively charts the postwar fate of the stately home.

In *The Mousetrap*, the young owners of Monkswell Manor, Giles and Mollie Ralston, keep chickens for eggs, chop firewood, and paint their own signage. Dinner is "two tins of minced beef and cereal and a tin of peas" (*The Mousetrap* 301) and, in the absence of "indoor" staff, Mollie notably carries a vacuum cleaner across the stage four years before the sight of a woman ironing caused a sensation at the Royal Court. Once the guests start to arrive they are a markedly displaced, transient, anonymous collection of solo travelers ("a queer bunch" the censor commented, knowingly, in his report [Lord Chamberlain's Office]), and a murder in their midst triggers a recognizably wartime paranoia, with even the happily married young couple suspecting each other.

The Mousetrap's subject matter is as hard-hitting as its setting is contemporary, being inspired as it was by a widely reported 1944 case in which a child died in foster care. The play's backstory concerns the "Longridge Farm case", in which a child similarly dies after being placed in foster care with his two siblings—a scenario, which, to London audiences in the early 1950s, would have stirred anxious memories of wartime evacuee children being placed in the care of strangers. This is underlined by reference to the child's father having been an "Army sergeant, serving abroad", and Mollie noting that

> If he came home, after being a prisoner with the Japs, perhaps, and having suffered terribly—if he came home and found his wife dead and that his children had gone through some terrible experience, and one of them had died through it, he might go off his head a bit and want—revenge! (336)

Although in the play the reason for the children's fostering is that (as with the real-life case of the O'Neill brothers) they were "brought before the court as in need of care and protection". (316), Christie's 1947 radio drama "Three Blind Mice", on which *The Mousetrap* is based, is more explicit in its wartime referencing: "It was 1940. Three evacuee children were billeted on the Greggs. One of them died as a result of criminal neglect and ill treatment. Their father was serving abroad with his regiment" ("Three Blind Mice"). Christie herself was familiar with the wartime fostering system, having handed over her own country house, Greenway (near Torquay), to a scheme for the accommodation of London child evacuees in the early part of the war; it was later requisitioned for use by the American navy.

In "Three Blind Mice", one character's mother was killed in the Blitz and another was married to a fighter pilot killed in action. When Christie expanded the half-hour radio play into a novella (published in America in 1950, two years before its eventual appearance as a stage play), this also contained numerous references to the immediately postwar setting. Of the young couple at the center of the story, Christie observes that "In a worrying, nerve-wracked world they had found the miracle of each other" ("Three Blind Mice" 44). Although the contemporary referencing is less explicit in *The Mousetrap* itself, it is still abundantly clear that we are in a "worrying, nerve-wracked world"; a world of rationing, regulations, and mistrust.

As Harold Hobson, former *Sunday Times* drama critic, commented in an article included in the play's fortieth anniversary brochure, "I am convinced that *The Mousetrap* would never have achieved the longest run in the history of theater had it not been, as well as a very exciting story, a parable of the social outlook of our times" (Hobson). Federica Crescentini has undertaken detailed research on this largely unacknowledged "Second Identity" of *The Mousetrap* as social commentary[10] and, in my view, Christie's real skill as a playwright lies in her ability deftly to deliver this in a manner acceptable to the censor, palatable to West End family audiences of the early 1950s, and within the considerable constraints of the "whodunit" format. "Kitchen sink" realism, by contrast, is relatively easy to achieve on the stage (or onscreen).

In 2016, *EastEnders* script writer Sarah Phelps, herself best-known as an adept practitioner of the "kitchen sink" genre, adapted Christie's very short story "The Witness for the Prosecution" (originally published in 1925 as "Traitor Hands") into a two-hour television drama. Despite the story itself not containing a single period-specific reference, Phelps expanded the piece—which Christie herself referred to as a "mere sketch" (*An Autobiography* 515)—into a multilayered examination of post–First World War British society, thereby doing much to perpetuate the myth of Christie's work being "forged in the fires of the First World War". Phelps takes as her starting point "foppish" solicitor Mayherne's "little dry-as-dust cough that was wholly typical of him" ("The Witness for the Prosecution" 1), clearly intended by Christie to be nothing more than an affectation, and has the character coughing up blood as the aftereffects of exposure to mustard gas in the trenches. "From the first moments the legacy of the First World War leaked into every scene and emotion like mustard gas into a trench, poisoning everything it touched", wrote O'Donovan, a reviewer for the *Daily Telegraph*.[11]

Agatha Christie herself, however, in her own definitive 1953 adaptation of the story for the stage, evidently did not see it as having any resonances with the First World War. She instead elected to set her play very specifically in post–Second World War Britain, and this is reflected in key elements of the narrative. In the short story, the enigmatic Romaine is an actress from Vienna; but in the play we assume that she is German. She has married her first husband, a German, in Leipzig and she later meets and marries Leonard Vole in Berlin, where he is part of the army of occupation; in Billy Wilder's classic 1957 film, billed as being based on "Agatha Christie's international stage success", Tyrone Power's Vole (despite his American accent) is with the RAF. In the play, Romaine explains that Vole "got me out of the Russian zone and brought me to this country" (*Witness for the Prosecution* 397).

Romaine's subsequent courtroom artifice ultimately relies on QC Sir Wilfred Robarts's observation that "nine out of twelve in a jury box believe a foreigner is lying" (389). Without being explicit about it, Christie, by making her German, has skillfully played on the postwar prejudices of her audience as well as those of the jury. The reference to the "Russian sector" is significant, too. The lover who Romaine invents is clearly intended to be an Eastern bloc spy: "I can come to you without any fear of endangering the valuable work you are doing in this country", she purportedly writes to him, "I know the Cause and the Party comes first" (451). In 1953, Cold War paranoia was at its height, and two years previously the trial of Russian spies Ethel and Julius Rosenberg in the United States had grabbed headlines.

Christie was again effectively creating "immersive" theater to huge dramatic effect; just as her wartime audiences sat in their seats in fear that they might themselves at any moment become the victims of an unseen enemy, in *Witness for the Prosecution*, Christie masterfully plays on the prejudices and paranoia of the era to convince the audience to make the same mistake as her fictional jury. The idea that members of the audience could be seated onstage to make up the numbers in the courtroom, as in the 2017 London revival, is nothing new, and was in fact suggested by Christie herself in her "Author's Note" to the 1954 published edition (370).

Just as the audience is primed to turn against Romaine, so they are inclined to empathize with the predicament of Vole: "Doing my army service unsettled me a bit … Since I've come back to this country I can't seem to settle down properly. I don't know really what I want to do" (376). However, critically, the implication is that Vole (who is described as being "about twenty-seven" [373]) has been undertaking obligatory national service as part of the postwar army of occupation rather than himself having been a wartime combatant; so, when the tables suddenly turn, we don't discover that our misplaced sympathies have been with a villain who is potentially also a damaged war hero.

Witness for the Prosecution was Christie's proudest achievement as a dramatist; to such an extent that she resisted the republication of the original short story in case it disappointed fans. This, though, was not the first of her works that she had re-set into a post–Second World War context; at the end of 1950 she had undertaken a similar exercise with *A Daughter's a Daughter*, production of which had been abandoned in 1939 on the outbreak of war. The drama unfolds in a London flat, which widowed Ann Prentice shares with her daughter, Sarah, and setting the final act in "the present" now neatly placed its opening scene at the end of the war. Sarah is portrayed as returning from service with the WAAF (rather than, as previously, a skiing holiday) and her suitor Jerry is a demobbed Squadron Leader. Christie's daughter Rosalind, whose husband died in action a year after the birth of their son Mathew, had toyed with the idea of joining the WAAF, and in 1943 Christie wrote to Max saying that she was thinking of "writing a play about a W.A.A.F. (…spy drama!)" (Correspondence).

The rewrites add a sense of postwar displacement to the characters' efforts to redefine themselves in a period of accelerated social change. The spoilt Sarah objects to her mother's fiancé, to whom she takes an instant, jealous dislike, not helped by his view that "Girls take on a job just like men do nowadays" (*A Daughter's a Daughter*). Jerry's new status as a demobbed airman means losing a sequence in the original script in which he reports having been fired from his job for impersonating a "frightful old Jewboy" (*A Daughter's a Daughter*) who visits his employer; although audiences were clearly not intended to empathize with Jerry's dilemma, Christie seems to have appreciated that it was no longer acceptable even for her characters to adopt the casual anti-Semitism that was prevalent in her own Edwardian youth. Despite the updates, which work well, *A Daughter's a Daughter* received only one week of performances in Christie's lifetime; at the Theatre Royal, Bath in 1956, where it was presented as a play by "Mary Westmacott", having been novelized by her in 1952 using the pen name she reserved for her noncrime fiction.

Although we are clearly engaging with a distinctly post–Second World War mores in various Christie novels, it was in the theater—where she could directly engage her audience in an immersive group experience—that her success was more directly accountable to her abilities to connect with their wartime and postwar concerns. As a dramatist, Christie was not content simply to include wartime and postwar dramatic tropes in her work, and neither was she "Austenesque", or notably "displaced" or "delayed", in her approach, as scholars have suggested. Instead she experimented radically, incorporating the collective agency of contemporary audiences into the theatrical dynamic itself, by immediately and directly engaging with their shared experience of the Second World War. In her three defining works as a playwright (*And Then There Were None*, *The Mousetrap*, and *Witness for the Prosecution*), she achieved this to astonishing dramatic effect.

During the First World War, Agatha Christie, who had been born a Victorian, married her first husband and wrote her first detective novel. During the Second World War, she became a woman of the twentieth century, hugely broadening her personal, sociopolitical, and intellectual frame of reference and writing (as Mary Westmacott) her masterpiece *Absent in the Spring*, "The one book that has satisfied me completely" (*Autobiography* 498). But, most significantly, Agatha Christie went into the Second World War a best-selling Golden Age detective novelist and emerged as a hugely successful modern playwright—one of the most extraordinary realignments of a literary career ever achieved by a writer.

Notes

1 Short, silent weekly newsreels played in cinemas during the First World War, along with full-length, government-sponsored propaganda features; but the BBC did not start radio broadcasts until 1922.
2 Rebecca Mills discusses the Blitz further in her chapter in this volume (Chapter 9).

3 For a detailed investigation of the work of ENSA and other wartime theatrical activity, see Anselm Heinrich's "Theatre in Britain During the Second World War".
4 In the period under discussion, both the book and the play were known in the UK by their original title, *Ten Little ──*. In the United States at this time, the book was known as *And Then There Were None* and the play as *Ten Little Indians*; although the US publisher's and producer's motivation for retitling them remains open to question. For the history of the title's evolution see Julius Green's *Agatha Christie; A Life in Theatre*, 157,180–82,186–87, 517–20.
5 The Agatha Christie Family Archive holds a copy of this book, signed by each of the actors in the original production on the page referring to their character's mode of death.
6 See J. C. Bernthal's chapter in this volume for more on "And Then There Were None" (Chapter 5).
7 The only extant copy of Agatha Christie's original text of her dramatization appears to be that held in the Lord Chamberlain's Plays collection at the British Library.
8 In 2014, I discovered what appear to be the only three extant copies of Agatha Christie's own 1945 adaptation of *Towards Zero* in the archives of the Shuberts, the Broadway producers who had successfully presented *Ten Little Indians* in 1944. In 1956, an entirely different adaptation of *Towards Zero*, written largely by Gerald Verner and with minimal input by Christie, received its London premiere. See Green, *Agatha Christie; A Life in Theatre*, 218–27, 417–28.
9 Some set photographs are also held in the Peter Saunders Archive.
10 See Crescentini's contribution to the present volume (Chapter 7).
11 O'Donovan's review is typical of popular criticism in attributing a layer of "sophistication" to this adaptation, which he assumes to be absent from Christie's own work, believing it to be a reworking of "Christie's hit 1950s stage drama" rather than the short story, which is its source.

Works Cited

Brine, M. E. "Civilian Casualties of the Bombing of Torquay". *Devon Heritage*, 31 Jul. 2009, devonheritage.org/Places/Torquay/Civiliancasualtiesofthebombingoftorquay.htm Accessed 17 Dec. 2017.

Burke, David. *The Lawn Road Flats: Spies, Writers and Artists*. Boydell Press, 2014.

Christie, Agatha. *An Autobiography*. 1977. Harper, 2011.

──. Correspondence Collected in the Agatha Christie Family Archive. Archive Trust c/o Agatha Christie Limited, London. Accessed 2013–2014.

──. *A Daughter's A Daughter* (play). Typescripts: Agatha Christie Archive, c.1939/c.1950.

──. *The Hollow*. 1952. *The Mousetrap and Other Plays*. HarperCollins, 2011, pp. 173–284.

──. *The Mousetrap*. 1954. *The Mousetrap and Other Plays*. HarperCollins, 2011, pp. 285–366.

──. "Ten Little ──. ". Typescript: Lord Chamberlain's Plays Collection, British Library, 1943.

———. *Three Blind Mice* (radio play). BBC Typescript. Agatha Christie Archive, 1947.

———. "Three Blind Mice". 1950. *Three Blind Mice and Other Stories.* William Morrow, 2012, pp. 1–81.

———. *Towards Zero.* 1945. Typescript in the Shubert Archive, New York.

———. *Verdict.* 1958. *The Mousetrap and Other Plays.* HarperCollins, 2011, pp. 541–622.

———. *Witness for the Prosecution*, 1954. *The Mousetrap and Other Plays.* HarperCollins, 2011, pp. 367–458.

———. "The Witness for the Prosecution". ["Traitor Hands"] 1925. *The Witness for the Prosecution and Other Stories.* 1948. New York: William Morrow, 2012, pp. 1–28.

Favret, Mary A. *War at a Distance: Romanticism and the Making of Modern Wartime.* Princeton University Press, 2010.

Gale, Maggie B. *West End Women: Women and the London Stage, 1918–1962.* Routledge, 1996.

Green, Julius. *Agatha Christie; A Life in Theatre.* 2015. HarperCollins, 2018.

Heinrich, Anselm. "Theatre in Britain during the Second World War". *New Theatre Quarterly*, vol. 26, no. 1, 2010, pp. 61–70.

Hobson, Harold. "Peter Saunders". St Martin's Theatre, *The Mousetrap Story.* St Martin's Theatre, 1992, p. 5.

Johnson, Kathryn. "'The Lord Chamberlain Regrets'". *English and Drama*, The British Library, 1 Oct. 2016, blogs.bl.uk/english-and-drama/2016/10/the-lord-chamberlain-regrets-.html Accessed 17 Dec. 2017.

Jones, Edgar. "Air-Raid Casualties in the First World War". *History of Government*, 19 Jan. 2015, history.blog.gov.uk/2015/01/19/air-raid-casualties-in-the-first-world-war Accessed 17 Dec. 2017.

Light, Alison. *Forever England: Femininity, Literature and Conservatism between the Wars.* 1991. Routledge, 2005.

Lord Chamberlain's Office. "Reader's Report for *The Mousetrap*". 17 Sep. 1952, *The Mousetrap* Correspondence File, Lord Chamberlain's Plays Collection, British Library. File ref: 1952/4570. Accessed 2013–2018.

Mills, Rebecca. "England's Pockets; Objects of Anxiety in Christie's Post-War Novels". *The Ageless Agatha Christie: Essays on the Mysteries and the Legacy*, edited by J. C. Bernthal, McFarland, 2016, pp. 29–44.

"The Mousetrap Designers". St. Martin's Theatre, *The Mousetrap Story.* St. Martin's Theatre, 1992, p. 87.

O'Donovan, Gerald. "The Witness for the Prosecution, Part 1 Review: A Mysterious Slice of Christmas TV Heaven". *The Telegraph*, 26 Dec. 2016, telegraph.co.uk/tv/2016/12/26/witness-prosecution-part-1-review-mysterious-slice-christmas Accessed 7 Jan. 2017.

"Rules of the People's Entertainment Society". Co-operative Press Ltd, 1942. *The People's Entertainment Society Archive*, National Co-Operative Archive, Manchester. Accessed 2014.

St James' Theatre. Program for *Ten Little ———*. 1943.

Weinberg, Kate. "How WW1 Shaped Agatha Christie—and Poirot". *The Telegraph*, 14 Sep. 2014, telegraph.co.uk/culture/books/11092925/How-WW1-shaped-Agatha-Christie-and-Poirot.html Accessed 17 Dec.2017.

7 "There Are Things One Doesn't Forget"

The Second World War in "Three Blind Mice" and *The Mousetrap*

Federica Crescentini

In 1947, the BBC broadcast the radio drama "Three Blind Mice", written by Agatha Christie in response to a request from Queen Mary on the occasion of her eightieth birthday. The author then donated her fee to the Southport Infirmary Children's Toy Fund. "Three Blind Mice" deals with the revenge of a man who had been abused as a child, and is set contemporarily, shortly after the Second World War. Subsequently, Christie developed the plot into a novella of the same name, published in 1948, and then into a theatrical play, *The Mousetrap*, performed for the first time in 1952. Julius Green observes that, "[t]o London audiences in the early 50s, this scenario would have stirred recent memories of wartime evacuee children being placed in the care of strangers, and of the inevitable anxieties caused thereby" (305). Moreover, in the opinion of Christie's official biographer, "*The Mousetrap* is underpinned by no less a theme than the catastrophic effects of childhood neglect" (Thompson 2011). In this chapter, I analyze the coded references to conflict present in the novella and the stage play, and evaluate their significance in terms of war and its material effects, social identity, and mental health in each text.[1] These topics are all represented by the expression "There are things one doesn't forget" (*The Mousetrap* 345), contextually related to personal identity harmed and changed by the war, but also applicable to every situation that provokes damage in the human being.

"Three Blind Mice"

The opening of "Three Blind Mice" presents a disrupted postwar England and creates the disquieting atmosphere that hovers until the end; the prose allows the author to explain the grievous situation after the Second World War more explicitly than the play. At the same time, Christie frames the narration with the classic elements of the detective fiction genre and includes comic scenes. This combination creates an odd but pleasant atmosphere of alternation between gruesome features and humorous relief, which function as a diversion, concealing the details connected with the conflict.

The story opens in London, where a woman is strangled in her home; later on, the action moves to Scotland Yard. Despite these introductory scenes, a house in the country is the focus of the plot. The principal setting, Monkswell Manor, connects past and present with its garden "terribly overgrown since the war, because there's been only one old gardener left" ("Three Blind Mice" 3). It becomes the start of a new life for a young married couple, who decide to transform it into a guesthouse due to the necessity of finding a job and of having a place to live. The situation connotes postwar austerity and the immediate housing crisis, when "A widely-expressed desire to re-establish marital and family life in the years after the war [...] in reality saw countless young couples compelled to live with their parents or other relatives" (Langhamer 349). Moreover, the manor house had been modernized before the war, and this aspect duplicates a true-to-life detail: in 1943 and in the postwar world, the presence of a bathroom in the house was a major social dividing line (Langhamer 350). Private domestic service, one of the traditional frontiers of status and class, had been obliterated by the war, as historian Jose Harris notes (26); the absence of servants is clearly expressed in the story. While Molly takes on a traditional female role of doing the housework, Giles represents the "increasingly active masculine role within post-war domesticity" (Langhamer 357). He carries the coal, paints the board by the gate (albeit with a spelling mistake), and helps the guests with their luggage.

Despite their organized new lifestyle, the couple feels lost and confused in terms of the law and legal structures. Indeed, when Molly receives a phone call from the police, without managing to find out the reason for the contact, she anxiously discusses the event with her husband. What emerges is a specific picture of economic and political traits of the postwar period, arising from the worried question: "What have we done?" (29). A subsequent flow of doubts and conjectures regarding food and clothes indicates complication and confusion surrounding legal procedures; the couple's preoccupation results in an expression of discontent at the extensive level of prohibited actions ("Three Blind Mice" 30). Giles also notes, in discussion with Sergeant Trotter, that the guests should possess identity cards and ration books (42). The number of legal and moral doubts reflects the fact that rationing was considered as a restriction of personal liberty within the Ministry of Food (Summerfield 258); in fact, besides high wartime taxation, nearly all the essential materials were rationed in postwar Britain, including petrol, butter, bacon, sugar, meat, cheese, tea, sweets, and personal clothing (Harris 19–23). Appeals for fuel economy are cited at the beginning of the novella and the successive remarks indicate the fiction's close reflection of real conditions. Furthermore, the quaint Mr. Paravicini is a suspected law-breaker dealing with the black market, reflecting the evidence of widespread participation in the black market and resentment against government controls (Harris 19).

Social Identity

Personal identity was unsettled by the war, and consequently social identity was disrupted along with it. Molly's fears and Mrs. Boyle's dislocation are discussed here as they evoke the sense of personal uncertainty, uncertainty toward others, and the loss of connections and social roles, with damage to social exchange as well.

Despite possessing a modernized private home in a period characterized by buildings destroyed by the bombings, Molly uncovers a strange feeling, conveyed through the use of free indirect discourse:

> The house felt suddenly very quiet and empty [...] she had never before been so conscious of being alone in it. [...] she jumped—*a strange man* was coming through the snow. [...] *a strange man*, walking into the empty house. [...] then, suddenly, illusion fled. ("Three Blind Mice" 5–6, emphases added)

Christie experiments with narrative voice here, using the long dash to express both suspense and Molly's tension, and conveying the fragmented thoughts of a young woman unexpectedly scared in her private space. It should be a place of safety and happiness; however, it is also a temporary residence for paying guests and thus for strangers, who seem to have no parents, no relatives, nor a place to truly call home, and who thereby alter the daily life and the intimacy between husband and wife. This home-sharing might remind the readers of the temporary homes organized during the war in order to give people a place to live. In the story, set after the end of the conflict, cohabitation maintains the quality of an ensemble of strangers forced together by the necessity for accommodation. Furthermore, despite the presence of Molly, the house is described as "empty" and her inability to recognize her husband is a significant precursor to the ensuing fear of a "strange man". Such an introspective moment invites an uncannily familiar feeling, a sense of something that should be perceived as familiar but, for reasons yet to be discovered, gives instead a feeling of strangeness and hence proves disquieting.

Developing this concept and employing opposing perspectives, Christie shows that security and safety in the postwar period are absent even in marriage; indeed, Molly progressively loses her trust in Giles. This estrangement between husband and wife has been engendered by the social conditions after the Second World War. The couple knew each other only a fortnight before getting married: "in a worrying, nerveracked world, they had both found the miracle of each other" (44).

Sergeant Trotter reinforces the insecurity about their relationship by presenting a different point of view, reminding Molly that people tend to accept the identities of others on the basis of words, since in the postwar context it is difficult and sometimes impossible to verify people's backgrounds.[2] The uncertainty about Giles as other from herself, other from her opinion of him, is latent in Molly's mind from the beginning of the story. The "miracle of each other" has thus become the nightmare of the stranger, possibly a killer. The actual "illusion" is the trusting relationship they (do not) have; the choice of words enhances the sense of alienation: "She was always making fresh discoveries about *this husband of hers*. He said so little about himself" (2, emphasis added). Since Molly does not know Giles truly, she experiences detachment from her identity of his wife: "there was just herself, Molly Davis, playing a role that did not yet seem a very natural role to play. Her whole life, at the moment, seemed unreal—Giles seemed unreal. She was playing a part" (6). Furthermore, she hides a past event regarding herself, thus even her own identity is unclear. Molly has been traumatized: her fiancé was a young pilot killed in action (63). Her story reflects the tragedy of women who hoped for marriage and were instead left with the presence of loss in their lives. Death is a key element of the genre, but here it is doubled by the subject matter of war, debated via various aspects.

Despite the de-familiarization toward her role, her husband, and her new house, the young woman finds a haven in the kitchen: "So, from immemorial time women *had cooked* food for their men. The world of danger—of madness, receded. Woman, in her kitchen, was *safe* [...]" (58, emphasis added). This place conveys the opposition between reality and safety: Molly feels protected in the room, which reminds her of the simple, comforting everyday things, whereas outside stands a reality of mortal danger. In her mind, safety (kitchen) and reality (Manor) result as almost opposing concepts; nonetheless, in the novella mortal reality and soothing everyday things (also, theoretically reassuring identities such as Giles or the Sergeant) are connected and coexisting. Therefore their separation in Molly's mind becomes almost paradoxical and this is reflected in the young woman's behavior every time that she forgets, or suddenly remembers, her duty of cooking: "And that reminds me, I must go and put the potatoes on" (41). Moreover Molly recalls the kitchen's function using the past (see emphasis in the above quote), while in the present she forgets to cook not only for Giles and for the guests, but even for herself. In this perspective the kitchen loses its basic function to become her private *locus amoenus*. The postwar present, combining destabilization, mortal danger, and everyday life, emotionally breaks through her logical thinking, thus creating the paradox of separation and forgetfulness. In the kitchen Molly is warned by Sergeant Trotter (57–58), exchanges secrets with Christopher (60–65), and becomes openly suspicious of Giles (66–68). These familiar/unfamiliar and normal/abnormal binaries are related to every character and emerge where the two parts coexist, materially (kitchen) and mentally, creating general alienation and an interior fracture in Molly, in the young guest Christopher, and in the culprit.

The reason for this anomalous situation lies in the aftermath of the Second World War, which brought destabilization to everyday life and roles that had been definite and certain. Therefore, uncertainty taints everyone in this novella, and every aspect of personal and common life. The postwar context enhances the already mysterious atmosphere of a Christie text, and adds possible secret scenarios to the plot. One of the most irritating personalities at Monkswell Manor is Mrs. Boyle, a former billeting officer whose role has also been destabilized by the war, though in an unexpected fashion:

> The end of the war had left Mrs. Boyle marooned [...] War activities had suited her down to the ground [...] And now all that exciting hustling life was over. (25)

Mrs. Boyle is the only female character who has been actively involved in the war effort, and she regrets the end of the conflict; she represents the concept that for some conscripted women the war brought excitement, travel, career opportunities, and a general enhancement of status (Summerfield 1984).[3] Nonetheless, women throughout the workforce were largely confined to repetitive and menial positions (Harris 26). Mrs. Boyle represents an exception in the conditions of women's agency, and so for her, the new reality is hard to accept:

> [H]er former private life had vanished. Her house, which had been requisitioned by the army, needed thorough repairing and redecorating before she could return to it, and the difficulties of domestic help made a return to it impracticable. (25)

Similarly, Christie's own Greenway House had become a nursery for evacuated children and then had been taken over by the United States Navy (*Autobiography* 484–90); Mrs. Boyle's situation thus recalls the fact that "over the whole war period more than four million mothers and children were evacuated [...] the vast majority to the homes of private citizens in the rural counties" (Harris 22). Her words also reflect reality in terms of private life. Christie herself specifically observed that after the end of the war "came the business of picking up the pieces, all the bits and pieces scattered everywhere—bits of one's life" (*Autobiography* 507). As a result, the civilian identity of Mrs. Boyle is detached from her war identity, perhaps her true one, which has ended with the beginning of peace. Mrs. Boyle is no longer listened to and respected, her severe manners and her continuous criticism toward the Manor and its inhabitants reveal a frustration due to the fact that, after the war, she is no longer powerful and has no authority over other people. She is utterly alone.

Although the setting of the story is the postwar period, the characters' thoughts of wartime recur throughout. Their actions and reflections are constantly oriented backward until the murderer is finally discovered; even the culprit's motivation look backward, to wartime violence. The menace, then, is the past, for two reasons: the old murder of a child and the specter of the conflict. Long descriptive passages, specifically regarding the war and the aftermath, reflect the social situation and its accompanying sense of helplessness: no stable place to live, no servants to help, no close friends, or accustomed work.[4] The characters feel alone, deprived of their previous social position and roles, sometimes with consequences on their mental health.

Christie famously hides clues in plain sight, inserting ideas to misdirect the attention of the reader. At the same time, her technique illustrates the characters' peculiarities as they are reflected in each other's thoughts; for example, Major Metcalf is the object of Giles's speculations: "Demobilized, probably, and no job to go to" ("Three Blind Mice" 27). Demobilization is another consequence of the conflict; the sadness of the Major's alleged condition is only part of the war heritage. Indeed, a remark about Christopher explains his peculiar psychology: "'He tells me he was buried during an air raid for forty-eight hours before being dug out', said Major Metcalf" (47). These comments are related to the plot and at the same they time depict an estranged and harmed society. Christie's heterogeneous group of characters illustrates changes across different social classes and backgrounds, through contemplative moments about past events. One of the most delicate and tragic elements is illustrated during a private conversation between Molly and Christopher. The latter confesses having a false identity and refuses to reveal his true name because it is not important, since he is a deserter from the army (61), letting the reader reflect on the negative opinion of deserters. Then the young man, with his suspicious behavior, explains the reason for his escape:

> I wasn't afraid—no more than anyone else [...] It was – my mother ... she was killed—in an air raid. Buried. They—they had to dig her out. [...] I suppose I went a little mad. (62)

Christopher hides solitude and desperation behind an attitude of persistent childishness, enhanced through the pauses and repetitions in his speech, signs of nervousness. Furthermore, his mental damage affects him so deeply that his mood changes suddenly (50); he tells two different tales about the air raid, and due to this behavior, he is reckoned the killer. In "Three Blind Mice", after his revelation, Molly encourages him to start again even though he feels hopeless; however, Mollie in *The Mousetrap* states that he should go on just as usual (331), giving their conversation a feeling of pessimism and sadness absent in the novella. This difference is due to the play of past identity between the innocent Molly Davis and the ambiguous Mollie Ralston. Being personally involved in a child's death, Mollie cannot pronounce words of hope because canceling her past behavior is impossible.

Central to the murderer's motivations is a story of child abuse, which took place during the Second World War (38–39). The plot was inspired by the real murder of Dennis O'Neill, a young boy who with his brother Terence had been abused and tortured by his foster parents. On 9 January 1945, Dennis died of "acute cardiac failure following violence applied [...] while in a state of under-nourishment due to neglect". There had also been "a serious lack of supervision by the local authority" (Great Britain Home Office 1945, A2). The case led to the Children Act of 1948[5]; Terence wrote a memoir book, *Someone to Love Us*, testifying of their suffering and the lifelong consequences of the brutality they faced. All the references to war and its consequences in the novella, then, can be considered as a sort of admonition, especially with regard to the murder of Dennis and the violence against Terence, as part of a history that must be remembered and never underestimated in its gravity, in order to provide actual justice and prevention of crime. "Three Blind Mice" is not merely escapist fiction; it explores humanity itself as subdued and damaged by the absence of justice in war but, in a best-case scenario, eager to start afresh.

The symbol of this concept is the killer, a young man who has formerly described himself as an army deserter. The alleged "homicidal maniac" (41) has killed two people responsible for the death of his brother. The last designated victim is Molly, whose identity has been confused with that of her sister, a schoolmistress who refused to help Georgie. When Molly demonstrates her complete innocence, though, the culprit states that it does not matter (78), remarking that his brother was an innocent person, but was murdered anyway, and the same fate will meet Molly. Hence the killer is both mad and cruel. He recognizes the difference between Molly and her sister, but he chooses to ignore it. Nonetheless, after preventing him from killing Molly, Major Metcalf, who is actually Inspector Tanner from Scotland Yard, shows mercy and treats him as a wounded human being. *The Mousetrap,* however, shows a change in the final part, which will be discussed in the next section.

"Three Blind Mice", then, is completely shaped by the aftermath of the Second World War. Despite its conventional framework, it is gloomy and more tragic than the stories in the Golden Age style, with its in-depth representations of grief, madness, doubt and alienation. Michael Holquist argues that:

> [T]he new metaphysical detective story [...] is not concerned to have a neat ending in which all the questions are answered, and which

can therefore be forgotten. [...] If, in the detective story, death must be solved, in the new metaphysical detective story it is life which must be solved. [...] [The metaphysical detective story] sees the potential for real violence [...] in the phony violence of the detective story. (153–56)

The novella reflects these ideas; the potential for real violence in this case is doubled in terms of both the actual murder and a possible future violence. Moreover, the lack of a neat ending is evident in the fact that Giles's past remains unknown to his wife and to the readers, while Christopher and Mr. Paravicini continue with their extravagant behavior. The novella has a peculiar history and a peculiar identity, reflected in the dualities of its characters. Even though the prose is rich in descriptions and background context, the ending offers a quick reconciliation between husband and wife. The feeling of relief is obscured by two key elements: the inappropriate gifts they have chosen for each other and the unresolved tension in Molly about her role, since she once again forgets her cooking (81). The conclusion thus suggests a sense of incompleteness, which is unusual in the denouement of a detective story. This incompleteness, then, refers to the story within the story, symbolizing the still uncertain life in the postwar years, where the unknown is likely to remain so, indicating a nebulous future built on a devastated past, from which it is not always possible to recover or even to reconcile, with the personal self or with other people. As the novella shows in the end, people can only hope for a better future.

The Mousetrap

The Mousetrap is the "longest running theatrical production of any sort in the history of the world" (Green 323) and has been performed without interruption since it opened in London's West End in 1952. As the characters try to hide their secrets, the play reveals details about the period when the action takes place. The recurring comic moments balance the dramatic situation: an isolated house in a desolate, unsafe postwar England, during winter at its peak. At Monkswell Manor, people of dubious identity are threatened by the tune and the words of a nursery rhyme, which becomes a symbol of both menace and childhood.

According to Beatrix Hesse (50), *The Mousetrap* is one of the few crime plays of the 1950s to immediately reflect the living conditions of postwar England. Moreover, for the first ten years, the audience was restricted to adults only (Thompson 2011), a precaution that confirms the presence of seriously disquieting features. Since the play is an adaptation, the change in medium allows for analysis of the same thematic areas of the novella, according to a theatrical perspective, which emphasizes the war clues in different ways.

The drama presents information about the historical era through clothes, manners, and dialogue on stage. It has an audiovisual impact due to the performance, which is ephemeral given the fleeting nature of theatrical representation. The dramatic text, therefore, is a source of specific elements: for example, in Act I, Giles and Mollie (as her name is now spelled) disagree about the identities of their guests. While Mollie accepts their good addresses at face value, her husband is more suspicious and hints that some of the guests could be criminals hiding behind forged references (*The Mousetrap* 282–83). The discussion is proleptic and displays an uneasiness associated with the postwar years. As Jessica Gildersleeve concludes, *The Mousetrap* is "important for its depiction of the anxious atmosphere of Britain in the years of recovery and change following World War II" (122).

More details about these years of change are given within the dialogue. Giles and Major Metcalfe both participated in the conflict, and their immediate complicity becomes apparent (288–89), even though it is only a superficial comradeship and not a motive for real trust. Christopher Wren has imagined Mollie as whom he probably considers a standard identity of that era: "a retired General's widow, Indian Army [...] terrifically grim and Memsahibish" (*The Mousetrap* 284). On the contrary, she and Giles are young and "struggling to set up a business in the post-war age of ration books austerity" (Green 305). Furthermore, the original prologue of *The Mousetrap* presented a conversation between two workers about marriage, accidents, and psychology. Julius Green has pointed out:

> Here is a unique attempt by Agatha Christie to portray working-class characters who are not domestic staff of some sort in their working environment. [...] This sort of material [...] does show that she was not unaware of the directions in which theatre was heading and not unwilling to dip her toe in the water. (308–09)

In *The Mousetrap*, Christie has preserved the theme of war and its aftermath, inserting even into this adaptation modern elements; Gildersleeve has remarked how specific dialogues display a peculiarly modern and modernist anxiety (119). Indeed throughout the play, the anxiety and fear of the unknown, of the difficulty and impossibility of knowing the other, are dominant concepts. Besides, the reactions to the appearance and behavior of the peculiar Christopher, Miss Casewell and Mr. Paravicini indicate the fear of people who do not correspond to the concept of normality, in the sense of conformity with established norms or standards. What the characters do not understand generates alarm and suspect. As a consequence, Giles definitely reckons Christopher a thief (293) and a homicidal maniac (334). While Miss Casewell and Christopher have British origins, Mr. Paravicini has an Italian surname and he never reveals his name; he therefore arouses more suspicion than the others. This concept recalls the idea of citizenship opposed to that of the stranger. The reciprocal suspicion between the characters allows reflection on the implications of belonging to the same nation: here, it does not guarantee reciprocal trust.

The fact that Miss Casewell has lived abroad inspires a discussion about living conditions in England, which is similar but not identical to the novella.

MRS. BOYLE: I suppose conditions are much easier abroad.
CASEWELL: I don't have to cook and clean—as I gather most people have to do in this country.
MRS. BOYLE: This country has gone sadly downhill. Not what it used to be. I sold my house last year. Everything was too difficult. (298)

The war hints, then, are presented as a background to the detective story; the "usual political crisis" (291) appears in the paper. The play mentions some laws of the time; Mollie and Giles worry about nylons from Gibraltar, their wireless radio license, and the unavoidable restrictions of the period (301). As is the case in the novella, the surface level appears to be the detective fiction, but the deeper level replicates sociopolitical and economical features of the postwar years. Since the two levels are profoundly connected, the clues regarding the war are never misplaced or inappropriate.

The Mousetrap shows almost the same characteristics of "Three Blind Mice", though expressed differently. A key thematic link between the two, then, are the concept of "stranger" and "strangeness". The dialogues and the (anti)social behavior of the characters bring an uneasiness typical of postmodernist writing; as Laura Marcus notes, "Postmodernist writing, and metaphysical detective story in particular, give us not familiarity but strangeness" (250). Even when polite social talk is attempted, it fails due to the different personalities and the lack of reciprocal understanding. The people in Monkswell Manor speak without truly communicating with each other, except for some introspective scenes between Mollie, Christopher, and Katherine Casewell. Indeed, behind its apparently familiar Golden Age frame, *The Mousetrap* is full of strangeness (as already noted by Gildersleeve and Green), starting with its characters, who appear to be strange and are strangers to themselves, because they hide their past and thus their true identities. Strangeness remains part of their personal relationships since they do not create bonds. Christopher Wren, Miss Casewell, and the mysterious Mr. Paravicini, who externally resembles Hercule Poirot, are emblematic of the strange identities, which give the play a disquieting allure.

Christie also modified some personalities in adapting the novella. Here, Mrs. Boyle is a former magistrate and Mollie a former teacher.

Miss Casewell, missing in "Three Blind Mice", has a fundamental role in the play: she recognizes Sergeant Trotter as her lost brother. Moreover, she and Mrs. Boyle enter into a brief political discussion:

MRS. BOYLE: No, indeed, the lower classes seem to have no idea of their responsibilities.
CASEWELL: Poor old lower classes. Got the bit between their teeth, haven't they?
MRS. BOYLE: (*Frostily*) I gather you're a Socialist. (298)

The dialogue, with the italics enhancing Mrs. Boyle's contempt toward whom she reckons "socialist", brings a tense political dispute, briskly relieved by a change of subject. Nonetheless the uneasiness continues: an attentive reading suggests that inside the isolated manor hides the uncanny familiar, symbolized by the estranged relationship between Mollie and Giles. Despite their reciprocal jealousy, she actively suspects him, while he tries to protect her, and observes: "You're different all of a sudden. I feel as though I don't know you anymore". "Perhaps you never did know me" is his wife's shocking reply (*The Mousetrap* 335). This leads to a disturbing question: who is the other, both in the sense of identity and in the sense of "who is the real stranger?" It is alarming and when associated with the social problem described by Trotter, definitely proves how the war has entered into the intimacy of human beings:

TROTTER: Especially since the war. Homes broken up and families dead. [...] Girl just marries her man. Sometimes she doesn't find out for a year or two that he's an absconding bank clerk, or an army deserter or something equally undesirable. (328–29)

Due to the play of identity among the characters, the entire plot is based upon misleading, which duplicates the act of performing. Furthermore, the deceit staged by the supposed victims insinuates a moral doubt: since they are guilty and morally guilty, should the culprit be considered a mere homicidal maniac, or is he trying to restore the justice, which has actually been missing from the very beginning?

One of the fundamental themes of the play connects mental health and memories and finds expression in the words of Miss Casewell: "I was thinking ... Ice on a bedroom jug, chilblains, raw and bleeding—one thin ragged blanket—a child shivering with cold and fear" (300). The dramatic text provides a recurring use of the verbs "remember" and "forget": when Katherine confronts Mollie about the past, the former appears resolute in refusing to think about it, even though she admits to having an unhappy childhood (314). On the contrary, Mollie is uncertain and her inner tension results in this attitude. When Katherine manages to calm the killer by reminding him of their shared infancy, she highlights the duplicity of memories, as present in the action both as a haunting force and as a saving energy. Trotter is trapped in the past by his memory while his sister is projected toward the future.

Mental breakdown is also suggested in a remark regarding their father:

MOLLIE: If he came home, after being a prisoner with the Japs, perhaps, and having suffered terribly—[...] and found his wife dead and his children had gone through some terrible experience, and one of them had died through it, he might go off his head a bit and want—revenge! (326–27)

This perspective enhances the devastation of a human being. The connection between madness and revenge inspires the question: can an act of vengeance be a sign of mental illness? The absence of justice, itself a fault, can provoke revenge and show an extremely fragile border, which not necessarily only mad people trespass. The contemplative moments evoke the extreme fragility of human beings, the psychological and emotional wounds, some of them irremediable. Christie here reminds that war and people can kill in different ways and physical death is only the last stage. Christopher Wren and the culprit are the best example since they have both become deserters from the Army, mentally unstable and desperate.

The murderer is the most complicated character in the action, and as previously observed, his role of detective suggests a connection with the metaphysical detective story, where "the detective confronts himself with unsolvable mysteries, associated with his interpretation of reality and with a never-ending search for his identity" (Darconza 44; translation by Crescentini). Despite being a fake sergeant, he actually is a sort of detective, since all his actions are performed to find the truth about his trauma. His detection is his own life, his raison d'etre, which he is unable to understand, and he therefore identifies it with the concept of revenge. This is illustrated by his declarations: "Prison wasn't bad enough for her" followed by "I'll kill them all when I grow up—because grown-ups can do everything they like" (352–53).

Since in the play Mollie is not entirely innocent, the audience's implied moral judgment of the killer is not as clear-cut as in the novella. Thus, his detection is a forlorn pursuit of the complete self and his decision to kill all the culprits highlights the concept of social, collective responsibility, connecting *The Mousetrap* with the noir genre. According to Darconza, in fact, "The noir genre [...] inspires reflections [...] on responsibility and connivance of every one of us [...] on the fragile boundary which separates normal people from the psychopaths we risk becoming in a moment" (14; translation by Crescentini). Significant power dynamics and a hierarchical relationship emerge: Mrs. Lyon, Mrs. Boyle, and Mollie are three women with powerful roles since they represent, respectively, the institutions of family, law, and education. Nevertheless, all of them have failed, betrayed, and ignored their roles. When confronted with the truth, they give different explanations. Mrs. Boyle declares: "I can hardly be held responsible. We had reports from welfare workers" (*The Mousetrap* 312). Mollie states that she was involved in the tragedy due to her role of teacher and firmly denies her responsibility, implying that she could not have saved the little boy (*The Mousetrap* 354). Nevertheless she actually could have helped him—it is not a false supposition on the part of Trotter. Mrs. Lyon, the homicidal foster mother, is murdered at the very beginning of the play. According to Gildersleeve, "since both the judge and the teacher are women, they are suggested to have failed their socio-maternal function to protect the vulnerable child" (121); this statement can also be applied to Mrs. Lyon.

Moreover, the plot has a mirrored structure: three culprits and three victims: the "three blind mice" are doubled by the circular subversion of roles, where the guilty people become the prey. Their attitude of self-exculpation is remarkable since it exhibits how powerful characters have not used their power properly, that is to help and protect people who needed care and justice. Here, power hurts, absolves itself, or does not act at all. Hence it is appropriate that the use of the verb "ignore" is a theme, in its meanings of pay no attention (Mollie), neglect (Lyon), and not consider (Boyle). The only one who opposes and punishes the unpunished guilty women is a mentally ill man: in doing so he diminishes the figure and the role of the real policeman, who is not much developed as a character, has very little space in the action, and neither solves the problem, nor openly arrests the culprit. The murderer here gains the role usually attributed to the detective, although he acts to restore a broken order via illegal punishment. The meaning of justice in this story is a point of reflection and according to Trotter, a matter of points of view rather than objective social order.

Conclusion

"Three Blind Mice" and *The Mousetrap* have titles that predict an act of revenge: the former due to the nursery rhyme associated with Bloody Mary (Evers 101), the latter because of its provenance from William Shakespeare's bloody tragedy, *Hamlet*. Both Hamlet and Trotter are haunted by the past; while Hamlet pretends to be mad, however, Trotter pretends to be sane. The basic question of detective fiction is "whodunit?" According to the first level, the Golden Age frame, the culprit is Trotter, nevertheless in the second level of "Three Blind Mice" and *The Mousetrap* the question is "who is responsible for what happened to Trotter?" The answer is the law (Boyle), the education system (Mollie), and family (Lyon/Gregg-Stanning): these "three blind mice" here represent something awful. Hence the plot is connected with a real problem, child neglect, and abuse; however, there are no children in the fiction and this absence symbolizes the trouble brought by the war: one of them is dead, the other two have become damaged adults, and the only character who always acts like a child is a traumatized man.

As this chapter indicates, the adaptations of the original radio-drama are centered upon the Second World War and its social, physical, and psychological consequences. Christie explores the themes of infant abuse, trauma, memory, investigation, and responsibility, experimenting with genre and identity and creating a character who is at the same time victim, killer, and detective. These elements suggest that memory affects human beings, and a memory affected by the war almost always incurably damages those who suffer from it, and also, in different ways, their community.

Considering the previous analysis, "Three Blind Mice" is darker than the play, while *The Mousetrap* is an example of "upbeat drama", which lightens topics without removing their seriousness.[6] Both stories rely on abiding subjects that are at once contemporary and unresolved; moreover, they induce further reflections on the importance of taking care of other human beings who, like everyone, need and deserve attention, equality, care, and protection. Crime and war cancel these principles and readers and spectators, focusing on the features analyzed in this collection, should perhaps notice how this specific production emphasizes the value of humanity against all that is beastly, crude, and ruthless.

The novella and especially the play are not merely directed backward; they illustrate fears, anxieties, and problems that are both real and contemporary. They represent a remembrance of past events and a reminder of what has to be taken into consideration regarding human lives. As the most damaged character states: "There are things one doesn't forget" (*The Mousetrap* 345).

Notes

1 For more on Christie's wartime theatrical work, see Julius Green's chapter in this volume (Chapter 6).
2 For further consideration of this postwar lack of verifiable identity, see chapters by Christopher Yiannitsaros (Chapter 8) and Sarah Martin and Sally West (Chapter 1).
3 This is a similar situation to that of demobilized WREN Lynn Marchmont in *Taken at the Flood* (1948); see Rebecca Mills's chapter for further discussion (Chapter 9).
4 For more on the servant problem, see Christopher Yiannitsaros's chapter in this volume (Chapter 8).
5 An Act demanding the creation of separate departments in local authorities to deal with children at risk (The National Archives—The Cabinet Papers, no page number).
6 "Upbeat drama" tries to translate "drammaturgia in levare", a phrase used by Anna T. Ossani in her analysis of *L'ora della fantasia*, a comedy written

by Anna Bonacci (1944), which became worldwide famous especially after Billy Wilder's filmic version *Kiss Me, Stupid!* (1964). See Anna T. Ossani, Tiziana Mattioli, and Anna Bonacci. *Biografia per immagini*, Rimini: Raffaelli Editore, 2014, p. 180.

Works Cited

Christie, Agatha. *An Autobiography*. William Morrow, 1977.

———. *The Mousetrap and Other Plays*. William Morrow, 1993.

———. *Three Blind Mice and Other Stories*. William Morrow, 1950.

Darconza, Giovanni. *Il Detective, il Lettore e lo Scrittore: l'evoluzione del Giallo Metafisico in Poe, Borges, Auster*. Aras Edizioni, 2013.

Evers, Liz. *Here Comes a Chopper to Chop Off Your Head – The Dark Side of Childhood Rhymes & Stories*. John Blake, 2014.

Gildersleeve, Jessica. "'We're All Strangers': Postwar Anxiety in Agatha Christie's *The Mousetrap*." *Clues: A Journal of Detection*, vol. 32, no. 2, 2014, pp. 115–23.

Great Britain, Home Office. *Report by Sir Walter Monckton*. H. M. Stationery Office, 1945.

Green, Julius. *Curtain Up- Agatha Christie: A Life in the Theatre*. Harper, 2015.

Harris, Jose. "War and Social History: Britain and the Home Front during the Second World War." *Contemporary European History*, vol. 1, no. 1, 1992, pp. 17–35.

Hesse, Beatrix. *The English Crime Play in the Twentieth Century*. Palgrave Macmillan, 2015.

Holquist, Michael. "Whodunit and Other Questions: Metaphysical Detective Stories in Post-War Fiction." *New Literary History*, vol. 3, no. 1, 1971, pp. 135–56.

Langhamer, Claire. "The Meaning of Home in Postwar Britain." *Journal of Contemporary History*, vol. 40, no. 2, 2005, pp. 341–62.

Marcus, Laura. "Detection and Literary Fiction." *The Cambridge Companion to Crime Fiction*, edited by Martin Priestman, Cambridge University Press, 2003, pp. 245–67.

Summerfield, Penelope. "Women, Work and Welfare: A Study of Childcare and Shopping in Britain in the Second World War." *Journal of Social History*, vol. 17, no. 2, 1983, pp. 249–69.

———. *Women Workers in the Second World War: Production and Patriarchy in Conflict*. Routledge, 1984.

The National Archives. The Cabinet Papers, "Protection of Children." www.nationalarchives.gov.uk/cabinetpapers/themes/protectionchildren.html Accessed 22 Jun. 2018.

Thompson, Laura. "*The Mousetrap*: Agatha Christie's Adult Masterpiece." *The Telegraph*, 28 Dec. 2011. www.telegraph.co.uk/culture/theatre/theatre-features/8975426/The-Mousetrap-Agatha-Christies-adultmasterpiece.html Accessed 22 Jun. 2018.

Welshman, John. "Evacuation, Hygiene, and Social Policy: The Our Towns Report of 1943." *The Historical Journal*, vol. 42, no. 3, 1999, pp. 781–807.

8   Displaced Persons
A Murder Is Announced and the Condition of Postwar England

Christopher Yiannitsaros

There are places in the fiction of Agatha Christie that are marked by a distinctiveness of characterization arisen from the studied attention the author pays to the geography and sociology of her characters. This chapter is concerned with one such place, which is the characterization of Mitzi—the housekeeper at Little Paddocks in Christie's "Miss Marple" novel *A Murder Is Announced* (1950). What makes the characterization of Mitzi so uncommon is that, in a move significantly not found elsewhere in her work, Christie makes the housekeeper at Little Paddocks a Central European Jewish refugee who arrived in England during or shortly before the Second World War to escape Nazi persecution. Discussing the representation of Jewishness in Christie's fiction, Merja Makinen points out that her Jewish characters are nearly always either "minor shady underworld crooks", her example being Boris in *The Mystery of the Blue Train* (1928), or "fabulously wealthy" like Sebastian Levinne and his parents in *Giant's Bread* (1930), a novel written under the name Mary Westmacott (177). This observation further augments Mitzi's exceptionality in terms of Christie's fiction, as she falls absolutely outside this dichotomy that usually prevails. As a Jewish wartime refugee, Mitzi is unique even in terms of a demographic already comparatively rare in its representation within by Christie. My argument is that, within *A Murder Is Announced*, Christie uses the trope of the "displaced person"—who functions as an "uncanny" fragment of an incomprehensible and frightening historical whole—as a means of articulating the increasingly dystopian reality of life lived in immediate postwar England: a reality in which neither people, information, nor widely held national narratives are to be trusted.

Uneasy Neighbors: A Murder in the (Imagined) Community

Published only five years after the close of the Second World War, the wartime displacement and subsequent relocation of persons (in a loose, general sense) is a phenomenon explored in Christie's novel. An advertisement in the local newspaper stating that a murder will happen

Displaced Persons 125

at Little Paddocks one particular autumn evening leads—directly or consequently—to three deaths in the fictional English village of Chipping Cleghorn. As Miss Marple and Inspector Craddock sit in the garden of the local vicarage (where the former is staying) and discuss Rudi Scherz's murder, the elderly sleuth knowingly compares the pre- and postwar English village, hoping to provoke Inspector Craddock into realizing what it is *in particular* that perturbs him about the mystery at hand. Filtered through the external narrator, Inspector Craddock comes to realize that, ultimately, the inhabitants of Chipping Cleghorn "were just faces and personalities [...] backed up by ration books and identity cards—nice neat identity cards with numbers on them, without photographs or fingerprints" (115). Craddock is therefore quite right in his thinking that the flaw with the compulsory identity cards introduced in Britain under the 1939 National Registration Bill is that, although these cards listed the name, age, address, sex, and occupation of each card holder, they did not include any kind of image, or something as uniquely individual as a fingerprint, and thus could easily be forged. As such, there is a certain dark irony in that this wartime government intervention into the domestic life of the population was intended to make the country more knowable and safe, but instead functioned to make it even more frighteningly anonymized: an "uncanny" inversion of the fantasy of what a nation ought to be.

With this in mind, in *A Murder Is Announced*, we find a deliberate playing about on Christie's part with the idea of what Benedict Anderson, much later in the twentieth century, would famously come to term the "imagined [...] community" (6): the idea of England *as a nation*, with all the resonances of kinship implicated within that term. Anderson debunks the seeming naturalization of the nation as a concept, instead underscoring its facilitation by religious redefinition across Europe, the birth of the industrial age, and the accretion of the middle classes and of literacy levels, all as recently as the eighteenth century. He goes on to suggest that, above all else, the reason why a nation is a community imagined rather than a community actualized is that for a person to think of themselves as belonging to a particular nation, there is a "deep, horizontal comradeship" implicated between this person and all the other individuals who share the same marker of national identity, encouraging emotional affinity purely on the basis of shared nationality (7). In the communities that Agatha Christie imagines, however, one's fellow countryman can be as treacherous as any dangerous "foreigner", and part of the reason why the mystery plaguing Chipping Cleghorn is such a lengthy one to untangle (and certainly the longest of Christie's "Miss Marple" capers), is that there are numerous characters who are living in the village under an assumed identity.

As Charles Osborne jocularly puts it, "at the end of *A Murder Is Announced* there are more cases of false identity than there are dead bodies at the end of *Hamlet*" (241). However, rather than seeing this as an (ab)use of narrative coincidence, as Osborne's jocular tone would seem to imply, my argument is that this deliberately responds to an epistemological crisis that characterizes postwar English society: an understanding that these people act precisely as disruption to the fantasy of a cohesive national identity. It is eventually discovered that the killer of Scherz, Dora Bunner, and Amy Murgatroyd is the respected pillar of the community, Letitia Blacklock. However, the woman known to her friends and neighbors as Letitia Blacklock is actually her sister Charlotte Blacklock, who has assumed her sister's identity since Letitia's death just after the end of the Second World War. Her reason for doing so is that she might claim the vast fortune that is due to befall Letitia after the death of Belle Goedler, who is the ailing wife of Letitia's former employer. At the same time, however, Charlotte's lodger, Phillipa Haymes, and her distant cousin, Julia Symmons, turn out to be the disinherited twins Pip and Emma—the two people who stand to inherit the Goedler fortune in the unlikely case that Belle Goedler should outlive Letitia Blacklock. Having been separated as toddlers, both women have, under slightly different auspices, descended upon Chipping Cleghorn with the eventual hope that, when she comes into her inheritance, the woman they know as Letitia might be persuaded to make her distant relatives an allowance. Both women subsequently realize the impossibility of making a clean breast to Letitia owing to the way in which their deception will be perceived considering Scherz's shooting at Little Paddocks, and thus both decide to maintain the deception until absolutely necessary shortly before the novel's *dénouement*.

Such plots could almost have been plucked from a nineteenth-century sensation novel and, indeed, there is irony in the modernity of postwar England, with its neat and tidy ID card system, which can actually be seen to facilitate a retrogressive spiral toward the chaos and disrupted legacies of Gothic sensation. In fact, Christie's characterization of Charlotte Blacklock has a lot in common with both the Gothic and sensational villains of previous centuries, particularly in that all her attempts to master the increasingly pandemoniac events of the novel are always ultimately undone. Charlotte is forced into a self-perpetuating cycle of having to take more and more extreme measures: first firing gun at Rudi Scherz, then poisoning Dora Bunner, strangling Amy Murgatroyd with her own washing, and finally being arrested while attempting to drown her housekeeper in the kitchen sink. Indeed, pushed to extremities by her paranoia, the shift that occurs from weaponry specifically designed to kill to whatever implement may be nearby and convenient absolutely exemplifies the escalation of Charlotte's desperation and the psychological decline that accompanies such an agitated condition. While, from her debut novel onwards, Christie's fiction has always foregrounded the possibility of one's neighbors harboring villainous, cases of fraudulent identity, as a specific crime, are few and far between specifically in her rural fictions of the 1920s and 1930s. Thus, the context of the Second World War, its concomitant displacement of persons, and government attempts to negate the effects of such displacement in the form of National Registration, appears to allow Christie, in postwar works such as *A Murder Is Announced*, to explore the ways in which this seemingly new instability in rural identities might impact upon the more significant crime of murder.

This Servant Problem: Wartime Horror in the Home

Christie's principal means of engagement with wartime displacement, however, does not concern the villainous schemes of the novel's murderer, but her housekeeper, Mitzi. Referred to, derisively, as a "Mittel Europa refugee of some kind" (48), Mitzi acts as a disruption to the fantasy of imagined community in a somewhat different way. Having been popularly used to connote an undesirable state of rootlessness since the beginning of the Second World War, the term "displaced persons" was escalated to become a specific legal classification in 1944, as Mark Wyman discusses (25). Owing to the diversity of wartime backgrounds, the spectrum of people who came to be legally certified as "displaced" is broad and, in Wyman's words, included among others, "thousands whose war years were spent with the anti-Nazi resistance—guerrilla units hiding in the marshes of northeastern Poland, loosely linked bands raiding in the Italian Alps" (34). However, most commonly, and certainly the sense in which the term is used by various characters to refer to Mitzi in *A Murder Is Announced*, the "displaced persons" of the Second World War are people of Jewish extraction who were forced to flee their homes in Central Europe and emigrate to countries such as Great Britain after Adolf Hitler came into power in Germany in 1933. These refugees arrived in the United Kingdom either directly or in a roundabout way, usually from Germany or Austria, although some originated slightly further afield, in countries like Czechoslovakia or Hungary (Snowman xvi).

Under the rule of the Nazi party, Hitler's "Aryanization" program intensified in the years following 1933, eventually spreading to Austria, which was successfully annexed by Germany in 1938. In terms of Hitler's scheme of Jewish persecution, of particular consequence was the event that began on the night of 9 November 1938, continuing into the early morning of the following day; it has now come to be referred to as *Kristallnacht*, or "Night of the Broken Glass", and consisted of a series of coordinated attacks on Jewish property and communities in Germany and Austria, the scope of which was previously unsurpassed during the Nazi's political reign.[1] As Tony Kushner suggests, although many German and Austrian Jews had affidavits of support that would have eventually allowed them to emigrate to America, it was swiftly realized that, in the wake of *Kristallnacht*, it was through deeply "unwise" to sit and to wait for one's American quota number (569). The answer, therefore, for many Jewish people seeking to escape the situation in their own countries was emigration to the United Kingdom via a domestic services permit.

Chronicling changes in British domestic servitude across the twentieth century, Pamela Horn argues that in the early decades of the twentieth century, white, non-British servants only "formed a smaller specialty sector of the domestic labour force" (203). However, this was to change significantly by the close of the Second World War, owing to the fact that, from April 1938 onward, "a special category of refugee domestic workers" were granted entry into the country "under permits issued by the Home Office [...] and following investigation by the Central Committee for Refugees, the Jewish Aid Committee and the International Solidarity Fund" (Horn 213). It is estimated that around 14,000 women, 1,000 girls, and a few hundred married couples used just such permits to flee both Germany and Austria (Horn 214), suggesting that admission to the United Kingdom in a domestic service role was one of the preferred methods of escaping ethnic persecution for a significant number of Central Europeans of Jewish descent, particularly those who were women. Indeed, this is precisely the backstory that is suggested by Christie in her characterization of Mitzi, whose exact country of origin is never explicitly stated; however, her famed goulash that she cooks for the household on the day of the holdup gestures toward Hungary (although this is hardly conclusive) (26). Indeed, in the pages dealing with *A Murder Is Announced* in one of Christie's working notebooks from the second half of 1948, Mitzi is listed by the author as a "persecuted Polish girl" (Christie qtd. in Curran 177). Rather than exact provenance, instead, the key point is very much her status both as domestic servant and as refugee from Nazism. On the morning of Scherz's death, shortly following the family's first glimpse of the ominous newspaper notice, Mitzi bewails to her employer:

> I do not wish to die! Already in Europe I escape. My family they all die—they are killed—my mother, my little brother, my so sweet little niece—all, all they are killed. But me I run away—I hide. I get to England. I work. I do work that I never—never would I do in my own country... (25)

In addition to suggesting the upset and fear caused by the murder announcement, Mitzi's lament, tellingly described by the narrator as a "constant refrain" (25), reflects the historical reality that, far from affording these victimized persons the salvation it initially seemed to, undertaking domestic servitude in a foreign country was often a further agonizing experience for the already traumatized evacuees.

In 1939, *Housewife Magazine* put forth to its readers "The Case for a Foreign Maid", nonchalantly highlighting the situation in Europe as an opportunity to be seized upon (quoted in Delap 78). Alison Light points out that although the number of female domestic servants in Britain had been in decline from the 1890s onward, it is really with the new employment opportunities for working-class women that came about after the close of the First World War that led to the birth of the "service problem" among the British upper classes and middle classes (179). She argues that the demographic of British women who in the previous century would have seen entry into live-in service as their most obvious employment option, in the interwar years "increasingly had other options", particularly in the clerical, retail, and leisure industries (178). Given how real a sea change the decline in servitude thus represented, deeply affecting—for better or worse—the everyday reality of the vast majority of British women, the popular literature and culture of the period duly reflects this social anxiety. As Nicola Humble describes:

> We find in the magazines, cookery books, and fiction of the years between the wars what amounts to a hysterical worry among the middle classes about the decline in the number of servants and the difficulty of getting—and keeping—good ones. (115)

However, given that near total erasure of the live-in servant as a fixture of the British middle-class household as the 1940s and 1950s progressed (Humble 124),[2] this obsessive anxiety about servants is even more prominent within the middlebrow fictions of the postwar era and *A Murder Is Announced* is certainly a case in point in this regard.

Christie's readers are directed to the "service problem" remarkably early in the novel, when Mrs. Swettenham, reading the morning paper, comments to her adult son, Edmund, that "Selina Lawrence is advertising for a cook again. [...] She hasn't put her address, only a box number—that's *quite* fatal" (10). The issue augmented further when the Swettenhams' own Mrs. Finch enters the dining room to clear away breakfast and is not only prevented from doing so by late-rising Edmund not having yet finished, but "sniff[s]" and withdraws from the room in offense on catching sight of his reading of the *Daily Worker* (11). After his mother attempts to reprimand him for reading socialist newspapers at the breakfast table, upsetting the servants, Edmund nonchalantly retorts, "I don't see what my political views have to do with Mrs. Finch" (11). However, for the middle-class Swettenhams, at this deepest point in the crisis in domestic servitude, the political *is* deeply personal. For as Mrs. Swettenham wisely informs her champagne-socialist son, "Mrs. Finch does matter. If she takes a dislike to us and won't come, who else could we get?" (11).

Thus, when the *Housewife Magazine* describes the Nazi persecution of Jewish people as a golden "opportunity" for British householders, this is precisely because the women who have been forced to flee from their homes in Central Europe have essentially been forced into the undesirable vocational roles increasingly rejected by working-class British women. As Kushner suggests, the seemingly philanthropic sentiment on the part of well-to-do English men and women in aiding the rescue of Jewish women was, in reality, "not incompatible with exploitation" (566). Many English householders were, at least in part, enticed into "helping" Jewish evacuees by the prospect not only of filling the vacancies for live-in domestic staff but, specifically, of getting the most for their money: exploiting a powerless social group without possible means of objection or access to recourse. Whether employed by an exploitative or genuinely sympathetic employer, what is key to note is that only a small fraction of the émigrés arriving in Britain at this time had previously been employed as domestic servants in their own countries. In fact, the majority of these refugee servants were women of middle-class or professional status, many of whom were accustomed to keeping servants themselves (Horn 217). Thus, one thing that nearly *all* refugee servants have in common is that their having to undertake work as a domestic servant was a form of degradation.

In *A Murder Is Announced*, when Mitzi launches a tirade against the blonde-haired, blue-eyed Phillipa Haymes, accusing her of being a Nazi, we in fact learn that Mitzi has been privileged to have an "expensive university education" achieving a degree in economics (63). Moreover, as earlier suggested, Mitzi makes crystal clear that, since arriving in England, she has been expected to do work that she would have been considered too educated to undertake in her home country. Even during those brief moments in which Mitzi is in an uncharacteristically placid mood, a slight note of resentment at the plight she has faced manages to seep through. This can be seen when Patrick Symmons raises a toast to Mitzi to thank her for making her signature chocolate cake for Dora's birthday tea party:

"Here's to the best cook in the world." said Patrick.
Mitzi was gratified—but felt nevertheless that a protest was due.
"That is not so. I am not really a cook. In my country I do intellectual work."
"Then you're wasted," said Patrick. "What's intellectual work compared to a *chef d'oeuvre* like Delicious Death?" (162–63)

Although there is clearly at least a vein of genuine care and affection in his remarks, in suggesting that her intellectual faculties pale in significance when brought up against her culinary proficiency, the hedonistic Patrick has clearly missed (or chosen to ignore) the point. In fact, hardly the most sensible character in the novel, we learn elsewhere that practical joker Patrick once "sent Mitzi a postcard saying the Gestapo was on her track" (95). Thus, for Mitzi, as for her real-life counterparts, the experience of displacement is incarnated not only as a geographical phenomenon, but also as a social phenomenon. As Horn summarizes, not only were these Jewish women "traumatised by events in their own country and deeply worried about relatives left behind, but they experienced feelings of humiliation and social dislocation at being reduced to what they saw as the status of domestics" (217). Even within the context of the one institution in which these foreign servants *should* have obtained both empathy and a sense of solidarity, their incoherent social, linguistic, and cultural situation—their "out-of-placeness"—was even further augmented. In 1938, a National Union of Domestic Workers was established, which, despite its initially slight membership, outright refused to consider applications from non-UK natives (Light 251; Horn 215). These hardened attitudes toward refugees in service demonstrate the fact that they were thought of as not being owed the same rights afforded to those who, in terms of social status, were their direct "native" counterparts. Moreover, such attitudes are very much reflected in Christie's novel, and are shown, for instance, through the friction between Mitzi and the novel's other servant characters: a friction arisen from xenophobic distrust on the part of the English characters, and deep resentment on the part of Mitzi. When Inspector Craddock visits Dayas Hall, looking for Phillipa Haymes, he has an impromptu tête-à-tête with the estate's gardener, known as Olde Ashe. Through Ashe, Craddock learns that the opinion of Mrs. Huggins, who works as the daily charwoman at Little Paddocks, is that "Mitzi's mixed up in" the attempted holdup. He continues that Mitzi has an "[a]wful temper" and that she "gives herself" "airs"; "Called Mrs. Huggins a working woman to her face the other morning" (69).

Playing on the well-established phrase of "The Servant Problem", in the same year as the publication of *A Murder Is Announced*, Christie's contemporary Marghanita Laski penned a short but pithy article for *Spectator* magazine, cunningly titled "*This* Servant Problem" (emphasis mine), as Delap discusses. Marked by language deeply implicated in ongoing post-Enlightenment debates regarding what Kate Ferguson Ellis refers to as the "typological conception of 'domestic happiness'" (ix), in her article Laski outlines her rationale as to why the mere presence of a European refugee housekeeper makes "an easy natural atmosphere around the home [...] unattainable" (371). As such, it is largely unsurprising that Laski's primary concern with refugees acting as servants in English households is not so much to do with practical matters: that, as I earlier mentioned, owing to their middle-class and professional social status in their home countries, these women were largely untrained in the household matters they were now forced to daily undertake (although she does at least touch on this). Instead, Laski's chief reason as to why domestic happiness cannot be achieved with a refugee from Nazism employed in service is because of the collective sense of shame that they educe within the household. Laski insists that "they are frequently capable of far more intelligent work, and everyone feels a sense of guilt at harnessing a race-horse to a dray" (371). It is fair to suggest, in light of this, that people such as Mitzi—"displaced persons" employed as servants in English households—have an element of the "uncanny" about them, posing a threat to normative modes of postwar domesticity. They have the capacity to rupture a given household's collective psychological boundaries between sanctified interior space and the exterior world of political upheaval, violence, and persecution. Through occupying the position of a "fragment" dislodged from its appropriate locale and from its appropriate chronology, within postwar English middle-class society, the Jewish refugee servant threatens to efface any meaningful geographical distinction between "here" (England) and "there" (Central Europe), or any temporal delineation between "then" (the Nazi party's political reign) and "now" (the postwar period). Those that encounter Mitzi are therefore forced to contemplate the frightening historical "whole" that they are actively trying to forget. Ultimately, Mitzi's disquieting presence in the village of Chipping Cleghorn serves to debunk this English community's constructed fiction of having moved past the horrors of the Second World War: that they have, as Mrs. Swettenham puts it strikingly early within the novel, "got over all that" (11).

People Like You: Bodies, Reading, and Postwar Identities

Mitzi's situation at Little Paddocks functions, in a very physical way, to keep the trauma of the Second World War alive. As such, it is unsurprising that even the movements of her body are characterized by their violent intensity. It is widely considered that to propagate the "easy natural atmosphere" of the domestic sanctuary, servitude must be simultaneously present yet almost invisible. Mitzi, however, singularly refuses to disappear into the backdrop of domestic interiority, and her movements throughout Little Paddocks are as disruptive as possible. This is reflected in her *penchant* for making "dramatic entrances", in one case "flinging open" the door of the lounge so forcibly that she almost knocks Inspector Craddock to the ground sideways (225). Ultimately, the displacement Mitzi has experienced owing to Jewish persecution has rendered her culturally "unreadable"; that the other characters in the novel, including the third-person narrator, have no easy, ready narrative through which to interpret her traumatic past experiences. This, I argue, is one of the reasons that the novel's descriptions of Mitzi are so contradictory and disjointed. Upon Mitzi's entrance into the story, the reader is given a vivid and intense snapshot of her physicality:

> Through the door surged a tempestuous young woman with a well developed bosom heaving under a tight jersey. She had on a dirndl skirt of a bright colour and had greasy dark plaits wound round and round her head. Her eyes were dark and flashing. (25)

Given that, at least *structurally* speaking, Mitzi is somewhat of a tangential character, such close, considered attention to her physical appearance, countenance, and mannerisms could be considered both unusual and largely unnecessary. Moreover, the most striking aspect of the description itself is the incoherence of Mitzi's outward appearance: the jarring, uneasy coalescence of those aspects of her appearance, which are clearly attractive (the heaving bosom, the vivid eyes), and those which are very much unattractive (the gaudy outfit, the greasy hair). There is, in fact, an emphasis on Mitzi's clothes throughout the novel, such as when she decides to wear a combination of green skirt and purple jumper "not becoming to her pasty completion" (62). The fact that Mitzi seems to *always* be wearing clothes that do not flatter her works to reinforce her situation of displacement. They remind the reader of the fact that the clothes that would suit her presumably had to be abandoned in Europe along with the great majority her possessions, and that the garments that currently adorn her she has either had to purchase, or perhaps have been given in an act of charity, since arriving in a new country. This again makes explicit that Mitzi's body cannot be properly "read" by the community within which she now finds herself: that the apparatus required to interpret Mitzi's traumatized body somehow eludes the residents of Chipping Cleghorn. Resultantly, the villagers' encounters with Mitzi must always be disquieting encounters that threaten any form of complacent domesticity in operation within their "sleepy" English village during peacetime.

In fact, Christie's representation of racial prejudice in *A Murder Is Announced* further illuminates the village of Chipping Cleghorn as far from having, to appropriate the psychoanalytic terminology, properly processed or "worked through" the trauma of the preceding era of bloodshed and carnage across Europe. David Kynaston notes a noticeable revival in British anti-Semitism in the immediate postwar climate, documenting that several British cities had anti-Semitic riots in the year prior to the publication of *A Murder Is Announced*, "triggered by lurid headlines about the hanging in Palestine of two captured British sergeants but also involv[ing] a widespread belief that it was Jews who were responsible for running the black market" (270). With this in mind, it is telling that Christie gestures toward an assumed link between Jewishness and criminality within her novel. By virtue of the fact that they are "both foreigners" (49), Mitzi is unrelentingly suspected, both by the police and by other characters in the novel, of being somehow involved with Rudi Scherz in the attempted shooting of her employer.

However, rather than replicating anti-Semitic attitudes without comment, I argue that Christie in fact utilizes Mitzi to challenge ideas of a collective English national identity and a dominant model of postwar Englishness that would preclude people of other national and ethnic backgrounds. In the regard, the opening chapter of the novel is significant. Organized as a sequence of vignettes, its importance springs from the fact that the sequence presents four individual households in close geographical proximity—The Swettenhams, The Easterbrooks, Miss Hinchcliffe and Miss Murgatroyd, and The Harmons—reading the same advertisement in the *Chipping Cleghorn Gazette*, at more or less the same time:

> *A marriage is announced*—no, a *murder*. What? Well, I never! Edmund, *Edmund*, listen to this… (12, emphasis original)
> "Archie," said Mrs Easterbrook to her husband, "listen to *this*. […] Archie, do listen["] (13–14, emphasis original)
> "In the *Gazette*," [Miss Murgatroyd] panted. "Just listen—what can it *mean*?["]. (16, emphasis original)
> "Oo, scrumptious!" said Mrs Harmon across the breakfast table to her husband, the Rev. Julian Harmon, "there's going to be a murder at Miss Blacklock's." […].
> Mrs Harmon […] handed the *Gazette* across the table. (17)

Anderson argues that the popularization of the newspaper in eighteenth-century Europe represents a critical milestone in the development of the modern concept of nationalism, owing to the fact that the newspaper was one of the discursive forms that "provided the technical means for 're-presenting' the *kind* of imagined community that is the nation" (25; emphasis original). Indeed, newspapers are of particular importance in the process of marking out the parameters of the community, on both local and national levels. Not only do they bring the reader details of what other people within the same community or nation are up to, thus further supplementing the sense of "knowing" people that is so important to the manufacturing of a national kinship, but, moreover, they inevitably get read by large numbers of people at the same temporal moment (in the case of *A Murder Is Announced*, over breakfast). Thus, not only are a nation's individuals connected along a spatial plane, they are also connected through existing at the same notch along a chronological timeframe. Christie's vignettes depicting the breakfast-time reading of the *Gazette* in *A Murder Is Announced*, is therefore a prime example of what Anderson terms the "confidence in […] steady, anonymous, simultaneous activity" that can foster such powerful feelings of affinity in members of the same nation (26).

However, Christie's novel does not just unthinkingly reproduce these formative mechanics of nation-building (in the first instance, her unsubtle flagging-up of these processes could itself be construed as a form of resistance). Rather, through its depiction of Mitzi as a "displaced person", *A Murder Is Announced* critiques the mechanisms through which national identity is acquired and venerated, as what Christie does in the novel is reverse the situation, underscoring the ways in which the uprooted and nationally incongruous Mitzi *herself* belongs to an imagined community of persons. While still posing as Letitia, Charlotte Blacklock tells the novel's detective characters that her housekeeper "has a kind of persecution mania" (57) and not to be overly suspicious of Mitzi because she is known to lie: that "her atrocity stories have grown and grown until every kind of unpleasant story that has ever appeared in print has happened to her or her relations personally" (57). Instead she points out that Mitzi did see at least one her relations killed, and upon reflection, thinks that "a lot of these displaced persons feel, perhaps justly, that their claim to our notice and sympathy lies in their atrocity value and so they exaggerate and invent" (58). The "exaggeration" and "invention" implicated in Mitzi's remediation of her experience of the Nazi regime directly parallel the imaginative acts that must be perpetrated to augment one's sense of belonging to a national community.

The key point is the emphasis Christie places on the act of reading in the interpolation of national identity: that it is precisely the process of reading stories about people "like you" (whether English or Central European Jews) that allows you to *imagine* yourself as part of a community whose constituent members must, however abstractly, somehow have a connection deep-down. It is therefore highly significant that the novel's most racially "other" character—the person so unequivocally out-of-place in the novel's middle-England setting—experiences through her reading of war atrocity stories a process of self-identification, which so strikingly parallels that which the novel's "native" characters experience when they "eagerly [...] plunge..." into their morning papers (9). Ultimately, despite all the ways in which, consciously or otherwise, the Second World War has worked to consolidate the fantasy of a cohesive English-cum-British national identity, *A Murder Is Announced* articulates a noticeable awareness of precisely of the fictional basis of that fantasy, thereby working to debunk any kind of narrative of national "superiority" on England's part at this specific—and specifically traumatized—historical moment. Ultimately, the condition of postwar England as articulated by Christie's novel is a condition of fractured identities and "uncanny" haunting.

Notes

1 In terms of the scale of this "orgy of destruction", Read and Fisher document that, in the first twenty-four hours alone "at least 7,500 stores, 29 warehouses and 171 houses were destroyed; 191 synagogues were razed

by fire and a further 76 physically demolished; 11 Jewish community centres, cemetery chapels and similar buildings were torched and another three gutted" (73).
2 Also see Light, *Mrs. Woolf and the Servants* (313).

Works Cited

Anderson, Benedict. *Imagined Communities: Reflections of the Origin and Spread of Nationalism*. 1983. Verso, 1991.
Christie, Agatha. *Giant's Bread* (as Mary Westmacott). 1930. HarperCollins, 2017.
———. *A Murder Is Announced*. 1950. HarperCollins, 2005.
———. *The Mystery of the Blue Train*. 1928. HarperCollins, 2015.
Curran, John. *Agatha Christie's Secret Notebooks: Fifty Years of Mysteries in the Making*. HarperCollins, 2010.
Delap, Lucy. *Knowing their Place: Domestic Service in Twentieth-Century Britain*. Oxford University Press, 2011.
Ferguson Ellis, Kate. *The Contested Castle: Gothic Novels and the Subversion of Domestic Ideology*. University of Illinois Press, 1989.
Fisher, David and Anthony Read. *Kristallnacht: Unleashing the Holocaust*. Penguin, 1989.
Horn, Pamela. *Life below Stairs in the 20th Century*. Sutton, 2003.
Humble, Nicola. *The Feminine Middlebrow Novel, 1920s to 1950s: Class, Domesticity and Bohemianism*. Oxford University Press, 2001.
Kushner, Tony. "An Alien Occupation? Jewish Refugees and Domestic Service in Britain, 1933–48". *Second Chance: Two Centuries of German-Speaking Jews in the United Kingdom*, edited by Werner E. Mosse, JCB Mohr, 1991.
Kynaston, David. *Austerity Britain: 1945–51*. Bloomsbury, 2007.
Laski, Marghanita. "This Servant Problem". *Spectator*, 24 Mar. 1950.
Light, Alison. *Mrs Woolf and the Servants*. Penguin, 2008.
Makinen, Merja. *Agatha Christie: Investigating Femininity*. Palgrave Macmillan, 2006.
Osborne, Charles. *The Life and Crimes of Agatha Christie: A Biographical Companion to the Works of Agatha Christie*. 1982. HarperCollins, 2000.
Snowman, Daniel. *The Hitler Émigrés: The Cultural Impact on Britain of Refugees from Nazism*. Pimlico, 2003.
Wyman, Mark. *DPs: Europe's Displaced Persons, 1945–51*. 1989. Cornell, 1998.

9 Detecting the Blitz
Memory and Trauma in Christie's Postwar Writings

Rebecca Mills

While Agatha Christie's writing in the 1920s hints at the continuing psychological and social wounds of the First World War, and some of her 1930s novels foreshadow the bombings and destruction of the Second World War,[1] war is largely absent from her prolific 1940s output. Motifs of lingering trauma and threat from the skies vanish almost completely, and the glancing references to aero planes and danger that do appear are detached from historical specificity. During the Second World War, Christie published thirteen detective novels (and wrote two others to be published later), and a literary novel as Mary Westmacott.[2] Apart from the spy thriller *N or M?* (1941), set on the British coast and dealing with Fifth Columnists and the threat of submarines, none of Christie's prose explicitly engages with the Second World War. This distancing becomes all the more significant as Christie was living in London at the time, at the epicenter of the Home Front. Indeed, in October 1940, Christie's London home at 48 Sheffield Terrace was bombed. There were no fatalities, but Christie and her household had to move; this destruction and upheaval are contained within a single page of *An Autobiography* (1977), suggesting an unwillingness to return to the events. Nevertheless, this bombing resurfaces, barely disguised, in the Poirot novel *Taken at the Flood* (1948), where it has tragic and traumatic consequences that continue to destabilize and threaten lives and identities in peace time.

It is this dynamic of absence and resurfacing, and the forms and implications of this resurfacing, that I examine here via structures of trauma and memory. References to the Blitz and its personally and nationally disruptive effects occur with decreasing frequency between 1948 and the posthumous publication of Christie's autobiography in 1977. This chapter, then, maps this diffusion; I argue that these glancing but recurring references to the Blitz offer a clue to themes of memory, identity, and trauma across Christie's body of work, and particular insight into Christie's textual response to war.[3] To some extent, therefore, the generic elements of Christie's corpus—the murders, investigations, and resolutions of the detective story—are decentered here by conflating the Westmacotts, the mysteries, and *An Autobiography*. Nevertheless, this approach is not incompatible with generic narrative structures. In her article on reading detective fiction as a way of processing her grief over the death of her mother, Sally R. Munt notes that

> Freud argued that repetition is a form of recollection, which takes place in the realm of the symbolic (i.e., in representation). We cannot move forward until we understand the past. Reading detective novels compulsively is a return to death on two levels: in the story we investigate it, and each time we reach the end of a narrative, we experience a kind of imaginative death, as we close the pages. (143)

I would suggest that this "return to death" is a process shared by detective fiction writers as well as readers, and that Christie embeds the repetition of the traumatic event of the Blitz within the repetitions of the detective novel. Christie's fictionalized references to the Blitz become increasingly allusive—and elusive—with time, even as the brevity and stoicism of her autobiographical accounts obscure the record of her full experience.

While Christie's fiction has never dealt with war and its victims as explicitly as that of her contemporary Dorothy L. Sayers, whose detective Lord Peter Wimsey suffers from shell shock and flashbacks to the trenches, traces of twentieth-century conflicts and the wounds of war are detectable across her writings. Between *N or M?* and *Taken at the Flood*, the danger of airplanes surfaces occasionally, but is detached from wartime significance. Secret service agent Anthony Browne in *Sparkling Cyanide* (1945) poses as a saboteur in aero plane and armament manufacturing, but there is no heightened urgency assigned to these industries. In *The Moving Finger* (1942), the significantly named *Jerry* (slang for Germans in the Second World War) Burton is a pilot badly injured in an air crash, but the novel is not set in wartime. Similarly, in *The Body in the Library* (1942), wheelchair-bound patriarch Conway Jefferson's family was killed in an aero plane accident that left him "like a man who's lost half himself—and I'm not speaking of my physical plight!" (74), but this occurs eight years before the beginning of the novel. These novels, therefore, transpose the danger of airplanes in the Second World War into accidents for flyers and passengers rather than hostile enemy action targeted at civilians on the ground, but the anxiety generated by the Blitz is evident in the link between airplanes and bodily and psychological traumas.

The Blitz, then, inhabits the margins of Christie's work, but aerial bombardment, an act of violence unique to wartime, does inscribe its traces across genres, modes, and author identities—erased, displaced, and disguised during the war, but resurfacing *after the war* in detective fiction, life writing, and the Mary Westmacott novels, diffused across authorial identities. It is precisely this slipperiness and peripherality that interests me here, and its implications for how memory and amnesia, as well as the passage of time, are presented in a way that counters the orderly clarity of Christie's Golden Age detective narratives

This repetition and reemergence across categories, then, evokes Roger Luckhurst's observation that "Trauma violently opens passageways between systems that were once discrete, making unforeseen connections that distress or confound" (3). *Taken at the Flood* begins with an air raid in London; the Westmacott *The Rose and the Yew Tree* (1948) is set during the "black period" ("Prelude") immediately after the Second World War and recalls air raids, bombs, and evacuation. The Blitz is remembered in the standalone crime novel *Crooked House* (1949) as an event that brought incompatible family members under the same roof.

In all of these novels, then, the Blitz conveys instability and social anxiety, as well as material destruction and threats of injury and death. But this "breach of borders" is also temporal; examining references to the Blitz uncovers not only unstable memories and identities but also "unforeseen connections" to the central trauma of Christie's life—her mother's death in 1926, rapidly followed by her divorce from Archie Christie and then "disappearance." As biographer Laura Thompson recounts, on Friday 3 December in 1926, Christie left her car by a quarry and took a train to Harrogate. A nationwide manhunt ensued; Christie was discovered at a spa hotel eleven days later, booked in as Tessa Neele, the name of her husband's paramour. The official explanation, reinforced by her then-husband Archibald Christie, was illness and amnesia (186–219). These events are almost completely ignored in *An Autobiography*, but elements reappear in both Westmacott and Christie novels; as Thompson suggests, the Westmacott identity allowed Christie to "go wherever she wanted, into every idea that had ever fascinated her, even into the recesses of her own past" (366). These traumas, I suggest, are recontextualized within the collective memory and the physical and psychological wounds of war.

My intention here is not to diagnose Christie herself with any psychological disorder, or to suggest that the shifting sequences of repression and resurfacing across her work are deliberate or conscious. Psychological "trauma" and posttraumatic stress disorders are not terms or concepts that Christie herself has used. The etymology of "trauma" is Greek, meaning "wound", and until the late nineteenth century was used for physical damage. In 1894, the term made a shift to psychology and is currently generally understood, according to the *Oxford English Dictionary*, as "A psychic injury, esp[ecially] one caused by emotional shock the memory of which is repressed and remains unhealed; an internal injury, esp[ecially] to the brain, which may result in a behavioral disorder of organic origin." Both psychological and the physical traumas can be identified across Christie's work, as can repressed memories and mechanisms for their conscious or involuntary recovery. She was also familiar with shell shock, now considered a form of posttraumatic stress disorder (PTSD).[4] Indeed, in the Westmacott novel *Unfinished Portrait* (1934), a one-armed veteran compares shell shock to his injury:

> I know something about nerves and mind. Three of my best friends were shell-shocked in the war. I know myself what it is for a man to be physically maimed—I know just what it can do to him. I know, too, that one can be mentally maimed. The damage can't be seen when the wound is healed—but it's there. There's a weak spot—a flaw—you're crippled and not whole. (13–14)

The imagery of wounds here echoes the original meaning of trauma, but it is also significant that the narrator is not addressing a fellow veteran—his listener is a suicidal woman, wounded by her divorce and bereavement and trying to disappear in a foreign country.[5] Domestic emotional injury, then, is diagnosed via a disorder specific to the First World War, even as psychological wounds are grounded in the memory of the Blitz after the Second World War.

Christie's preoccupation with the wounds of war and their destabilizing effects also appears in her crime fiction; in *The Murder of Roger Ackroyd* (1926), a character remarks of a troubled youth and murder suspect that,

> "But, of course, one must remember that Ralph was in several air raids as a young boy. The results are apparent long after, sometimes, they say. People are not responsible for their actions in the least. They lose control, you know, without being able to help it. [...] Like shell-shock, you know." (120)

In her examination of Lord Peter Wimsey's shell shock and its social context, Ariela Freedman notes that, "[w]hile shell-shock victims were heroes, they were also suspect as potential criminals. If they had been subject to one lapse in judgement during the war, they may be susceptible to similar lapses in civilian society" (376). This anxiety about a lingering and unpredictable psychological weakness persists in Christie's work, but after the Second World War, she often linked the potential psychological and social disruption of this wound to women and civilians, particularly those who endured the Blitz, as well as male veterans.

The Blitz, then, can be read as a traumatic event, and the absence or temporal distancing of the Blitz in the wartime texts between *N or M?* and *Taken at the Flood* as a break in a narrative caused by latency, or delay in fully processing an experience, reinforced by cultural and social pressure—as well as editorial interventions from publishers and literary agents. Gill Plain comments that during the Second World War, the success of detective fiction as fantasy lies less in its ability to create another world than in its ability to provide a resolution. [...] The solution of the mystery, the provision of an answer through the courage and intelligence of the individual detective, is a central fantasy of wartime survival. (*Women's Fiction* 17).

Christie faced commercial pressure to edit her wartime work in an escapist direction; even if Christie had wanted to negotiate the war contemporaneously and directly, both the prevailing cultural attitude and the specific interventions of Christie's agents and publishers encouraged repression, and thereby perhaps compounded the original wartime trauma narrative, leading to its return.

From a psychoanalytical perspective, Christie's textual narratives and representations of trauma as they relate to the Second World War reveal that flashbacks and ellipses on a formal narrative level reflect delays and disruptions on psychological and epistemological levels.[6] Cathy Caruth's articulation of Freud's ideas of latency, later termed belatedness, is useful for examining these structures of trauma:

> The pathology consists [...] solely in the structure of its experience or reception: the event is not assimilated or experienced fully at the time, but only belatedly, in its repeated possession of the one who experiences it. To be traumatized is precisely to be possessed by an image or event. [...] Indeed, modern analysts as well have remarked on the surprising literality and non-symbolic nature of traumatic dreams and flashbacks [...] It is this literality and *its insistent return* which thus constitutes trauma and points toward its enigmatic core: the delay or incompletion in knowing, or even in seeing, an overwhelming occurrence that then remains, in its insistent return, absolutely true to the event. (4–5; emphasis original)

The return of the original event is generally considered to be involuntary. The repeated references to the Blitz and its related keywords—air raid, bomb, flying bomb—from *Taken at the Flood* onward, therefore, I regard as moments of return, or flashbacks, in which the detached and displaced allusions to airplanes and air crashes of the wartime novels are relived in their real context, reattached to the trauma of the War. Stephen Knight observes that

> Christie's [1939–1945] wartime mysteries superintend contemporary battles from a distance and with an Austenesque pattern of radical displacement, not recognizing the war as itself, but representing its effect in terms of disruptions to the normal balance of gender and social power. (163)

The term "displacement" here echoes the deferral of experiencing the traumatic event, as does the idea that Christie's work shows only limited and "metaphorical" (Hartley 170) engagement with the war. This displacement is only temporary, however, as I have argued elsewhere in terms of Christie's use of material culture to reify the psychological and social disruptions of the war.[7] Here the psychological and experiential delay in fully recognizing the war appears across Christie's work not only as an explicit discussion of social change, but also on a narrative level in the return of the war through flashbacks.

Flashbacks in psychological terms mean the "recurrence of a memory, or the experience of reliving an episode from the past" (Colman 287) and can be linked to posttraumatic stress disorder. In narrative terms, Luckhurst describes the flashback as "an intrusive, anachronic image that throws off the linear temporality of the story" (180). Narrative flashbacks reflecting psychological flashbacks recur across Christie's genres and authorial identities, as well as between fictional and autobiographical writing, which supports the notion of "insistent return" but also offers a rationale for considering these texts to inhabit a shared psychological and mnemonic terrain for the purposes of this investigation. This is not to say they make a cohesive whole; as Jane Robinett has observed, "[t]raumatic experience produces narrative structures that are fractured and erratic, structures which will not sustain integrated notions of self, society, culture, or world" (297).[8] Indeed, the very title of *Unfinished Portrait* suggests a break in narrative—a lack of closure. *Taken at the Flood* breaks away from the generic mysteries and murders of Christie's interwar titles,[9] suggesting a more profound unrest and division with its title and epigraph from Shakespeare's *Julius Caesar*: "There is a tide in the affairs of men. / Which, taken at the flood, leads on to fortune;" (IV.2.268–69). The preceding lines in Brutus's speech situate the threat and volatility suggested by the "flood" of the epigraph and title within war: "Our legions are brim-full, our cause is ripe: / The enemy increaseth every day;" (IV.2.265–66). Victoria Stewart mentions Christie only briefly in her discussion of memory/amnesia and war in thrillers and detective fiction, but her argument is relevant here:

> Amnesia, and the recovery of memory, can serve as a means of representing the fragmentation and uncertainty of wartime experience, [...] even where the gaps in memory (and therefore the plot) are eventually filled, there is often residual anxiety about the viability of such an urge to completion. (93)

These narrative structures, then, as well as the "insistent return" of these flashbacks across Christie's work, challenge the resolution and return to equilibrium that has been considered essential to the detective fiction genre.

These processes of displacement and repression, then, as well as social commentary, are certainly present across Christie's work, underpinning her oblique and allusive relationship with her immediate environment and its hazards. The reemergence of the symbolic and cultural imaginary of the Blitz in Christie's postwar writings, as well as its physical psychological damage, suggest a "residual anxiety", but also that the memory of the war, particularly the air raids, is the locus for a slippery conjunction of the personal and the national. As Roger Luckhurst points out, "Trauma has become a paradigm because it has been turned into a repertoire of compelling stories about the enigmas of identity, memory and selfhood that have saturated Western cultural life" (80); this repertoire can be read in Christie's challenges to solid and situated identity, as well as official and generic narratives of memory.

"Funny business this blast"

When *Taken at the Flood* is read in tandem with *An Autobiography*, a narrative of latency emerges. The air raid that kills patriarch Gordon Cloade and destroys his house in the novel parallels the blast that destroyed Christie's Sheffield Terrace home in 1940; indeed, the Campden Hill location of *Taken at the Flood* adjoins Sheffield Terrace. Christie recalls in her autobiography:

> Events happened in confusing order. I remember Sheffield Terrace was bombed on a weekend when we were away from London. A landmine came down exactly opposite it, on the other side of the street, and completely destroyed three houses. The effect it had on 48 Sheffield Terrace was to blow up the basement, which might have been presumed the safest place, and to damage the roof and top floor, leaving the ground and first floors almost unharmed. My Steinway was never quite the same afterwards. (503)

An Autobiography emphasizes damage to property rather than the psyche, shifting from a mention of Christie's "horror at being trapped underground" (503) and consequent refusal to use shelters to the more practical difficulties in obtaining movers and storage in war. Nevertheless, the reference to the Steinway, as Merja Makinen has commented in conversation, is not merely flippancy, stoicism, or regretting damage to an expensive possession—Christie was very musical, and in her late teens dreamed of becoming an opera singer. Instead of dwelling on the upheaval to her "real life" caused by the bomb, Christie therefore mourns an alternative future and life.

The fictional explosion is placed in 1944 rather than 1940, but the novel echoes the structural damage caused by the Sheffield Terrace explosion precisely, in accordance with the "literality" noted by Caruth in the belated return of the traumatic event. Major Porter comments of Gordon Cloade's death: "Funny business this blast. Never know what it's going to do. Blew the basement in and ripped off the roof. First floor practically wasn't touched" (2). In *Taken at the Flood*, David Hunter survives because he slept in his first-floor bedroom rather than the air raid shelter in the basement, as Christie was in the habit of doing; this story is recounted to Poirot in the "Prologue", as he and a friend are waiting in the underground shelter of "The Coronation Club" during an air raid. "Club bore" Major Porter gives a rambling account of Gordon Cloade's marriage to David Hunter's sister, Irish possible bigamist/gold-digger Rosaleen, Cloade's subsequent death in the raid, and her inheritance of his wealth, which meant that Cloade's family was excluded from his legacy. Significantly, in both writings, the safety of the underground shelter is shown to be a myth—and *Taken at the Flood* goes on to develop this theme by exposing the fragility of shelter offered by home, family, and structures of inheritance, while presenting danger and uncertainty as attractive.

The carnage of *Taken at the Flood*—three servants were killed as well as Gordon Cloade—did not occur at Sheffield Terrace, but its *possibility* is the traumatic event that was not fully experienced or understood at the time, especially as Christie and her husband were away from their home during the explosion and did not witness the destruction. Consequently, the event returns in fictional form. Caruth observes that

> What one returns to, in the flashback, is not the incomprehensibility of the event of one's near death, but the very incomprehensibility of one's own survival. Repetition, in other words, is not simply the attempt to grasp that one has almost died, but more fundamentally and enigmatically, the very attempt to claim one's own survival. (25)

The repetition of the damage to the basement and the imagining of the potential catastrophe that would have occurred had Christie and her household been present, then, can be understood as an attempt to negotiate survival. The air raid in the "Prologue" of the novel is in fact the *third*—Sheffield Terrace, Campden Hill, Coronation Club. The episode in the shelter ends with "This was in the autumn of 1944. It was in late spring, 1946, that Hercule Poirot received a visit" (5–6). In his evaluation of "the mechanics of trauma's narrative spur", Luckhurst invokes narratologist Gerard Genette's "taxonomy of time slippages", including the "accelerated time" of ellipsis (83); here the slippage from 1944 to 1946 not only suggests the trauma of the air raids, but also shows that their effects continue.

The war may officially have been over by 1948, when *Taken at the Flood* was published, but in a sense, it cannot be over. As R. A. York points out, "The book is pervaded [...] by the memory of deaths in the war, the sense of the missing young men: [Gordon Cloade's niece] Lynn's fiancé Rowley [Cloade], who has stayed at home [...] is haunted by guilt at having survived" (135).[10] As a counterpoint, demobilized WREN (Women's Royal Naval Service officer) Lynn misses the travel, danger, and purpose of her war service. This psychological continuation of the war, signposted by the prologue's ellipsis between the air raid of 1944 and Poirot's invitation to investigate Rosaleen Cloade in 1946, is echoed in the ambiguity of the novel's end, where neither the romantic subplot nor the requirements of justice is conventionally fulfilled, and order is not restored. Poirot knows that Rowley committed manslaughter, and Rowley knows that he knows, and is left to anticipate arrest. Rowley renews his romance with Lynn by attempting to possessively strangle her; she is content with both the threat of future physical violence and Rowley's possible imprisonment: "I've never, really, *cared* very much for being safe—" (279), she states, having found a way to continue the thrill of the war—or doomed to repeat its trauma.

"Events happened in confusing order"

Memory and timelines are central to detective fiction. Investigations depend on witnesses remembering precisely where they were and what they saw at a certain time; criminals must keep worlds of falsehoods in their minds. The detective must map a precise sequence of events and scenes. Indeed, as Stewart observes, the genre of detective fiction is "predicated on the idea that past events must be recalled in a timely and appropriate manner in order that present events might be elucidated" (88). Similar to Robinett's observations of trauma in narrative structure, Luckhurst writes, "No narrative of trauma can be told in a linear way: it has a time signature that must fracture conventional causality" (9). By using the Blitz to embed uncertain memory and non-linearity within her postwar narratives, Christie challenges the very possibility of these generic mnemonic feats, even as the temporal disruptions of trauma challenge the restoration of order implied by the investigations of the detective. Lyndsey Stonebridge describes the effect of trauma on perceptions of time as follows:

> Central to trauma theory is the idea that an impression can be both experienced and forgotten (sometimes in the same instant). Trauma thus divides the mind not only from itself, but also splits it in time: there's a lag, a snatch, in the experience of the traumatized that pulls them out of linear chronology. (196)

This division is visible in the temporal slippage between the "Prologue" and first chapter of *Taken at the Flood*, but also in the tension between the externally imposed pressure to forget, and the impossibility of forgetting, that resonates throughout the novel. Rosaleen was traumatized by the bombing at Campden Hill that killed Gordon and left her "suffering from blast" (2), as Major Porter notes. Lynn's mother, Gordon's relative, remarks with passive-aggressive sympathy: "Of course...the poor girl was blitzed and had shock from blast and was really frightfully ill and all that, [...] she's never really quite recovered. [...] sometimes, she looks quite half-witted" (23). As in *Unfinished Portrait*, mental and physical traumas are blurred, although Rosaleen meets no empathetic wounded veteran. Lynn, at ease with "the mines at sea, the bombs from the air, the crisp *ping* of a rifle bullet as you drove over a desert track" (111; emphasis original) but struggling with peacetime, scorns Rosaleen's nerves, until David observes:

> "Fear isn't logical. When you've suffered from blast—"
> Lynn was suddenly ashamed—contrite. She said: "I'm sorry. I'd forgotten."
> With sudden bitterness David cried out: "Yes, it's soon forgotten—all of it. Back to safety!" (115)

This is barely two years after the Campden Hill bomb, but there is a division between those who suffered directly from the Blitz, and those who did not, and are able to move forward and forget.

Lynn can look back on the war with nostalgia; Rosalind remains temporally and mentally caught within the epicenter of the horror:

> "That was when the bombs were there—the bombs." She shivered, closed her eyes. "I'll never forget—never..."
> "Yes, you will." [David] took her gently by the shoulders, shook her slightly. "Snap out of it, Rosaleen. You were badly shocked, but it's over now. There are no more bombs. Don't think about it. Don't remember." (58)

David attempts to cancel out Rosaleen's traumatized repetition of "the bombs" and "never" with his own insistent repetition of "don't", but unsuccessfully; Rosaleen continues to be "possessed" (to use Caruth's term) by the explosion. The horror of her current situation is that there is no way to escape the temporal "lag" of the traumatized and rejoin a linear chronological narrative—indeed, she is eventually killed when David inserts morphia into one of her sleeping pills and is thus out of time forever. But Rosaleen cannot move forward because she was knocked unconscious, and therefore did not fully experience the event—she experiences it *belatedly*, hence the insomnia, "vacancy", and "shivers."

There is another reason why she cannot fully process this traumatic event. Rosaleen Cloade, wife of Gordon, was killed in the blast, as was everyone in England who knew her, and David Hunter persuaded another woman to take her place; as Stewart observes, this illustrates "the fragility and uncertainty of wartime relationships" (87). But the significance in terms of trauma is deeper than this, as Eileen Corrigan, a rural Irish Catholic housemaid, is living Rosaleen Cloade's life, and therefore *Rosaleen*'s narrative of trauma. Eileen comments to David of Rosaleen Cloade's wealthy and privileged life: "It's quite true, David, it is like a dream—or like something on the pictures" (60), suggesting that she is not fully present or awake in Rosaleen's life: literally "not all there." Eileen/Rosaleen's trauma, then, is doubly weighted, and informed by her class and social performance. As a rural housemaid from County Cork, Eileen Corrigan might have been able to properly grieve and understand her experience; as Rosaleen Cloade, supposed to be of "Old Irish landed gentry" (79), widow of Gordon Cloade, she is expected to forget and move forward.

Complementing the desire for escapist and insulating rather than realistic detective fiction during the war was the prevailing impulse to encourage a culture and narrative described by Amy Bell as "civilian steadfastness" (161); she writes, "The British public regime of stoicism created a wartime urban culture of psychological tension civilians sought to minimize or repress their fears except in moments of intense terror" (155). *Taken at the Flood* opens by affirming life as usual; at the Coronation Club: "[T]he fact that an air raid was in progress made no difference to normal procedure" (1). "Careless talk costs lives" was emblazoned on posters, and while it explicitly refers to passing on dangerous information to the enemy, the slogan implicitly promotes a culture of silence and withholding. Similarly, in the interests of civilian morale, the government made it an offense to "spread alarm and despondency"; Christie comments in *Taken at the Flood*: "For young Mr. Mellon [Poirot's friend] enjoyed creating alarm and despondency in such places as it was not forbidden by the Defence of the Realm Act" (5). Bell notes that during the Blitz, some writers displaced psychological fears onto the body—the mind could embrace stoicism, but "[t]he body was a terrain difficult to control" (159). In *Taken at the Flood*, it is foreigners who are allowed these psychosomatic reactions—Poirot recalls sitting "very sick in my stomach" during the air raid at the Coronation club (184). Similarly, the Irish Eileen/Rosaleen has shivers and insomnia, embodying her trauma. To be British, however, is to be steadfast. Christie remarks on the routine of war in the *Autobiography*: "'Oh dear, there [the bombers] are again!' I would mutter, and turn over" (503).

The traumatized, then, interrupt the linear passage of time; they are reminders of weakness, the horrors of the war, the fragility of the border between body and mind, and the breach of trauma. This is perhaps why, after 1948, Christie's mentions of the Blitz become increasingly oblique and distanced, insulated by layers of narrative, third-hand rather than lived experience. Rather than directly affecting secondary or even tertiary characters, the air raids and their consequences resurface in memories and anecdotes that link postwar present to a wartime past. Indeed, as Stewart remarks, "Even when [memory loss] takes a more peripheral role, it is often an index of the anxieties arising from the conditions of wartime" (86). An anecdote in the Poirot novel *After the Funeral* (1953) is repeated almost exactly in the standalone Cold War thriller *Destination Unknown* (1955). In both stories, a woman sustains a head injury during in an air raid, followed by concussion. She then makes a journey, and wakes up in hospital with amnesia, unaware of where she is or how much time has passed— "out of linear chronology", as Stonebridge writes. This repetition of anecdotes is significant in itself as a flashback suggesting the insistent return of Blitz-related trauma across texts, but also because the recounted sequence, I suggest, is a repetition of the emergence and updating of *the* trauma in Christie's own life narrative, in an updated form—in *Unfinished Portrait*, psychological wounds and disruptions were linked to shell-shock, whereas here amnesia, dislocation, and lost identity are framed by the war and the Blitz.

In *After the Funeral*, middle-aged Miss Gilchrist served as companion to Cora Abernethy; she murdered Cora with a hatchet, and then posed as Cora at a family funeral; she performs and then discards Cora's identity with padding and wig. Later she strikes another character on the head; her victim is hospitalized with concussion. Miss Gilchrist, maintaining her guise as chatty companion, links this incident to the war:

> "A woman I knew had concussion during the war," said Miss Gilchrist conversationally. "A brick or something hit her as she was walking down Tottenham Court Road—it was during fly bomb time—and she never felt anything at all. Just went on with what she was doing—and collapsed in a train to Liverpool twelve hours later. And would you believe it, she had no recollection at all of going to the station and catching the train or anything. She just couldn't understand it when she woke up in hospital. She was there for nearly three weeks." (239)

Miss Gilchrist is obsessed with the loss of her teashop during the war, which she views as bereavement, referring to the teashop as "a war casualty" (40). She recycles her stories about the teashop throughout the novel, unable to move forward. This anecdote, then, reveals a recurring anxiety of the fragility of the body and the memory, but it can also be related to Miss Gilchrist's own fundamental disorientation regarding her loss. During the war, people would speak of being overseas, or putting their furniture in storage and lives on hold, "for the duration", considering the war a temporary suspension or break in their lives and by extension their narratives. Miss Gilchrist cannot resume her life after this break without her teashop; her habit of talking in ellipses emphasizes this fragmentation: "I had a small tea-shop at one time, you know—but then the war came—it was all very unfortunate" (107). Miss Gilchrist's murder and performance of Cora Abernethy, then, can be read as an attempt to recover her own true identity, breached by the trauma of the war: "'Five thousand pounds,' said Poirot, 'would have rented and equipped a *tea-shop*...'" (280; emphasis original). The murder, however, only results in a loss of memory and psychic disintegration: "'She's gone definitely over the edge since she's been in prison [...]She spends most of her time making the most elaborate plans to run a chain of teashops'" (285). Like the woman in her anecdote who suffered concussion during an air raid, Miss Gilchrist is disorientated and detached from linear chronology.

The same conjunction of Blitz, concussion, unexpected journey, and amnesia is repeated in *Destination Unknown*, also related to head wounds and dislocated identity. Divorcee Hilary Craven is in Morocco, posing as Olive Betterton, a woman killed by injuries sustained from an aero plane crash on her way to join her husband in a mountain lair where a mysterious agency is holding the best scientists of the West. Hilary was originally supposed to be on the airplane that crashed, planning to commit suicide by overdosing on sleeping pills after her husband's desertion and daughter's death. The British Secret Service offers a more "sporting form of suicide" (239) and trains Hilary in the minutiae of Olive's life to take her place. Hilary relies on a tale of concussion caused by the crash to cover any lapses in memory or agreed procedure expected by the mysterious agency. She explains her uncertainty about her schedule to a hotel manager, and he responds:

> "Ah, yes. [The loss of memory] is the result of the concussion. That happens once to a sister of mine. She was in London in the war. A bomb came, she was knocked unconscious. But presently, she gets up, she walks about London and she takes a train from the station of Euston and, *figurez-vous*, she wakes up at Liverpool and she cannot remember anything of the bomb, of going across London, of the train or of getting there! The last thing she remembers is hanging up her skirt in the wardrobe in London. Very curious these things, are they not?" (60)

Even as Miss Gilchrist's anecdote foreshadows her eventual loss of memory, here the anecdote reflects Hilary's journey to a "destination unknown" as well as her performed amnesia. Similarly to *After the Funeral*, therefore, this anecdote represents the resurfacing of the fragmented narratives of national trauma, while echoing the uneasy situation of the protagonist caught within a break in narrative and chronological "lag" after a personal trauma. Miss Gilchrist attempts to resolve this fracture through murder, and Hilary through suicide. Nevertheless, while Miss Gilchrist ends the narrative in a break from time and reality, Hilary survives to move forward. After her time in the "dream world of unreality" (231) as Olive Betterton, comparable to the disorientated state of the concussion victims in the anecdotes, she notes: "Oh, I feel as if I've woken up out of a nightmare" (269)—her suicidal impulses are left behind "just as unreal as anything else" (269). Hilary's journey ends conventionally in romance.

The structural violence, disorder, and damage of the Blitz, then, inflict physical wounds, which cause amnesia and temporal disorientation. Concussion, as a "general medical condition" (Colman 217), would seem to preclude any underlying dissociative or amnesiac disorders related to psychological trauma. Indeed, the official narrative of Christie's own disappearance and resurfacing foreshadows how *Destination Unknown* and *After the Funeral* ground amnesia and dislocated narrative within a physical root cause. In 1926, when Christie was discovered in Harrogate under an assumed name, Archie Christie's statement linked illness to amnesia: "My wife is extremely ill, suffering from a complete loss of memory. Three years have dropped out of her life. She cannot recall anything that has happened during that period" (quoted in Thompson 215). In 1928, responding to accusations of hoaxing the public and wasting police resources, Christie described the events of the night she went missing, blaming a combination of insomnia and "high nervous strain" resulting from her recent bereavement, and aimless driving in her car during which she hit her head, followed by the memory loss and assumed identity as Mrs. Tessa Neele (quoted in Cade 157).[11] Only a brief euphemistic allusion to the event exists in *An Autobiography*: "There could be no peace for me in England now after all I had gone through" (364).

Thompson notes the recurrence of this narrative in *Destination Unknown*, suggesting that it exemplifies Christie's "quite extraordinary freedom" to "reveal what she liked, knowing that she was hidden from view" (404). This allusion, however, is framed within a discussion not only of the dissolution of her marriage, but also a meditation on memory. Christie epigraphs a chapter in this section with a quotation from Keats: "What shall I do to drive away/Remembrance from mine eyes?" going on to comment, "But should one drive it away?...I must recognize it because it is *part* of me. But there is no need to dwell on it" (361). The epigraph suggests willful repression, whereas the commentary suggests the voice of experience, a narrative of "working through" the trauma and resolution—in both senses of the word—in *An Autobiography*. Leading up to this resolution, the appearance of these anecdotes in fiction suggest traumatic repetition, a collision of personal and national trauma and perhaps an attempt to belatedly "fully realize" one through the other, the psychic wound through the physical wound of concussion. Despite this insistence on physical and medical trauma rather than psychic traumas in both the life narratives and the fiction, then, a sense of posttraumatic dissociation—"partial or total disconnection between memories of the past, awareness of identity and of immediate sensations, and control of bodily movements" (Colman 2017)—pervades *Taken at the Flood*, *After the Funeral*, and *Destination Unknown* on both individual and collective levels, challenging official narratives of memory and identity.[12]

"All the others are—what shall I say—fluid?"

The contextualization of these traumas and complex negotiations of memory within the language and events of the Blitz blurs the boundaries between individual and collective injury, as well as between physical and psychological wounds. Cinema scholar René Bruckner discusses how the blunt force trauma of concussion leads to a switch in identity in films such as *Mulholland Drive* (2001); this connecting of concussion to disrupted identity forms a startling parallel with the motifs of concussion and performed identities of *Taken at the Flood*, *After the Funeral*, and *Destination Unknown*, although in the novels the change in identity is performed rather than organic. Bruckner's discussion of the space in which these traumatized women are situated, therefore, is relevant here:

> But this terrain in which the narratives' accident victims find themselves is too contingent and unstable to be categorized simply as space, no matter how open. It can be described as nonspace—placeless, deterritorialized, fantasmatic— but, more pointedly, as a productive kind of post-traumatic temporality. (376)

If "accident" is understood to include psychological as well as physical catastrophe here, Eileen/Rosaleen inhabits this space, along with Miss Gilchrist/Cora Abernethy, Hilary Craven/Olive Betterton, and the "Mrs. Christie" of Archie's narrative; indeed, Eileen/Rosaleen and Hilary/Olive both mention the unreal, dreamlike nature of their performed posttraumatic existences. This "nonspace" could also be extended to encompass the whole of Christie's postwar England. In *Mrs. McGinty's Dead* (1952), Inspector Spence remarks to Poirot:

> You know what things are nowadays. The war stirred up everyone and everything. The approved school where Lily Gamboll was, and all its records, were destroyed by a direct hit. Then take people. It's the hardest thing in the world to check on people. Take Broadhinny—the people in Broadhinny we know anything about are the Summerhayes family, who have been there for three hundred years, and Guy Carpenter, who's one of the engineering Carpenters. All the others are—what shall I say—fluid? (204)

152 *Rebecca Mills*

Without official records, without firm, rooted pasts, after the temporal rupture and shock of the war, England itself is in a fluid, unmoored, traumatic state—like the concussion victims—and like Rosaleen Cloade, keen to detach from past horrors but unable to escape them. Luckhurst suggests that "Trauma is a piercing or breach of a border that puts inside and outside into a strange communication" (3); we see this inside/outside shift in the shaping influence Christie's interior emotional terrain has on the fictional world of her postwar writing, as well as in the language and structure exterior events and pressures offer Christie's real-life narratives. While trauma narratives in Christie's texts are fragmented between authorial identities, dotted across decades, and placed within fiction and memory, what emerges is, indeed, a "strange communication" that offers some sense of a capacity to create order out of temporal and emotional chaos.

Notes

1 *Hercule Poirot's Christmas* (1939) refers to bombings in the Spanish Civil War, for example.
2 During the war, Christie also wrote a memoir of her husband Max Mallowan's archaeological expeditions (and as Julius Green discusses elsewhere in the present volume, she also wrote and adapted work for the theater).
3 For more on trauma in Christie's post-war work, see Jessica Gildersleeve's "Nowadays: Trauma and Modernity in Agatha Christie" (2016). Gildersleeve draws on Caruth's notion of trauma to argue that "Christie's late Poirot novels figure an anxious desire to protect against the possibility of traumatic return, a gothic plot in which the terrible secrets and crimes of the past return to haunt the present" (97). Gildersleeve's focus is on the resurfacing of crime as an indicator of post-war uncertainty and "to counter the rural or domesticated nostalgia typical of Golden Age detective fiction" (101) rather than the resurfacing of the war itself.
4 The concept of posttraumatic stress disorder was developed during the later stages of the Vietnam War and entered the lexicon of psychiatry in 1980. See, for example, Ben Shephard's *A War of Nerves: Soldiers and Psychiatrists 1914–1918* (2002).
5 Thompson and other biographers and scholars have noted correspondences between *Unfinished Portrait* and Christie's life narrative.
6 For more on flashbacks and 1940s writing, see Stewart's *Narratives of Memory* (2006).
7 See Mills, "England's Pockets: Objects of Anxiety in Christie's Post-War Novels" (2016).
8 Robinett challenges what she calls Caruth's idea of the 'fundamental "inaccessibility of trauma" (291) and an inevitable incompatibility of trauma and narrative, using two war narratives (*All Quiet on the Western Front* by Erich Maria Remarque and *The Sorrow of War* by Bao Ninh) to suggest "studies of the cognitive, physiological, psychological, and behavioural implications of expressive writing corroborate what readers of literature have long suspected: writers often turn intuitively to writing as a way of confronting and surviving trauma suffered in their own lives" (291).

9 See, for example, *The Mysterious Affair at Styles* (1918), and *The Murder at the Vicarage* (1930).
10 Lucy Hall and Gill Plain suggest that Rowley Cloade is also haunted by "the emasculation of not being permitted a combat role" (122–23).
11 For more on attempts to reconstruct the events and motivations related to Christie's disappearance, see Jared Cade's *Agatha Christie and the Eleven Missing Days* (2006) and Andrew Norman's *Agatha Christie: The Disappearing Novelist* (2014). Both Cade and Norman note the conjunction of concussion followed by pretended amnesia in *The Secret Adversary* (1922), and the biographical references of *Unfinished Portrait*, but do not connect them to war or Christie's post–Second World War novels.
12 Norman suggests that Christie herself suffered from "dissociative fugue", which would mean the narrative of post-concussion amnesia was an exaggeration or distortion of the truth.

Works Cited

Auden, W. H. "The Guilty Vicarage: Notes on the Detective Story, by an Addict." *Harper's Magazine*, May 1948. https://harpers.org/archive/1948/05/the-guilty-vicarage/ Accessed 13 Mar. 2018.

Bell, Amy. "Landscapes of Fear: Wartime London, 1939–1945." *Journal of British Studies*, vol. 48, no. 1, 2009, pp. 153–75.

Bruckner, R. T. "Lost Time: Blunt Head Trauma and Accident-Driven Cinema." *Discourse*, vol. 30, no. 3, 2008, pp. 373–400. *Project MUSE*, muse.jhu.edu/article/364471 Accessed 13 Mar. 2018.

Cade, Jared. *Agatha Christie and the Eleven Missing Days*. Peter Owen, 2006.

Calder, Angus. *The Myth of the Blitz*. Pimlico, 2008.

Caruth, Cathy. *Trauma: Explorations in Memory*. Johns Hopkins University Press, 1995.

Christie, Agatha. *Absent in the Spring* [as Mary Westmacott]. 1944. HarperCollins, 1997.

———. *After the Funeral*. 1953. HarperCollins, 2010.

———. *Appointment with Death*. 1938. HarperCollins, 2016.

———. *An Autobiography*. 1977. HarperCollins, 1993.

———. *Crooked House*. 1949. HarperCollins, 2017.

———. *Destination Unknown*. 1954. HarperCollins, 2017.

———. *Hercule Poirot's Christmas*. 1938. HarperCollins, 2013.

———. *N or M?* 1941. HarperCollins, 2015.

———. *Sparkling Cyanide*. 1945. HarperCollins, 2008.

———. *The Body in the Library*. 1942. HarperCollins, 2016.

———. *The Moving Finger*. 1942. HarperCollins, 2007.

———. *The Murder of Roger Ackroyd*. 1926. HarperCollins, 2010.

———. *The Rose and the Yew Tree* [as Mary Westmacott]. 1948. Harper Collins, 2017.

———. *Taken at the Flood*. 1948. HarperCollins, 2015.

———. *Unfinished Portrait* [as Mary Westmacott]. 1934. Harper Collins, 1997.

Colman, Andrew M. *A Dictionary of Psychology*. 3rd ed., Oxford University Press, 2009.

Freedman, Ariela. "Dorothy Sayers and the Case of the Shell-Shocked Detective." *Partial Answers: Journal of Literature and the History of Ideas*, vol. 8, no. 2, 2010, pp. 365–87.

Genette, Gerard. *Narrative Discourse: An Essay in Method*. Cornell University Press, 1980.

Gildersleeve, Jessica. "Nowadays: Trauma and Modernity in Agatha Christie's Late Poirot Novels." *Clues: A Journal of Detection*, vol. 34, no. 1, 2016, pp. 96–104.

Hall, Lucy and Gill Plain. "Unspeakable Heroism: The Second World War and the End of the Hero." *Heroes and Heroism in British Fiction Since 1800: Case Studies*, edited by Barbara Korte and Stefanie Lethbridge, Palgrave Macmillan, 2016, pp. 117–34.

Hartley, Jenny. *Millions Like Us: British Women's Fiction of the Second World War*. Virago, 1997.

Knight, Stephen. "Murder in Wartime." *War Culture: Social Change and Changing Experience in World War Two Britain*, edited by Pat Kirkham and David Thomas, Lawrence & Wishart Ltd., 1995, pp. 161–71.

Luckhurst, Roger. *The Trauma Question*. Taylor & Francis, 2008.

Mills, Rebecca. "England's Pockets Objects of Anxiety in Christie's Post-War Novels." *The Ageless Agatha Christie: Essays on the Mysteries and the Legacy*, edited by J. C. Bernthal, McFarland & Co, 2016, pp. 29–44.

Munt, Sally R. "Grief, Doubt and Nostalgia in Detective Fiction or… 'Death and the Detective Novel': A Return". *College Literature*, vol. 25, no. 3, 1998, pp. 133–44.

Norman, Andrew. *Agatha Christie: The Disappearing Novelist*. Fonthill Media, 2014.

Plain, Gill. *Women's Fiction of the Second World War: Gender, Power and Resistance*. Edinburgh University Press, 1996.

Robinett, J. "The Narrative Shape of Traumatic Experience." *Literature and Medicine*, vol. 26 no. 2, 2007, pp. 290–311.

Shakespeare, William. *Julius Caesar*. The Royal Shakespeare Company, Palgrave Macmillan 2011.

Shephard, Ben. *A War of Nerves: Soldiers and Psychiatrists 1914–1918*. Pimlico, 2002.

Stewart, Victoria. *Narratives of Memory: British Writing of the 1940s*. Palgrave Macmillan, 2006.

Stonebridge, Lyndsey. "Theories of Trauma." *The Cambridge Companion to the Literature of World War II*, edited by Marina MacKay, Cambridge University Press, 2009, pp. 194–206.

Thompson, Laura. *Agatha Christie: An English Mystery*. Headline, 2007.

"Trauma, n." *OED Online*, Oxford University Press, Jan. 2018, www.oed.com/view/Entry/205242 Accessed 6 Mar. 2018.

York, R. A. *Agatha Christie: Power and Illusion*. Palgrave Macmillan, 2007.

10 "The Thrill When It Suddenly Went Pitch Black!"

Blackout Cultures in *A Murder Is Announced* and *The Mousetrap*

Roger Dalrymple

The plunge into darkness is something of a gift to the crime novelist. Dating back at least as far as Horace Walpole's *Castle of Otranto* (1764) and thus to the very origins of Gothic fiction, the topos of the darkness-plunge reliably evokes a thrill of sensation, beckoning the imagination to do its worst. When a sputtering candle is snuffed out in the draughty passage of a Gothic castle or faulty lamps darken a remote country house, the reader feels an accompanying sense of foreboding. More pragmatically, the plunge into darkness provides the crime novelist or dramatist with a convenient plot device. When all the lights go out, agency is obscured and the hand that wields the murder weapon is concealed. Imagination is heightened but perception confounded as the killer strikes under cover of darkness.

Unsurprisingly, Agatha Christie's crime fiction sports many of these darkness-plunges both on paper and on stage. *Black Coffee* (1930), *And Then There Were None* (1939), *Sparkling Cyanide* (1946), *The Mousetrap* (1952), and *They Do It with Mirrors* (1952) are just some of the texts in which the trope occurs. Yet what compels attention in a study of Christie at war is the way in which the motif takes on a deepened and shifting significance in the novelist's postwar works. No longer confined to recalling Gothic literary tradition, the darkness-plunge in post–Second World War Christie also confronts the traumatic memory of wartime blackouts and the threats that accompanied them. As we shall see with reference to *A Murder Is Announced* (1950) and *The Mousetrap* (1952), Christie's development of the motif moves to reclaim individual agency and moral responsibility after the long years of state-imposed blackout. This chapter will briefly sketch the historical context of the Second World War blackouts, and review the literary origins and development of the darkness-plunge, before exploring Christie's playful yet subtle reimagining of the motif and its meanings.

Christie and Blackout Culture

When exploring the darkness-plunge in Christie's work, it is salutary to remember that during the novelist's long writing career, the state twice immersed the entirety of her insular reading public in darkness.[1] Sporadically in the Great War, and then concertedly between 1939 and 1945, government regulations blacked out both town and city, the painted and boarded windows, thick curtains and dimmed car headlamps all designed to thwart the aerial navigation of enemy bombers. Christie was herself displaced and blacked out alongside her readership. With the outbreak of war, the holiday home Christie shared with husband Max Mallowan, Greenway House, was to become a refuge for child evacuees, its owners relocating to London so that Max could serve in the Home Guard and Christie could work at University College Hospital by day, and continue writing by night (Curran 309). Christie was thus located in an embattled London from an early stage of the Blitz, living first in Half Moon Street, then Park Place "with noisy sessions of bombs going off all around us" (Osborne 155) before a move to a house in Sheffield Terrace. When this property was promptly bombed out, Christie was to relocate once again, this time to Lawn Road in Hampstead, close to the Heath. From this besieged position, Christie had ample opportunity to reflect on the contradictory proposition the wartime blackout extended to civil society. While ostensibly offering shelter and protection, blackout equally exposed the populace to other forms of risk, opening up, as one commentator has said, "new wartime spaces of transgression, danger, and tension' (Wiggam 237).[2]

First, there was a greatly heightened risk of pedestrian trips, falls, and other accidents while navigating the darkened streets and skirting the lampposts and sandbags: "roads which people could have sworn they knew intimately became impenetrable mysteries" (Ziegler 68). Add the motor car to the equation, its single headlamp dimmed in line with regulations, and the perils were exacerbated. As early as October 1940, a dismayed House of Commons learned that the number of road deaths from traffic accidents had already doubled from the previous year (Wiggam 223); for a period in December 1940, there were forty fatal road traffic accidents recorded in London every day (Ziegler 68). Public zeal to enforce the blackout also led to further risks. Conflicts would arise when citizens resisted the dictates of Air Raid Patrol (ARP) wardens or, conversely, when members of the public took the law into their own hands to enforce blackout regulations on the noncompliant. Even public-spirited initiatives to "put that light out" could lead to disaster: when Metropolitan Police Constable George Southworth gamely scaled a drainpipe to the fourth floor of a Harley Street address to extinguish the sole light burning in the window, he slipped and fell to his death, another untallied casualty of the blackout (Ziegler 70).

As if these sources of peril were not dire enough, the blackouts would also provide cover for a range of criminal and nefarious activities. Black-market trading, looting, and theft all increased significantly during the metropolitan and provincial blackouts: for this was the era of "spivs, deserters and racketeers" as Donald Thomas's study of the period puts it. Illustrative headlines from the provincial press of the time report "Guardsman's Blackout Theft: Young Woman's Pluck" (*Wiltshire Times and Trowbridge Advertiser* 1942); "Blackout Theft: Youths who Snatched Bag at Seaforth" (*Liverpool Echo* 1939); and "Nottingham Man for Trial Charged with Blackout Raid and Theft" (*Nottingham Journal*, 1939). And in the dark, murder is easy. The *Newcastle Evening Chronicle* relates a "Murder in the Black-out" in Edinburgh in 1939. *The Lincolnshire Echo* proclaims the "Blackout Murder" of a police constable in 1940, while the *Newcastle Evening Chronicle* recounts the "Police Hunt in Bus Stop Black-out Murder" in 1942.

Christie's own circle was by no means untouched by blackout crime. The cozy London premises of the Detection Club (of which Christie was a founding member and future president) were broken into by thieves under the cover of darkness (Edwards 405), and in early 1942, its Soho environs were prowled by serviceman and serial killer Gordon Frederick Cummins, nicknamed "the blackout Ripper". Mercifully, Cummins exercised a shorter reign of terror than the Victorian killer after whom he was named, but sensational press reports exploited the connection and inspired at least two B-movies boasting a "blackout Ripper", the 1943 film *A Night for Crime* and a late entry in the Basil Rathbone version of the Sherlock Holmes series, *The Woman in Green* (1945).[3] Even the memoirs of the Scotland Yard Inspector who ran Cummins to ground shared this melodramatic tone, telling of a benighted London in fear of the lone killer:

> Not since those panic-ridden days in 1888, when Jack the Ripper was abroad in the East End, had London known such a reign of terror as that which existed in this war-time February, when night after night, death—fiendish, revolting, and gruesome—came to four unsuspecting women in the heart of the Metropolis. (Cherrill 186)[4]

Cummins's crimes epitomized the threats of the blackout: those same air raid shelters that were designed to provide safe haven from aerial bombardment could equally be places of vulnerability to other perils and threats. The "rowdyism and drunkenness", which, according to the contemporaneous press, would sometimes break out in air raid shelters were as nothing compared to the harm awaiting forty-year-old Evelyn Hamilton, Cummins's first known victim, her body discovered in a public air raid shelter in Marylebone in February 1942.[5]

Thus, blackout Britain was a contradictory place; "its role in protecting the safety of the community had profound implications for the sense of personal security" (Wiggam 194). Retreating behind curtains or below stairs, or hastening into the darkness of public air raid shelters, might afford relative safety from the skies, but there were other sources of danger close by. Moreover, the strictures of blackout culture severely curtailed the individual agency of the populace, effectively limiting free movement and showing "how the technology of war could alter the relationship between the state and the citizen" (Wiggam 237). Civilians were doubly disempowered: to be safeguarded from the sky-borne threat, they must embrace a state-imposed confinement in darkness or venture out to navigate a darkened city, exposed to a whole host of perils.

Literary Associations of the Darkness-Plunge

Before exploring how Christie's fiction reflects and then challenges this wartime inheritance in her use of the darkness-plunge, it is necessary to look back briefly to the earliest literary associations of the motif. As we have seen, the motif inheres in the very roots of Gothic fiction, appearing at a moment of high drama in Walpole's *Castle of Otranto* (1764) when the imperiled protagonist flees from her patriarchal oppressor through subterranean caverns: "she approached the door that had been opened; but a sudden gust of wind that met her at the door extinguished her lamp, and left her in total darkness" (91). Here, the darkness-plunge signifies a physical and moral vulnerability while also evoking the inner state of the heroine. An equally signature Gothic text, Ann Radcliffe's *The Romance of the Forest* (1791) develops the trope further, now casting a male protagonist into darkness: "he found himself in a narrow passage; but as he turned to pursue it, the damp vapors curled round him and extinguished the light" (54). Invariably, the light goes out at the end of a sentence or paragraph. It is the climactic moment—the fulfillment of a dreaded inevitability and the moment of catastrophe for the protagonist. It is the reader's cue to gasp with anticipation of whatever will happen next.

The darkness-plunge soon became a signature of Gothic tradition, its currency as stock motif confirmed by Austen's parody *Northanger Abbey* (1817) where the romance-reading heroine creeps about the chambers of the eponymous abbey, determined to find something sensational:

> The dimness of the light her candle emitted made her turn to it with alarm [...] Alas! It was snuffed and extinguished in one. A lamp could not have expired with more awful effect. Catherine, for a few moments, was motionless with horror. It was done completely; not a remnant of light in the wick could give hope to the rekindling breath. Darkness impenetrable and immovable filled the room.

A violent gust of wind, rising with sudden fury, added fresh horror to the moment. Catherine trembled from head to foot. (123–24)

From this point, the perpetuation of the motif into nineteenth-century sensation fiction such as Wilkie Collins's *The Woman in White* (1859) and subsequently into ghost stories was assured. Perhaps its apotheosis is H. G. Wells's ghost story "The Red Room" (1896):

> I turned to where the flames were still dancing between the glowing coals and splashing red reflections upon the furniture; made two steps toward the grate, and incontinently the flames dwindled and vanished, the glow vanished, the reflections rushed together and disappeared, and as I thrust the candle between the bars darkness closed upon me like the shutting of an eye, wrapped about me in a stifling embrace, sealed my vision, and crushed the last vestiges of reason from my brain. (178)

Here a daredevil narrator keeps vigil in a castle's haunted room and finds that the only thing to fear in the darkness really is fear itself. Susan Hill's *The Woman in Black* perpetuates the trope in the modern ghost story when protagonist Arthur Kipps is plunged into darkness in remote Eel Marsh House: "No light came on. The torch had broken" (167).

Reflections of Blackout Culture

From Gothic novels to ghost stories then, the darkness-plunge was a well-established literary trope before ever the crime novelists of the Golden Age began to exploit its atmosphere and plot-utility. Christie's own early uses of the motif, as in the early Poirot play *Black Coffee* (1930), make full use of these aspects. In this early outing for the Belgian detective, the onstage blackout is built into the diegesis of the narrative: the lights are extinguished so that a thief can return a stolen document under amnesty—though in the event a murder is committed under the cover of the darkness. A decade later, reflections of blackout culture begin to make their presence felt. We find them, for example, in the novel and subsequent stage play of *And Then There Were None* (1939, 1943), where Vera roams the upper rooms of Mr. Owen's murder mansion with a single candle for illumination:

> She made a step forward. The draught from the window caught the flame of the candle. It flickered and went out...
> In the dark she was suddenly afraid...
> "Don't be a fool," Vera Claythorne urged herself. It's all right. The others are downstairs. All four of them. There's no one in the room. There can't be. You're imagining things my girl. (179)

The stage adaptation of 1943, written and performed to blackout audiences, deepens this sense of the physical and moral panic associated with total darkness. Exclaiming "Why can't we have some light?" and flagging her lack of agency while roaming the darkened house, Vera continues:

> It's awful in the dark. You don't know where you are. You don't know where anyone is. (66)

Such reflections on darkness must surely have resonated for contemporaneous readers and audiences, certainly with those who watched the stage play from a darkened auditorium in the knowledge that at the play's end they must navigate the blacked-out city on their precipitous journey home. Indeed, Vera's self-talk in the novelized version and her blind panic in the dramatized version are paralleled suggestively in the contemporaneous account of one Irene Byers, who recounts losing her way outside London's Central Telegraph Office at the height of the blackout:

> I stood still, panic-stricken, then said firmly over and over again to myself, "I know this street absolutely well— don't be such an ass— walk forward quietly and you will come to Newgate Street. [...] But I felt damp with perspiration and quite exhausted. (Ziegler 68)

In Vera's and Byers's accounts alike, the perceived loss of agency and sense of disempowerment and disorientation are emphatically the same.

Blackout Subcultures and the Darkness-Plunge

If these instances of the darkness-plunge show the classic motif overlaid with associations of wartime blackouts, the early postwar texts *A Murder Is Announced* and *The Mousetrap* involve a more complex deployment of the motif. This time, Christie enacts the gradual reassertion of individual agency after the years of state-imposed darkness—the power of just one person to put out the lights. This reassertion of agency plays out against a surprising context, a now largely forgotten blackout subculture involving play and parlor games. This subculture, attested by sources in the wartime press, offers a ludic response to enemy action and enforced darkness. Through imagination and in play, it turns the threat of militarized murder from the skies into an innocuous domestic game of murder in the dark.

It is, after all, a parlor game that the readers of the *North Benham News and Chipping Cleghorn Gazette* are expecting after reading the celebrated notice that opens *A Murder Is Announced*:

> A murder is announced and will take place on Friday, October 29th, at Little Paddocks, at 6:30 p.m. Friends accept this, the only intimation. (5)

The intimation for the villagers is one of game play. Edmund Swettenham, Colonel Easterbrook, and Bunch Harmon all read the notice as announcing a game of "wink murder":

> [S]omebody's the victim and somebody else is a detective—and then they turn the lights out and someone taps you on the shoulder and then you scream and lie down and sham dead. (10)
> One person's the murderer, nobody knows who. Lights out. Murderer chooses his victim. The victim has to count to twenty before he screams. (11)
> I don't really like games that happen in the dark. They frighten me, and I do hope I shan't be the one who's murdered. If someone suddenly puts a hand on my shoulder and whispers, "You're dead," I know my heart will give such a big bump that perhaps it really *might* kill me! (13)

Surprisingly, this taste for wink murder and murder-themed parlor games appears to have been actively nurtured during the blackouts of the Second World War. Replete as the documentary sources are with blackout injunctions, air raids notices, and casualty lists, they also include surprising evidence that wartime blackouts were sometimes perceived as opportunities for play, and parlor games—for "an imaginative response to the darkness" (Wiggam 200). Thus, scattered among the 1940s press headlines of bomb damage and casualties, we also find signs that behind those blackout curtains and boarded windows of wartime Britain, parlor games were sometimes in full swing. The notebook entries for *A Murder Is Announced* reveal that a competing setting for the novel was at one point the London address of 20 Ennerly Park (Curran 175). The relocation to the country setting of Chipping Cleghorn in no way diminishes the memory of Blitz and blackout conditions, which were enforced equally on town and country; the haphazard jettisoning of bombs by returning enemy bombers meant villagers could know the effects of bomb damage as well as their urban counterparts. Morale-boosting notices and advertisements pepper the provincial press of the war years, assuring readers that "there are blackouts and blackouts", inviting them to join in "card games for the long black-out nights" or to gather to enjoy "light, warmth, music, games, refreshments and everything to dispel the miseries of a town in darkness".[6] Some of this game play would be on an apt theme. The assembled parties would sometimes play rounds of "wink murder" or "murder in the dark"—a parlor game whose precise origins are difficult to fix but which appears to have been codified, as we might expect, during the Golden Age of detective fiction.[7] A 1930 summary of the game's rules in *The Sketch* would appear to be one of the earliest examples:

> Murder is the game which has succeeded auction and contract as Society's latest indoor sport. In the following article, Mr. Rupert Grayson, Murder expert and detective-story writer, describes "ways" and method of play, so that our readers may enjoy a round of Murder after dinner. There are people who enjoy counting the shudders in life. The simple game of "Murder in the Dark" is innocently thrilling.

In *A Murder Is Announced*, Christie invokes this "innocently thrilling", ludic memory of blackout subculture alongside the wider array of wartime allusions and memories noted by Curran: "The shadow of rationing and bartering, deserters and foreign 'help', ration books and identity cards hovers over the book" (487). This ludic subculture, then, informs the manner in which the participants gather at Little Paddocks, the country house, for what they assume will be a game of murder in the dark. They are indeed plunged into darkness as expected, but in the event, an intruder brandishing a torch and, they assume, a weapon, holds the party up at gunpoint before he is mysteriously and fatally shot by an unseen hand.

An array of blackout and postwar allusions attends this murder in the dark. The absence of a fire in the Little Paddocks grate is attributed to fuel rationing; house-servant and wartime refugee Mitzi screams "like a siren" (66) after the murder; and the entire episode puts former Air Raid Patrol warden Hinch in mind of her old patrols. Reliving the gunshots, Mrs. Harmon avers, "I don't like bangs" (60) while Mrs. Swettenham eschews the more obvious wartime simile to liken the "real bullets, just whistling past our ears" to "the Commandos in the war" (56). Other subtle allusions to the Blitz (and this time to Allied air attacks) include mention of the provenance of the crucial shepherd and shepherdess lamps: they are made from Dresden china (128).

These evocations of the "innocently thrilling" ludic subculture sit side-by-side with more traumatic wartime memories such as Miss Marple's recollection of "a fly-bomb in London—splinters of glass everywhere" (184) and Mitzi's traumatized account of the fate of her brother in war-torn Europe, curtailed by Inspector Craddock who refuses to have this wartime memory brought too close to home:

> "My little brother—I see him killed before my eyes—I see blood in the street— people shot, dying, I—"
> "Yes," said Inspector Craddock. "Thank you very much." (48)

This instinct to repress and forget the privations of the Blitz and blackout are central to the novel's plot. The intruder at Little Paddocks is revealed to be Swiss national Rudi Scherz, one of the few individuals aware that householder Miss Blacklock is an imposter, younger sister Charlotte having assumed the identity and estate of elder sister Letitia who died in Switzerland. The deception that blackmailer Scherz has threatened to uncover has been made possible by the years of blackout and Blitz.[8] It is only because of the six years of wartime darkness and destruction of old ties, photographs, and documentary records that Charlotte is able to practice her deception and impersonate her sister to gain an inheritance—a stake for which she will commit the murder of Scherz and subsequently two of the villagers.[9] Inspector Craddock muses on how such frauds and assumed identities have increased since the war—with identities "borrowed from people who had met sudden death by 'incidents' in the cities" (87). Indeed, Charlotte could be said to embody this invidious legacy of wartime blackout and Blitz, her very name flagging the association. Suggestively, at the novel's end, vicar's wife Bunch Harmon uses the definite article to refer to Charlotte as "The Blacklock".

Yet, however, sinister the goings on in Miss Blacklock's sitting room (it is Charlotte who has fused the lights; it is she who has fired the fatal shot at Rudi Scherz), this ludic, parlor-game version of blackout involves only a temporary vulnerability and restriction of agency for the assembled guests. We have moved on from the years of state-imposed darkness and mass vulnerability of the populace. Once the crime is committed, game players of sufficient wit and insight will be able to penetrate the darkness. For Hinch, prompted to reconstruct the scene in her mind—"She wasn't *there*!" (218; emphasis original)—or for Miss Marple noting the significance of a frayed lamp cord, the parlor game can be played out to a normative end. Likewise, when the lights go out at Little Paddocks, the darkness is not imposed by the unseen hand of the state but by a sole hand flicking the light switch or fusing the Dresden china lamp. The darkness that falls is not as deep or as abiding; the forces unleashed not as universally deadly or unceasing. Instead of a faceless enemy state prosecuting a campaign of murder from the skies, just one malefactor is at work, with us in this very room, playing the parlor game by the familiar rules.

A Murder Is Announced thus seems to offer rapprochement between the competing conceptions of blackout culture bequeathed by the Second World War. On the one hand, the dark days of blackout have enabled the shifting of identities, the perpetration of fraud, and the masquerade of imposters preying on a public immersed in darkness. On the other, the evocation of the ludic, game-playing subculture of blackout enables a normative outcome and the unmasking of "the Blacklock", offering reassurance that when the lights go out in 1950s Britain, it is within the individual's power to find illumination and restored safety.

"Parlor Games!"

As brief coda, a look at *The Mousetrap* shows how Christie played out the same pattern, at much the same time, upon the London stage. In the archetypal murder-house setting of Monkswell Manor (a name evocative of the Gothic origins of the darkness-plunge motif), the lighting and dimming of lamps is safely within the purview of the occupants. Landlady Mollie lights the lamps and "wall brackets" twice in Act One, Trotter dims them before the "reconstruction" in Act Two and of course, the hand of the killer extinguishes them before the murder of Mrs. Boyle: *A hand shows through the open doorway and clicks the light switch. The lights suddenly go out* (326). Again, while there is evocation of blackout and Blitz and the disruption that they bring, not least in Trotter's speech to Mollie—"You'd be surprised, Mrs. Ralston, if you knew how many cases like yours we get. Especially since the war. Homes broken up and families dead. [...] There aren't any backgrounds nowadays" (338)—the ludic, "innocently thrilling" subculture of parlor-game ultimately predominates:

TROTTER: This isn't a game, sir.
CHRISTOPHER: Isn't it? Now there I think you are wrong. It is a *game*— to somebody. (357)

"Parlour games!" exclaims Paravincini when the trap is set. And indeed, in *The Mousetrap* as in *A Murder Is Announced*, the ludic elements are as pronounced as the element of mystery, bringing postwar reassurance that individual vulnerability in the face of just one malefactor is a much more welcome, even comforting, proposition than mass vulnerability in the face of wartime enemy action.

Conclusion: Murder in the Dark

In *A Murder Is Announced* and *The Mousetrap* then, Christie confronts the legacy of blackout and Blitz. She adapts the long-established darkness-plunge motif as a locus for postwar reassertion of individual agency amid shared memories of trauma and mass vulnerability. Indeed, Christie's treatment of the motif offers a modest but rewarding insight into the socio-literary function of postwar crime fiction and indicates something of the deeper significance of the perceived "coziness" of Christie's postwar narratives. Just as the notion of murder as puzzle could offer a hermeneutic of pattern and order to the postwar reading public, so in Christie's hands the specific motif of the darkness-plunge is tamed and called back from the darkest associations of blackout and Blitz to become something more ludic and even comforting. When the lights go out at Little Paddocks or Monkswell Manor, we are no longer at the mercy of the immobilizing darkness of a state at war, but threatened by just one criminal, close at hand, whose steps can ultimately be retraced, whose crimes can be unraveled.

Given all this subtle and allusive light-snuffing, the tribute paid by the St Martin's and Savoy Theatres on the night of Christie's 1976 passing is not only poignant but apt. For a full hour, both theaters dimmed their lights.

Notes

1 The lesser-known blackouts of the First World War are documented by Ian Castle's *The First Blitz: Bombing London in the First World War* (Osprey, 2015).
2 Wiggam's offers an exhaustive comparison of blackout culture in both Britain and Germany and this chapter is much indebted to its findings.
3 An influence can also be detected in Michael Powell and Emeric Pressburger's *A Canterbury Tale* (1944), which features nonfatal but nonetheless sinister blackout assaults on young women in Canterbury, their hair being covered with glue by a mystery assailant.
4 HO 144/21659 collates the main Home Office documentation on the Cummins case.
5 'Free Fights in Raid Shelters', *Daily Mirror*—Friday, 30 August 1940. A recent account of the case is provided by Simon Read in *The Blackout Murders* (The Cromwell Press, 2008).
6 "Card games for the long black-out nights", *Newcastle Journal*, Tuesday 10 October 1939; 'There are Black-outs & Black-outs', *Skegness Standard*, Wednesday 11 October 1939.
7 Given the well documented Victorian taste for sensation fiction, penny dreadfuls and true crime, we might expect "murder in the dark" to be of earlier origin but Patrick Beaver's exhaustive review of Victorian parlor games unearths no game more sinister than "Cat and Mouse" (*Victorian Parlor Games*, 1974).
8 Likewise, the plot of *Taken at the Flood* (1948), is set in motion by the fate of the wealthy Gordon Cloade, killed instantly when his house on Campden Hill is bombed *Taken at The Flood* (1948), as Rebecca Mills discusses elsewhere in this volume (Chapter 9).

Works Cited

Austen, Jane. *Northanger Abbey*. 1817. Wordsworth, 1993.
Beaver, Patrick. *Victorian Parlor Games*. Thomas Nelson Inc., 1974.
"Blackout Murder." *The Lincolnshire Echo*, 1 Mar. 1940.
"Blackout Theft: Youths Who Snatched Bag at Seaforth." *Liverpool Echo*, 15 Dec. 1939.
"Card Games for the Long Black-Out Nights." *Newcastle Journal*, Tuesday 10 Oct. 1939.
Castle, Ian. *The First Blitz: Bombing London in the First World War*. Osprey, 2015.

Cherrill, Fred. *Cherrill of the Yard*. The Popular Book Club, 1954.
Christie, Agatha. *And Then There Were None*. 1939. HarperCollins, 2003.
———. "And Then There Were None". 1944. *The Mousetrap and Selected Plays*, HarperCollins, 1993, pp. 1–78.
———. *Black Coffee*. 1930. Samuel French, 1934.
———. *A Murder is Announced*. 1950. Fontana, 1963.
———. *Sparkling Cyanide*. 1946. Fontana, 1960.
———. *Taken at the Flood*. 1948. Pan, 1965.
———. *The Mousetrap*. 1952. *The Mousetrap and Selected Plays*, HarperCollins, 1993, pp. 285–366.
Curran, John. *Agatha Christie's Complete Secret Notebooks: Stories and Secrets of Murder in the Making*. Rev. ed. HarperCollins, 2016.
Edwards, Martin. *The Golden Age of Murder: The Mystery of the Writers Who Invented the Modern Detective Story*. HarperCollins, 2016.
"Guardsman's Blackout Theft: Young Woman's Pluck." *Wiltshire Times and Trowbridge Advertiser*, 28 Nov. 1942.
Hill, Susan. *The Woman in Black*. 1983. Profile Books, 2011.
"Murder in the Black-out." *Newcastle Evening Chronicle*, 15 Sep. 1939.
Neill, Roy William (dir.). *The Woman in Green*. Universal Pictures, 1945.
"Nottingham Man for Trial Charged with Blackout Raid and Theft." *Nottingham Journal*, 26 Sep. 1939.
Osborne, Charles. *The Life and Crimes of Agatha Christie*. Contemporary Books, 1982.
"Police Hunt in Bus Stop Black-out Murder." *Newcastle Evening Chronicle*, 26 Mar. 1942.
Powell, Michael and Emeric Pressburger (dirs). *A Canterbury Tale*. Eagle-Lion Films, 1944.
Radcliffe, Ann. *The Romance of the Forest*. 1791. Oxford University Press, 2009.
Read, Simon. *The Blackout Murders*. The Cromwell Press, 2008.
"There are Black-outs & Black-outs". *Skegness Standard*, 11 Oct. 1939.
Thomas, Donald. *An Underworld at War: Spivs, Deserters, Racketeers and Civilians in the Second World War*. John Murray, 2003.
Thurn-Taxis, Alexis (dir.). *A Night for Crime*. Producers Releasing Corporation, 1943.
Wells, H. G. "The Red Room". 1894. *The Oxford Book of English Ghost Stories*, edited by Michael Cox and R. A. Gilbert, Oxford University Press, 2008, pp. 172–79.
Walpole, Horace. *Castle of Otranto*. 1764. Penguin, 2002.
Wiggam, Marc Patrick. *The Blackout in Britain and Germany during the Second World War*. PhD. dissertation, University of Exeter, 2011.
Ziegler, Phillip. *London at War 1939–1945*. Sinclair-Stevenson, 1995.

Notes on Contributors

J.C. Bernthal is a Panel Tutor at the University of Cambridge and the author of *Queering Agatha Christie: Revisiting the Golden Age of Detective Fiction* (Palgrave 2016). He is the founder and co-organizer of the International Agatha Christie Conferences.

Paula Bowles was born in North London, not far from HMP Holloway. From an early age she became fascinated with crime and the novels of Agatha Christie offered an opportunity to engage, from a safe distance. As an adult studying criminology, she realized that these early forays into Christie's world were the entry to a world of complex causalities and theories, which recognize crime as one of the most contentious and complex expressions of an organized society. Currently a Senior Lecturer at the University of Northampton, she introduces new generations of curious individuals to criminology.

Brittain Bright is an academic, professional tutor, and several other things. She teaches in English and Comparative Literature at Goldsmiths, University of London, and at Clean Prose London. She has written on various aspects of interwar detective fiction, including "The Revelations of the Corpse: Interpreting the Body in the Golden Age Detective Novel" with Rebecca Mills in *New Perspectives on Detective Fiction: Mystery Magnified* (Routledge 2015), edited by Casey Cothran and Mercy Cannon.

Federica Crescentini studied Foreign Languages and Literature at the University of Urbino, and obtained a Master's degree in Languages for Translation in 2015; *The Mousetrap* was the topic of her MA thesis. Federica is currently an independent scholar who will participate in the conference "Urbinoir 2019" at the University of Urbino, discussing amnesia and memory in "Three Blind Mice" and *The Mousetrap*. She recently wrote a chapter partially devoted to Christie in response to the project "To Prove a Villain: On the Performativity of 'Evil' Characters in Anglophone Literature".

Roger Dalrymple is Principal Lecturer in the Faculty of Humanities and Social Sciences at Oxford Brookes University. An educationalist and

English scholar, he is currently completing a book on the literary and cultural formation of the Dr. Crippen murder case of 1910.

Julius Green is a Fellow of the Birkbeck Centre for Contemporary Theatre, University of London. He read history at Corpus Christi College, Cambridge, and was Fellow Commoner of the College in 2014. In 2001 he produced the Agatha Christie Theatre Festival and in 2006 he created the Agatha Christie Theatre Company. He wrote the introduction to *The Mousetrap and Other Plays* (HarperCollins2011) and published *Agatha Christie: A Life in Theatre* (HarperCollins 2015). In 2017 he was a keynote speaker at *Agatha Christie: A Reappraisal* (Lucy Cavendish College, Cambridge). Other publications include *How to Produce a West End Show* (Oberon 2012).

Merja Makinen is the author of *Agatha Christie: Investigating Femininity* (Palgrave 2006) and essays and articles on Christie, including "Transforming Justice? Murder on the Orient Express 1934–2010" with Patrick Phillips, *Clues: A Journal of Detection* (2016); "Agatha Christie in dialogue with *To the Lighthouse*" in *The Ageless Agatha Christie: Essays on the Mystery and the Legacy*, ed. J.C. Bernthal (McFarland&Co 2016) and "Contradicting the Golden Age: Reading Agatha Christie in the Twenty-First Century" in *Criminal Moves: Modes of Mobility in Crime Fiction*, eds. J. Guiddal, S. King, and A. Rolls (Liverpool University Press 2019).

Sarah Martin is a PhD student and visiting lecturer at the University of Chester, working under the supervision of Dr. Sally West. Her thesis applies theories of psychogeography to Golden Age detective fiction, examining the role of the female detective. Sarah is on the Agatha Christie Conference committee. Recent publications include "Psychogeography and the Detective: Re-evaluating the Significance of Space in Agatha Christie's *A Murder Is Announced*" in *Clues: A Journal of Detection* (2018).

Rebecca Mills teaches crime fiction, celebrity culture, and other literary and media units at Bournemouth University. Publications on detective fiction include "England's Pockets: Objects of Anxiety in Agatha Christie's Post-War Novels" in *The Ageless Agatha Christie: Essays on the Mystery and the Legacy*, edited by J.C. Bernthal (McFarland&Co 2016) and "The Revelations of the Corpse: Interpreting the Body in the Golden Age Detective Novel" with Brittain Bright, in *New Perspectives on Detective Fiction: Mystery Magnified* (Routledge 2015), eds. Casey Cothran and Mercy Cannon.

Sally West is a Senior Lecturer in English at the University of Chester. Her original specialism was Romantic Literature, and she has published on the influence of the first generation of Romantics on the second (*Coleridge and Shelley: Textual Engagement* (Ashgate, 2007)). However, Sally has loved Golden Age detective fiction since stealing her mother's copy of Sayers's *Strong Poison* aged ten, and now teaches and researches in the area of crime fiction. She is currently working on the significance of physical spaces to the psychology of Patricia Highsmith's protagonists.

Christopher Yiannitsaros's AHRC-funded thesis *Deadly Domesticity: Agatha Christie's "Middlebrow" Gothic, 1930–1970* (University of Warwick 2017) examined Christie's use of the Gothic, particularly via her nineteenth-century interlocutors. He has published variously on women's twentieth-century "middlebrow" fiction and the Gothic, including journal articles on works by Molly Keane, Daphne du Maurier, and Agatha Christie. He also has an interest in the relationships between food and textual culture. With Mary Addyman and Laura Wood, he is co-editor of *Food, Drink and the Written Word in Britain, 1820–1945* (Routledge 2017). He is a qualified primary school teacher, living and working in London.

Index

The ABC Murders 35
The ABC Murders (BBC 2018) 6; *see also* Phelps, Sarah
Absent in the Spring 106; *see also* Westmacott, Mary
After the Funeral 36, 148–51
Agatha Christie: An Autobiography: Christie's disappearance 139, 150; First World War 96; Mary Westmacott 106, 137; Nazism 63; Second World War experiences 2, 68, 89, 97, 113, 137, 143, 147; theatre 97–9, 104
air raids 1, 3, 5, 6, 8, 9; blackout 156–8, 161–4; Christie's experiences 71, 97, 137, 143; in London 99–100; in *The Mousetrap* 103, 164–5; and narrative structure 54, 55; trauma 114, 138–41, 144–51; and wartime thrillers 64, 67
Akhnaton (play) 98
Allingham, Margery 4–6, 32
And Then There Were None 98, 159; meals 89, 91, 92; narrative structure 47, 49–53, 55, 58–60
And Then There Were None (play) 81, 89–92, 98, 99, 159
And Then There Were None (BBC 2015) 6; *see also* Phelps, Sarah
Appointment with Death 33, 49, 101
Appointment with Death (play) 101
anti-Semitism 63, 106, 133, 134
Austen, Jane 5, 96, 106, 141, 158

BBC 6, 50, 74, 106, 109
The Big Four 32
Black Coffee (play) 95, 155, 159

black market 17–20, 31, 84, 111, 133, 157
Bletchley Park 1, 2, 10, 71
Blitz *see* air raids
The Body in the Library 6, 138

capitalism 12, 19, 71, 72, 86
"The Capture of Cerberus" (1939) 63–8, 74, 76, 77
"The Capture of Cerberus" (1947) 64, 68
Cards on the Table 50, 58
Chamberlain, Neville 67, 98; Appeasement Policy 1, 50, 63
Christie, Archibald (Archie) 3, 96, 139, 150, 151
Churchill, Winston 1, 3, 10, 65, 67, 79
Cold War 2, 77, 105, 148
communism 2, 7, 71–3
Crooked House 139
Curtain: Poirot's Last Case 2, 47

A Daughter's a Daughter (play) 98, 105–7
Dead Man's Folly 34, 39, 40
Death Comes as the End 57
Death in the Clouds 49
Death on the Nile 46, 47, 101
demobilized soldiers 39, 101, 105–6, 114, 145; *see also* deserters; servicemen; veterans
deserters 17, 34, 40, 157, 162; in *The Mousetrap* 119–20; in *Three Blind Mice* 114–15
Destination Unknown: amnesia in 148–51; as wartime thriller 63, 71–2, 74–5, 77–8
Dumb Witness 33, 47

Index

Elephants Can Remember 73
evacuees 1, 103, 109, 128, 130, 156
Evil Under the Sun 6, 55

fascism 7, 54, 71, 74, 77, 97
Five Little Pigs 49

Gilbert, Michael 4
Giant's Bread 124, 136; see also Westmacott, Mary
Greene, Graham 5, 6, 32, 68, 98

Hallowe'en Party 73
Hitler, Adolf 1, 7, 57, 101, 127; in wartime thrillers 63–7, 69–79
The Hollow 57, 85, 86
The Hollow (play) 102

identity card 6, 17, 110, 125, 162

Jews 8, 63, 65, 106; Holocaust 9, 136; refugees 124, 127, 128, 130–3, 135; see also anti-Semitism

Knox, Dilly 1

Lorac, E.C.R. 4, 6
Lord Edgware Dies 85

Mallowan, Sir Max 3, 63, 67, 105; war work 70–1, 97, 98, 101, 156
The Man in the Brown Suit 58
Marsh, Ngaio 4, 6
Milton, John 63, 78
The Mirror Crack'd from Side to Side 20–5
The Mousetrap (play) 7–9; memory in 109, 114–22, 155, 160, 164; writing and staging 102–4, 106
The Moving Finger 5, 138
Mrs McGinty's Dead 6, 151
The Murder at the Vicarage 13–14, 16–17, 21, 46, 23–4
A Murder is Announced 8, 9; blackout 155, 160–4; displaced persons 124–5, 127–31, 133–5; rationing 84; village space 17, 19–21
Murder is Easy 50, 57
The Murder of Roger Ackroyd 50, 140
The Murder on the Links 32, 34
Murder on the Orient Express 47

The Mysterious Affair at Styles 2, 6, 30, 31
The Mystery of the Blue Train 34, 124

Nazism 1; Nazi policy 58; in cinema 77–8; refugees from Nazi-occupied territory 124, 127, 128, 130, 132; wartime thrillers 63–70, 72–6
N or M?: Nazism in 67–9, 71–4, 76, 78; wartime publication 1, 4, 6, 55, 64, 137–8, 140

One, Two, Buckle My Shoe 55, 57, 58

Passenger to Frankfurt 2, 63, 64, 71–3, 77, 78
Peril at End House 32
Phelps, Sarah 104
Phoney War 1, 63, 65

rationing 7, 8, 67; and meals 82–4; in plays 102, 103, 110, 117; in postwar village 17, 19, 20, 89, 125, 162
refugees 2, 8; in First World War 30, 31; in Second World War 68, 124, 127, 128, 130–2, 162
The Rose and the Yew Tree 139; see also Westmacott, Mary

Sad Cypress: meals 81, 82, 85, 86, 88–9; narrative structure 46, 49, 53–5
Sayers, Dorothy L. 4, 138
The Secret Adversary 2, 65
The Secret of Chimneys 57, 58, 65
servicemen 7, 30, 32–40, 105, 145, 157
shell-shock 35, 36, 138–40, 148
Sparkling Cyanide 138, 155; narrative structure 46, 47, 53, 54, 58–60

Taken at the Flood 6; air raids 137–45, 147, 151; ex-servicemen 37–9
They Came to Baghdad 2, 63, 71, 75, 77–8
They Do It With Mirrors 155
Three Blind Mice (radio play) 8, 103; memory 109–11, 114–15, 118–19, 121–2
Towards Zero 46, 47, 54–9, 61, 102

trauma 5–9; and air raids 135, 137–52, 155, 162, 164; and bereavement 112; and displaced persons 128, 131–3; and soldiers 35, 120; village space 11, 14, 17; in wartime thrillers 73, 74, 78

Unfinished Portrait 140, 142, 146, 148; *see also* Westmacott, Mary

Verdict (play) 35, 97
veterans 29, 33, 35–6, 38, 76; and nostalgia 140, 146

Westmacott, Mary 106, 124, 137–40
"The Witness for the Prosecution" 104
Witness for the Prosecution (play) 104–6
Witness for the Prosecution (BBC 2016) 104; *see also* Phelps, Sarah

Printed in Great Britain
by Amazon